SKIRTING THE ETHICAL

MERIDIAN

Crossing Aesthetics

Werner Hamacher

Editor

*Stanford
University
Press*

---

*Stanford
California
2008*

SKIRTING THE ETHICAL

Carol Jacobs

Stanford University Press
Stanford, California

Printed in the United States of America
on acid-free, archival-quality paper

Library of Congress Cataloging-in-Publication Data

Jacobs, Carol.
Skirting the ethical / Carol Jacobs.
p.   cm.—(Meridian, crossing aesthetics)
Includes bibliographical references and index.
ISBN 978-0-8047-5789-8 (cloth : alk. paper)
ISBN 978-0-8047-5790-4 (pbk. : alk. paper)
1. Literature and morals.   2. Ethics.
3. Motion pictures—Moral and ethical aspects.
I. Title.
PN49.J315 2008
809'.93353—dc22
2007014961

Contents

For Nadia and Tamara: in awe, and with endless gratitude.

Marx says—revolutions are the locomotives of world history. But perhaps it is entirely different. Perhaps revolutions are the grasp of the human race traveling in this train for the emergency brake.

—Walter Benjamin

Acknowledgments

This book gives me the occasion to thank the Baldwin family for their enormous generosity to Yale University in establishing the Birgit Baldwin professorship in Comparative Literature and most especially for their personal graciousness to me. I would like to think that something in what I have written here might be in the spirit of what Birgit had already so brilliantly devoted herself to in her graduate years at Yale. In any case, everything I have come to learn about Birgit Baldwin leads me to believe that a book that celebrates the possibility of an ethics bound up with the practice of literary theory might have some resonance with all that she was.

My great thanks to Werner Hamacher whose support for this project was unwavering from the very beginning and whose patience with respect to its completion was exemplary. To Joshua Kates for the great care and generosity with which he read. And to Richard Macksey, the guardian angel of my work for over three decades.

Chapter 1 first appeared as "'Dusting Antigone,'" *Modern Language Notes* 111 (December 1996): 889–917. Several pages of chapter 4 were published in a brief and different version and are reprinted by permission of the publisher from "Questioning the Enlightenment" in *New History of German Literature*, edited by David E. Wellbery, pp. 361–66, Cambridge, Mass.: The Belknap Press of Harvard University Press, Copyright © 2004 by the President and Fellows of Harvard College. Chapter 5 previously appeared as "What Does It Mean to Count? W. G. Sebald's *The Emigrants*," *Modern Language Notes* 119 (December 2004): 905–29; chapter 6 as "Playing Jane Campion's *Piano*: Politically," in *Modern Language Notes* 109 (December 1994): 757–85.

Prologue: Skirting the Ethical

Kein Mensch muß müssen.
No one must must.

       —Lessing, *Nathan der Weise*

What If . . .

What could such disparate texts and films as those read here, Sophocles' *Antigone*, Plato's *Symposium* and *Republic*, Hamann's "Aesthetica in nuce," Sebald's *The Emigrants*, and Campion's *The Piano*, possibly have in common? Spanning multiple genres and thousands of years, they initially find their place in classical antiquity, but with subsequent leaps move first to the eighteenth and then to the twentieth century, from Greece to Germany and then to New Zealand. Is it irreponsibility, then, that nevertheless gathers them together under the same cover? This would be a cover, after all, that fails to concentrate them into a single shape and under which, admittedly, all conclusions remain enmeshed in the intricacies of individual moments.

Even if it will not ultimately cover for them, it is impossible to miss the ethical call in each of these works, above all these works, so noted for their political and ethical positionings. Thus Antigone, challenging the rule of state, eloquently commits herself to the perfect divine law. The *Republic* images the ideal state and famously offers both a definition of justice and a meditation on "the good." Socrates culminates his speech in the *Symposium* by guiding the listener to "true virtue" destined to make one beloved by the gods (212a). In "Aesthetica in nuce" Hamann, too, invokes the name of his god, speaking in the name of Jesus Christ and closing that essay with a celebration of the Last Judgment. "*The Piano*" rehearses an immediately recognizable array of politically correct admonitions. And who could miss the moving and somber call to conscience of Sebald's narrator who brings us face to face with the Holocaust? No consideration of these works can avoid coming to terms with their leap-to-the-eye pronouncements. Taking them seriously, as they lie at the very crux of the matter, is where all understanding begins.

Yet, what if ethics were neither prescription nor action—even though this is the defintion of ethics from which one will never entirely escape? And, perhaps, rightly so. What if, in the most striking manner, major works of Western letters, even those most celebrated for taking an ethical and political stand, perform a resistance to just this understanding of it? How could one conceive an ethics that is not prescriptive, in which language does not simply tell us what to do? What if an ethics practiced by these writings as an act of resistance functions neither as prescription, simply, nor as its negation? What if this other version of ethics is bound to jam what traditional ethics presupposes about language, both language in general and the medium of its message? What if such disruptions were not the failure of the ethical but rather the beginnings of a redefinition of it as responsibility, another display of it, a nontyrannical ethical no longer irrevocably bound to a must? What if, precisely in those works we turn to, say, for a definition of the state or of the good (Plato's *Republic*, for example), or that we regard, on the other hand, as among the most noble and heroic challenges to state tyranny (Sophocles' *Antigone*, for example), something else is in question? What if this challenge were necessarily an affront to the exemplarity of these works, no matter how often we call on them to serve in that guise? What if at a certain juncture they refuse to serve as examples, so different is the particularity of their configurations on these issues? What if ethics is abruptly and punctually shifted in these works from the realm of the eternal *must be* to an ever renewed and ever new call that asks: What if?

The Language of Ethics . . .

Still, in another sense, one cannot but encounter the ethical head on. What could be more evident? It establishes boundaries, sets forth in a gesture of well-marked difference limits that must not be transgressed. What, if not the ethical, could we trust to speak to us straight out, couched in a language that says what it means, shining directly (like the sun that stands in for the good in Plato's famous passage) as the necessity of the must—or at least of the should be, the value of the good and the true? And if that is the case, if there is an ethical gravity to all these texts that seems to concentrate each individually into a single, graspable shape, a shape that makes them generalizable in turn as works *about* the ethical, this is a gravity which we dare not give in to, not now, not yet, even though it is most certainly what they are about.

We read here works that openly stake out ethico-political positions, but are no less bound to disrupt them. Six works that set up side by side, as parallel worlds, literal and letteral tyrannies: the power of the state, polis, or Reich, of patriarchy, of divine law and its unshakable judgment, for example, alongside unproblematic powers of representation[1] and prescription. Six works that at the same time skirt their own prescriptions, ethical and linguistic, by way of meditations that may, as in Plato and Hamann, speak directly about language, but which more incisively perform its complexities and thus question their own will to unmediated truth and moral certitude.

For, actually, there is also no way to avoid skirting the ethical. All direct hits turn out suspicious at best. Hitting on it won't do at all—except, perhaps, in the shadows, where Socrates, groping about, claims to find it in the form of justice (*Republic*, IV, 432b–e). However, as even he would ultimately admit, that still tends to leave us in the dark. Not that skirting the issue—what the chapters that follow inevitably perform—will lead to enlightenment. Not one of these essays can make that promise. Still, following where the texts meander, tracing their indirections, while cognizant, at a respectful distance, of where they more obviously lead, produces versions of the ethical and political critical to their understanding. Thus we will listen to the shrieks of birds in *Antigone* and the freakish clicks of a metal finger on keys in the *The Piano*. We will take the drunken Alcibiades at his word in the *Symposium*. We will resist the rapacious dialectic of Socrates, the drive to represent and recuperate in *The Emigrants*, and the strangely paired seductions of scholarly reference and theological judgment in "Aesthetica in nuce."

Conventional ethics takes form here, then, as (and is therefore implicitly bound to a concept of) language capable of saying what it means more or less directly and operating as a call to action. There is, however, another version of the ethical. It doesn't say what it has to say head-on. And yet this act of skirting is neither tangential, nor beside the point. It is precisely this mode of indirection that challenges the potential tyranny of an ethics that threatens to become unquestioned compulsion. This other version is at work in these texts—not as the definitive undoing of the straightforward ethical positioning—but as its disturbance.[2]

Parallel to the admonitions about what not to take at face value in Sophocles, Plato, Hamann, Sebald, and Campion, another is in order about what not to take seriously in the essays that follow. It is not a question of introducing another moment, another passage, another text, in order to substitute it for those openly assured ethical proclamations. Whatever is staged here, these are not rhetorical struggles with winners and losers. Alcibiades enters when Socrates has finished speaking, but his speech (to which our reading will turn) does not have a life all its own. Campion's film, we will emphasize, closes with no fewer than three endings, but we cannot settle for simply disregarding the apparent moral of the first with the onslaught of the others. And its final complex moments do not drown out the echoes of what precedes: they enter into relation with it. Hamann's essay cites an earlier work, the *Biblical Observations*, but the crisis there generated does not stand in place of "Aesthetica in nuce." It is not a matter of countering the ethics for which these texts evidently speak so much as of allowing, however indirectly, an ethics of another order, an ethics which is, to be sure, out of order, to erupt or break through as part of the picture. At a critical point in the *Republic* Socrates speaks of having to settle for the *paradeigma*, which we have written of as the *side-by-side*. And whereas Socrates may imply that the side-by-side is a compromise, it is that splaying, the dislocating disassemblage of irresolvable alternatives, that opens up a certain hope, the hope of emancipation from an otherwise inevitable absolutism of sorts.

The reader, then, should be wary of the somewhat triumphal tone that finds its way into several of the commentaries that constitute this book, tellingly at their close. There are suggestions (perhaps necessary, in any case strategic) of resistance, liberation, interruption, as "respons-ability," arriving at the last possible moment to transform what came before. These should not be taken as the decisive word. If something like liberation or response is at stake, no endgame is at hand. It must rather be thought as a force at play more or less throughout. Thus if *patriarchy* is famously at stake in Sophocles' tragedy, what challenges is not a *matri-archy* that, mimicking the enemy, becomes its other, the double that would reinstate power under another name and another gender. The motherhood at issue in *Antigone* does not trump the old regime so much as disturb it. It sidesteps or skirts the lineage and power of reproduction and sashays toward an ethics without chain of command. What kind of ethics could this be that doesn't go by the rules but rather goes by them and goes on to upset the ruling, that offers us no definitive shape, no pure idea, no absolute good, no access to heaven after all, no promise of spoils, no reassurance of source, no final judgment? And which, all that notwithstanding, is certainly no call to anarchy.

Moreover, why should the strange paths of these texts that both hit upon and also veer off from the most conventional modes of asserting the ethical and political pass by way of issues of language that could seem so very beside the point? Why do both the texts read as well as the commentaries that make up this book skirt and flutter by the gravity of a definitive ethics precisely while confronting an unsettling coming to terms with language? Thus, to give some singular examples: Socrates will celebrate the dialectical mode of argument, shaking himself loose from his earlier method of eristics. The mode of speaking is anything but irrelevant, for the city they are forming, he will remind his followers, is a city they make in speech. And the attributes of dialectic, the rules of its game, will prove entirely at one with the political aim, the polis they see taking form. Or, in Hamann's "Aesthetica in nuce," every reader is confronted with the opacity of a text that begs for the scholarly labor of footnotes to lead us to the spoils of obscure and hard-won points of reference. Those same scholars who undertake this task liken Hamann's text to typology, thus attributing to his linguistic form the theological promise of redemption which is also at stake in the content of his essay. In Campion's *The Piano* which so often comments on its own filmic materialism, the language of its representation is time and again linked to ethical crises. We view, for example, the performance of *Bluebeard*, a play with a pointed moral that parallels the plot of the film, in which the complexities of its staging confuse an audience into taking it as a call to ethical action. How shall we conceive the analogies among a conservative theorization and practice of language as communication, an ethics that compels, and the imposition of a politics based on identity?

I have traced the unnameable state of affairs in these texts, in which the disturbance of comfortable linguistic modes is oddly productive of the ethical and political, under many names: in Plato as figuration (*Symposium*) or analogy (*Republic*), as "'living underwater'" and the filmic in *The Piano*, in *The Emigrants* as "cross-pollination" and the disruption of contained delineation. For the renegade ethics toward which these works point, but which can never be isolated or approached directly, are caught up in ungovernable versions of representation. Ungovernable—which is not to say precisely that they overcome the rule of law. That conventional structures of representation cannot reign marks, not the failure of the ethical, but the opening toward, the (however tentative) eruption, into an emancipation from the must be. Perhaps this begins to explain that strange interjection in the exemplary work of German literary ethics, Lessing's *Nathan the Wise*, which forms the epigraph of this prologue: for how can it be that Nathan, that figure of wisdom, insists, in however offhand a manner, that no one should be compelled to "have to." "Kein Mensch muß müssen." What kind of an ethics is it that sheds the "must"?

Skirting Identity and a Call to Judgment

There is also that other sense of "skirting," toward which the heavy-handed pun of the book title reaches. For the political and ethical gestures read here are sometimes overtly and often famously bound up with the question of gender. Jane Campion's film, *The Piano*, is to all eyes, at least from a certain point of view, a feminist film if ever there was one. Hamann's best known work, "Aesthetica in nuce," directs us to a little celebrated corner of his opus in which the definitions of good and evil pivot around the virtue of a biblical heroine. The *Symposium* is conditional upon expelling women from the scene of discourse, though Socrates, in a speech which one tends to take as Plato's final word in the matter of love, ventriloquizes his female mentor. In the *Republic* we find Socrates forced to turn back and transvaluate the place of woman in the polis before his ideal state can be fully conceived (Book V). It is gender politics as well that are so often understood to govern Antigone's affront to the state: by Creon in the tragedy and by many of Sophocles' most striking readers—Hegel and Irigaray, for example—for whom the formation of the state and the ethical in general cannot but pass by way of woman.

In both Plato and Hegel one has to domesticate woman in order to establish the state. Socrates solves the problem by taking her into the polis on an almost equal footing. Hegel, repressing the power of "womankind" as the eternal irony of the community, declares her, along with the family, a mere steppingstone on the way to the state. Having accounted for the gender war, both Plato and Hegel are thereafter, however, unable to imagine a state without acts of aggression that define its borders with a barbarian other. Woman, it seems, was something of a place holder for a more generalized structure of otherness.

If in Plato and Hegel identity in the name of gender drifts to identity in the name of state, Sebald has a sense of their uncertain ground. He turns all this inside out or, perhaps better, blurs it. For, at least in *The Emigrants*, and however obliquely, Sebald walks a very fine line when it comes to identity politics. History positioned him to do something different. That he skirts the issue of the Holocaust, even as he invokes it, is what one all too readily chooses not to see. Coming to consciousness in a postwar Germany where the "'other'" had been all too effectively eradicated, he writes less of discord with or war against the foreign than of the inevitabilities of its aftermath. The enigmatic photos that riddle his texts have everything to do with his enterprise, and everything to do with their misunderstanding. These are documents of restoration, recuperation—reparations of sorts but also, in a final turn, as we shall see, of self-accusation: the accusation that the attempt to memorialize, to reinstate, might place the narrator in the position of a very different politics, one that identified, not in order to recover, but rather to differentiate and annihilate. Sebald's is a rare, if indirect, meditation on the difficult relationship among representation, identity, aggression, and the inadequacy of be good–feel good ethics, of the necessity of perpetual renegotiation of identity as well as truth. Identity, politics, ethics, the language of representation: they are not the same but they are all put into relation with one another, shot through, preoccupied, animated, and haunted by similar forces and issues.

Let us dwell for a moment on that final turn. Nowhere in Sebald's writings is the flickering function and danger of representation more striking than in the closing lines of *The Emigrants*. Alone in a room, the narrator resurrects the experience of seeing a photographic exhibition about the Litzmannstadt ghetto. He brings back in words (the image itself is not reproduced) the faces of three women weaving at a loom. He imagines how they might have been called. Could they be "Roza, Lusia, and Lea," prototypical Polish given names? or rather "Nona, Decuma, and Morta," the Parcae or fates of Roman mythology—with spindle, and thread and scissors? What takes place as one shifts from one set of musings to another, from the conjectured specificity of the first to the mythical power of the second? Sebald's text which has seemed so bent on bringing back the dead, on saving the ghostly sufferers of the past, a text that bolsters its meanderings in this endeavor with photographs from albums, newspapers, and goodness knows where, deadends in an image. It positions him as the ghetto photographer, an official obsessed with memorializing his own "'good'" works in service to the Nazi regime. The narrator who sets out, more or less, to wed himself with the woman in the middle (she was, he writes, somehow like a bride) and save the imaginary "Roza, Lusia, and Lea" stands challenged: first by a gaze from the photograph and then by the Fates, judged for repeating the act of re-production, representation: the savior become perpetrator. The narrator's life, his fate, his death are at stake, as is the significance of his textual endeavor in which the politics of identity cut both ways. Sebald observes his alter ego seeing and being seen—the viewer scrutinzed, accounted for, summed up. His watchfulness about representation and judgment calls for ours.

It is unsettling to come to terms with how the one becomes the other—the impassioned attempt to save that seems to drive not only *the Emigrants* but *Austerlitz* and much else in Sebald's work as well, transfigured into an object of critique. More troubling still, there is no easy way to account for the act of judgment itself. Is it the promise of calculable justice as in the *Republic*'s myth of Er, or is it an act of unjustified violence—or something else again? How to understand the limits of judgment, those it necessarily sets, its inevitable shortcoming, as well as its inevitability? And what does it mean to marginalize judgment in the name of liberation (as the essays that follow may seem to do), when it is precisely another version of judgment at the close of *The Emigrants* that successfully ruptures the narrator's ethical complacency? Are telos and interruption, perhaps, not so clearly distinguishable after all?

At the interruptive close of "Aesthetica in nuce" Hamann appends what he calls an "Apostille," a gloss, a critical commentary, marginalia to his text. It doesn't upend what came before so much as warn us of its vanity, while calling upon us as well to read more and read elsewhere in order to understand the critical insights of what he has been about. It is a refusal of the tyranny of unexamined language, a refusal of thought to settle. His is an admonition and an explanation after the fact. I put mine up front. That language is always articulated with—or, as we have said, productive of—the political and ethical is difficult to make out, if only because it formulates no-thing definitively. What follows is not a vigil over the defunct body of ethics so much as a bid for vigilance as the difficult practice of reading.[3] Perhaps at least this much is legible: if the ethical is something to be desired, we find ourselves perpetually compelled to revisit the inter-relation among ethics, the political, and the specificities of individual acts of interpretation, however illusive the spoils of such a struggle might be. This is the risk of every judgment call while also a call to judgment.

SKIRTING THE ETHICAL

§ 1   Dusting Antigone: Sophocles' *Antigone*

For millennia, now, we have stood sentinel: hoping to see her—to catch her in the act, to say plainly and clearly what Antigone is about. Yet no vigilance could be adequate to the task. History offers a long succession of separate, disconnected experiences of *Antigone*—impossible to gather together into a single completed shape. Hegel and Irigaray are exemplary in this regard, and not only because their readings are at odds with one another. For each, as we shall see, was already of at least two minds about Sophocles' play: in the words of the guard who reports to Creon: their "thoughts gave [them] many pauses, as [they] wheeled round in [their] tracks to return."[1] Moreover, unlike the heroine of the play, who, at the most critical moment, leaves no stroke, no impression, no sign, Hegel and Irigaray (and so many others besides) marked out their tracks most clearly for us to see. Perhaps, then, there is no way to break new ground. No matter.

The stakes for Hegel, as for Irigaray reading Hegel, are sexual difference, the relation between family and state, and the movement from matriarchy to patriarchy in the pagan world.[2] Grave issues. No doubt. And yet woman's place in all this, as Hegel would have it, leaves something to be desired in the realm of the serious. In *The Phenomenology of Mind*, toward the end of the section entitled "Ethical Action" ("Die sittliche Handlung"), in that most questionable of phrases, Hegel speaks of "Womankind" as "the eternal . . . irony of the community (*die ewige Ironie . . . des Gemeinwesens*, translation altered)."[3] Everything hinges, one could argue, on how one understands this phrase.

Irigaray takes it as the title for her essay on Hegel in *Speculum of the Other Woman*. No red-blooded woman, after all, can fail to enjoy the irony of wearing Hegel's slur as something of a crown. But just how eternal is this irony, of womankind, and above all of Irigaray? How eternal can irony be or, rather, in what sense can irony possibly be understood to be eternal? Is it a position to be maintained? Irigaray's essay, "The Eternal Irony of the Community," after all, is overcast with a certain pall of seriousness. Sophocles' play, on the other hand, is itself no comedy. No comedy and yet no tragedy from a certain point of view, from the point of view, namely, of certain questions that Irigaray herself poses, following in the footsteps of Hegel and taking a few sidesteps of her own. So how can we too follow—in the path of Irigaray, Hegel, Sophocles, and especially in the path of Antigone, which is not one?

No less preoccupied than Hegel before her, Irigaray returns again and again to *Antigone*—in *Speculum of the Other Woman*, in *An Ethics of Sexual Difference*,[4] in "The Female Gender" (*Sexes and Genealogies*). Refusing to identify with her, "So let me return to the character of Antigone, though I shall not identify with it" (*Ethics*, 115F, 118E), calling her "anti-woman," Irigaray regards Sophocles' figure, however tragic, as "a production of a culture that has been written by men alone" (*Ethics*, 115F, 118–19E). Antigone appears merely as "the desexualized representative of the *other of the same*" (*Sexes*, 125F, 111E). She functions in the service of, as the representative of, the male,[5] the only sex society recognizes, in a tradition that has always operated as though there were only one sex, which is not to say an equality of male and female.

> When engaged in redressing her brothers' crime, Antigone is no longer fulfilling her own task, her *affirmative* relationship to ethics, she no longer serves *her* gods. The female gender, in its singularity, has been lost in this character who resists but nonetheless submits, out of womanly—or maternal?—fidelity to the male gods and to war among men. . . . In order to wipe a stain away once more. What stain? Fundamentally, the stain of her consciousness, of belonging to the female race, of having a maternal filiation. (*Sexes*, 125F, 111E)

Antigone as traitor to the position of woman, to "maternal filiation," then, at least in the earlier works.

Yet two years after the publication of *Sexes et parentés*, in *Thinking the Difference*,[6] Antigone, it seems, has been rehabilitated or rather reformed, has at the very least assumed a new shape.[7] She is now "an identity or identification for many girls and women living today" (*Difference*, 84F, 70E); for Irigaray as well, who speaks of the identity of "[Antigone's] view and mine"[8] (*Difference* 87F, 72E). Defender of the cosmic and of the laws of social order, which are no longer at odds,[9] Antigone, for Irigaray, rises up from the ashes as a heroine whose fidelity to maternal genealogy has saved the day.[10]

Whose genealogy is this anyway? Is Antigone a production written by men alone, dutiful daughter of male writing, or rather she who asserts against all odds the vertical genealogical relation between mother and daughter? And are these the only alternatives? Were we to regard Antigone, as Irigaray once did, simply as the issue of male writing, it would make sense to recall what Irigaray herself had written—(and this accounts for much of what she has to say):

> I search for myself, as if I had been assimilated into maleness. . . . Rise again from the traces of a culture, of works produced by the other. Searching through what is in them—for what is not there. What allowed them to be, for what is not there. . . .
>
> Woman ought to be able to find herself, among other things, through the images of herself already deposited in history and the conditions of production of the work of man and not on the basis of his work, his genealogy. (*Ethics*, 17F, 9–10E).

If we search *Antigone* for what is at once in it and for what is not there, the figure produced by this reading might be neither anti-woman nor heroine. Let us say, enigmatically for the moment, that we will find Antigone not only dutiful sister and daughter, but also, as in the etymology that Robert Graves accords her name "in place of a mother."[11]

But first of all Hegel, the mother of all philosophers when it comes to these issues: above all Hegel, since it is in the place of Hegel, and in place of Hegel, that Irigaray might be seen to situate herself. The story he tells is that of the ethical order—an ethical world divided between two kinds of law, the human and the divine, between the law of the community, government, or nation, on the one hand, and the law of the gods that governs the family on the other. It is a world to be divided as well between man and woman.[12]

What constitutes, then, the ethical character of the family? Hegel rejects a merely "*natural* relationship" based simply on feeling or love, and rejects the "*accidental* relationship" of rendering assistance in a specific instance which can only produce a "particular effect" (*Phenomenology*, ¶ 451, 268–69). What constitutes the relationship of its members is that the ethical action "can only be related to the *whole* individual or to the individual *qua* universal."

> The deed, then, which embraces the entire existence of the blood-relation (*des Blutverwandten*), does not concern the citizen, for he does not belong to the Family, nor the individual who is to become a citizen and will cease to count as this particular individual; it has as its object and content this particular individual who belongs to the Family, but is taken as a *universal* being freed from his sensuous, i.e. individual, reality. The deed no longer concerns the living but the dead, the individual who, after a long succession of separate disconnected experiences, concentrates himself into a single completed shape, and has raised himself out of the unrest of the accidents of life into the calm of simple universality. (*Phenomenology*, ¶ 451, 269–70)

The particular individual of the Family who has previously passed through "a long succession of separate disconnected experiences" is taken as a *universal* being, freed in death from the accidents of life and from individual reality. As we go on to read *Antigone* Hegel's promise that the individual "concentrates himself into a single completed shape" will take on peculiar significance. What Antigone makes possible, then, according to Hegel, is the raising of Polynices to universal individuality. He is saved from being at the passive mercy of another and is returned into a being-for-itself.

This final duty toward the dead is the "perfect *divine* law" the "positive *ethical* action" (*Phenomenology*, ¶ 453, 271) of the Family. Hegel speaks of the Family "as a *natural* ethical community (*ein* natürliches *sittliches Gemeinwesen*)" (*Phenomenology*, ¶ 450, 268); still almost everything in the description of the family's ethical action poses it as a disruption of Nature.[13] For death "is a state which has been reached *immediately*, in the *course of Nature*, not the result of an action *consciously done*" (*Phenomenology*, ¶ 452, 270).

> Blood-relationship supplements, then, the abstract natural process by adding to it the movement of consciousness, interrupting the work of Nature and rescuing the blood-relation from destruction; or better, because destruction is necessary, the passage of the blood-relation into mere being, it takes on itself the act of destruction. Through this it comes about that the *dead*, the universal *being*, becomes a being that has returned into itself, a being-for-self, or, the powerless simply isolated individual has been raised to universal individuality. The dead individual, by having liberated his *being* from his *action* or his negative unity, is an empty singular, merely a passive being-for-another,

at the mercy of every lower irrational individuality and the forces of abstract material elements, all of which are now more powerful than himself. . . . The Family keeps away from the dead this dishonouring of him by unconscious appetites and abstract entities, and puts its own action in their place, and weds the blood-relation to the bosom of the earth, to the elemental imperishable individuality. (*Phenomenology*, ¶ 452, 271)

Antigone, whose name is never explicitly uttered, couldn't be more clearly at work here. Polynices, unburied, lies at the mercy of carrion birds and dogs. His sister strives to keep these lower irrational forces from dishonoring him "by unconscious appetites." She puts her own action "in their place" and weds her brother to the womb of the earth. What place is it that her action occupies and what has this to do with the bizarre rites Hegel hints at that wed Polynices to a certain womb? Her action interrupts the work of Nature and adds to what seems a purely natural death the movement of consciousness. This is the positive ethical action of the divine law. This is the law that Hegel lays down as that of the Family, the law that Irigaray will question and play with, a law that *Antigone* if not Antigone is not at all one with.

It is a law carried out by a sister for a brother. For Hegel, as for Antigone, unlike the relationship of husband and wife, unlike the relationship between parent and child, that between sister and brother is the unmixed relationship of family kinship, untainted by the transition (*Übergehen*) from one generation to the next or by a lack of similarity, an inequality (*Ungleichheit*) of the sides.

They are the same blood which has, however, in them reached a state of rest and equilibrium. Therefore, they do not desire one another, nor have they given to, or received from, one another this independent being-for-self; on the contrary, they are free individualities in regard to each other. (*Phenomenology*, ¶ 457, 274)

It is this moment of peace that Irigaray will call the "*Hegelian dream*" (*Speculum*, 269F, 217E), equilibrium between sister and brother, matriarchy and patriarchy, woman and man.

The war of the sexes would not take place here. But this moment is mythical, of course, and the *Hegelian dream* outlined above is already the effect of a dialectic produced by the discourse of patriarchy. It is a consoling fancy, a truce in the struggle between uneven foes, a denial of the guilt already weighing heavily upon the development of the subject. . . . Yet both sexes, male and female, have already yielded to a destiny that is different for each. (*Speculum*, 269F, 217E)

And, indeed, just when Hegel has insisted on equilibrium between brother and sister, insisted that they are free individualities with regard to each other, a certain consequence that has no apparent necessity, a radical distinction, indeed inequality (*Ungleichheit*) is made to follow:

> Consequently (*daher*), the feminine, in the form of the sister, has the highest *intuitive* awareness of what is ethical. She does not attain to *consciousness* of it, or to the objective existence of it, because the law of the Family is an implicit, inner essence which is not exposed to the daylight of consciousness, but remains an inner feeling and the divine element that is exempt from an existence in the real world. The woman is associated with these household gods [Penates] . . . (*Phenomenology*, ¶ 457, 274)

No sooner does Hegel insist on the equilibrium between brother and sister than man and woman part ways, the "difference of the sexes" (*Phenomenology*, ¶ 460, 276) already announced in the section's title: "The ethical world. Human and Divine Law: Man and Woman." Man will pass from the divine law, law of the family, that law which guarantees him the completed shape that Antigone's burial of Polynices is meant to bring about, from there to the human law, law of the community and of the state.

It is a nonreciprocal recognition which makes this passage possible, a nonreciprocity that leaves woman with only intuitive awareness and in the dark, that raises man to the "daylight of consciousness," that nonreciprocity on which Irigaray will insist and which she will ironize.

> For if the female one can recognize herself in the male one, who has therefore supposedly assimilated her, the reverse is not necessarily true. . . . She can guarantee that the son develops for himself (*pour soi*), independently of the couple that made him: she is the *living mirror*, the source reflecting the growing autonomy of the self-same. She is the privileged place in which red blood and its semblance harmoniously (con)fuse with each other, though she herself has no right to benefit from this process. (*Speculum* 274–75F, 220–21E)

> Hegel . . . affirms that the brother is for the sister that possibility of recognition of which she is deprived as mother and wife, but does not state that the situation is reciprocal. This means that the brother has already been invested

with a value for the sister that she cannot offer in return, except by devoting herself to his cult after death. (*Speculum,* 270F, 217E)

A nonreciprocity that valorizes the brother, to be sure.[14]

And yet, in Sophocles' play Polynices hardly moves from the divine law over to human law without a glitch. In Hegel, for that matter, the sister, it seems, hardly becomes head of the household and guardian of the divine law without staging a violent disruption herself. For Antigone, whom Hegel celebrates elsewhere as "the heavenly Antigone, that noblest of figures that ever appeared on earth,"[15] is transformed by the end of the section into a formidable menace.

> Since the community only gets an existence through its interference with the happiness of the Family, and by dissolving [individual] self-consciousness into the universal, it creates for itself in what it suppresses and what is at the same time essential to it an internal enemy—womankind in general. Womankind—the everlasting irony . . . of the community—changes (*verändert*) by intrigue the universal end of the government into a private end, transforms (*verwandelt*) its universal activity into a work of some particular (*bestimmten*) individual, and perverts (*verkehrt*) the universal (*allgemeine*) property (*Eigentum*) of the state into a possession (*Besitz*) and ornament for the Family. Woman in this way turns to ridicule the earnest wisdom of mature age which, indifferent to purely private pleasures and enjoyments, as well as to playing an active part, only thinks of and cares for the universal. She makes this wisdom an object of derision. . . . (*Phenomenology,* ¶ 475, 288)

The community comes into existence by interfering with the Family and thus with woman. It thereby creates for itself what is essential to it, its internal enemy—womankind. Woman changes, transforms, perverts (*verändert, verwandelt, verkehrt*)—always the prefix *ver-* to mark the non-dialectical alteration, opposition, expenditure, and deterioration). The object of her repeated assault is the universal which she perverts in the name of the private and the particular—all this on the part of that same figure whom Hegel necessarily called forth earlier as the force that transforms the particular individual into the universal individuality of a single completed shape.[16] Go figure!

The role woman plays is certainly not simple nor ever completed. Not in Hegel and not in Irigaray. All the less so in *Antigone.* And yet theirs is the ground I have set out to cover—an uneven, unpredictable topography—or, if not cover then at least to broach, to touch upon, perhaps to change, transform, and even pervert by casting an eye to the particular.

What particular? And how shall we go about it? Until now we have looked to the philosophers rather than to Antigone. Both Hegel and Irigaray glide unproblematically from the figure of Antigone to the role of woman in general. Would a return to the specificity of the Greek heroine accomplish a redefinition of woman and her position in the question of the ethical? In whose voice might we bring this about? In *Thinking the Difference* Irigaray suggests abstracting Antigone from the discourses that surround her and listening to what it is she herself has to say.

> Her example is always worth reflecting upon as a historical figure and as an identity or identification for many girls and women living today. For this reflection, we must abstract Antigone from the seductive, reductive discourses and listen to what she has to say about government of the polis, its order and its laws. (*Difference*, 84F, 70E)

To be sure, neither Irigaray nor Hegel confine their remarks to such listening. Moreover, if we regard Antigone less as a historical personage than as what Irigaray called her elsewhere, "a production of a culture . . . written by men" (*Ethics*, 115F, 118–19E), or more particularly as the production of Sophocles, the voice of the character Antigone can claim no privilege.

Still, in turning from Antigone's own pronouncements, in assuming that she cannot consciously articulate the grounds of her rebellion, are we not following in the path of Hegel? He warns us that she may perform the ethical act but, by dint of gender, can never become properly conscious of it. Hers is merely an "*intuitive* awareness of what is ethical" (*Phenomenology*, ¶ 457, 274). But what if something takes place in *Antigone* that sidesteps this progressive hierarchy, something that has little to do with either the intuition of the ethical assigned to woman or the consciousness of it reserved for man?

In interrogating the play as to the question of woman's place, more or less the repeated question of Hegel and Irigaray, there are less obvious figures to turn to than Antigone: to begin with a wise man and a fool, a blind man and he who stands watch, a seer and an incompetent sentinel, a blind seer and a blind seer. It is not that either of these voices, however male, more consciously grasps what woman or the ethical is about. Nor do they have any direct relationship to Antigone's will, much less her intuition or (lack of) consciousness. It is just possible, however, that the words we read offer an ethical performance, albeit with regard to an ethics entirely at odds with Hegel's conception, perhaps even at odds with that of Antigone, certainly at odds with the concept that binds ethics to self-knowledge. We might say, citing Irigaray, citing her words but, no doubt, not her intention, *"Language reverses all that the dialectic describes—and reciprocally"* (*Sexes*, 126F, 111E). Still, when Hegel spoke of *Antigone* as "one of the most sublime, and in every respect most consummate works of art human effort ever produced," he added, "Not a detail in this tragedy but is of consequence":[17] in this we are inclined to follow him.

Tiresias, who understands the present and foresees the future, situates the ethical crisis as a relation between the above and the below.[18]

> You have thrust below one of those above, arrogantly lodging a living creature in a tomb, and have kept here one of those below, a corpse dispossessed, dishonoured, impure. (1068ff.)

Creon has kept one of those from the underworld, Polynices, here in the world above, dead but not buried; Antigone, "one of those above," he orders buried although not dead.[19]

How shall we speak of these displacements, not only in the context of *Antigone* but also in the context of Hegel and Irigaray? From Hegel's point of view, it makes perfect sense after all, since

> the law of the Family is an *implicit, inner* essence which is not exposed to the daylight of consciousness, but remains an *inner* feeling and the divine element that is *exempt from an existence in the real world*. (*Phenomenology*, ¶ 457, 274; emphasis mine)

For Irigaray, however, things are hardly so simple, she who reminds us repeatedly that woman does not have a place: "What is sometimes difficult for women is to provide themselves with a *periphery*, a circumference, a world, a home" (*Ethics*, 104F, 106E). What does it mean that woman cannot provide herself with a periphery? Such assertions take on different significations at different points of Irigaray's texts. An essay such as "Volume-Fluidity"[20] (equally translatable as a volume that cannot be outlined, traced, described, "Volume without Contours"),[21] on the one hand, announces the placelessness of woman:

> So woman has not yet taken (a) place. . . . Woman is still the place, the whole of the place in which she cannot take possession of herself as such. . . . She

is not uprooted from matter, from the earth, but yet, but still, she is already scattered into *x* number of places that are never gathered together into anything she knows of herself, and these remain the basis of (re)production—particularly of discourse—in all its forms. (*Speculum*, 282F, 227E)

But if the opening paragraphs of the essay seem to lament woman's inability to take possession of herself, the essay goes on to offer the indefinition of woman as something of a celebration. Woman not having her place is not entirely a negative force in Irigaray. Now and again is the suggestion that woman implies precisely the redefinition of space—as a space that cannot be controlled, as a space that becomes fluidity, a matter of fluid mechanics as opposed to solid mechanics, as Irigaray will put it elsewhere.

> Woman is neither open nor closed. She is indefinite, in-finite, *form is never complete in her*. She is not infinite but neither is she *a* unit(y), such as letter, number, figure in a series, proper noun, unique object (in a) world of the senses, simple ideality in an intelligible whole, entity of a foundation, etc. This incompleteness in her form, her morphology, allows her continually to become something else, though this is not to say that she is ever univocally nothing. No metaphor completes her. (*Speculum*, 284F, 229E)

In "The Eternal Irony of the Community," situated just before "Volume-Fluidity" in *Speculum*, Irigaray writes of Antigone's place as follows:

> Their inherent duty is to ensure *burial for the dead*, thus changing a natural phenomenon into a spiritual act. One more step (into negation) and we see that it is the task of womankind, guardian of the blood tie, to gather man into his final figuration, beyond the turmoil of contingent life and the scattered moments of his Being-there. (*Speculum*, 266–67F, 214E)

How are we to read that site of the woman/heroine? Irigaray repeats for us what she reads in Hegel, that woman's place in relation to her blood-relative is to ensure the raising "into the peace of simple universality" (*Speculum*, 267F, 214–15E). Except that Irigaray adds something, a something that does not universalize or make whole the body of work she reads, an addition that opens up rather what the text seemed to be saying.

> Thus woman takes this dead being into her own place on his return into the self—a being that is universal, admittedly, but also singularly drained of strength, empty and yielded passively up to others. She must protect him

both from all base and irrational individuality and from the forces of abstract matter, which are now more powerful than he. Shielding him from the dishonoring operation of unconscious desires and natural negativeness—*preserving him from her desire, perhaps?*—she places this kinsman back in *the womb of the earth*. . . . (*Speculum*, 267F, 215E)

Woman takes the dead man "into her own place (*chez elle*)," which is also said to be the womb of the earth? If Antigone places her kinsman back in the womb of the earth, which kinsman is it and where precisely does she place him? From what desire does she preserve him? Does she preserve him? Is there only one womb and how does it coincide with a tomb? whose womb? whose tomb?

As Tiresias tells it the crisis of burial is double. For with regard to the issues of woman's place that play such a fluid (not to say contradictory) role in Irigaray's writing and in this tragedy about a woman who clearly doesn't know her place, *Antigone* is about both the space the heroine dies in and the space in which Polynices can find no proper burial.

This burial is a difficult rite to define. At times it seems a matter of placing him underground; at others it is described as forming a funeral mound. It is a burial that in any case requires placing earth over the body. To this we have an eyewitness, a bizarre witness who first arrives to tell Creon less what he has observed than what he did not see. He is a man who dares to speak "even if [his] words are worthless" (234), who, as Creon puts it, speaks by way of "effectively covering [himself] and fencing [himself] round in this matter" (241f.). A speech, then, about the inadequacies of both speaking and seeing. To Creon's question "What are you saying? What man dared do this?" (248), the guard replies:

> I do not know. For at the spot there was no stroke made by a pickaxe, no impression of a mattock. The ground was hard and dry, unbroken and unmarked by cartwheels; there was no sign who the culprit had been. And when the first day-watchman showed us this, it came as an unpleasant shock for us all. For the body was out of sight—not entombed, but lightly covered with dust, as if by one who was avoiding pollution. (249ff.)

A scene in which no stroke of instrument has been made, in which no impression has been left. The ground is left unbroken and unmarked, with no sign of the doer of the deed. Still, Creon, in posing his question, is certain of one thing, that the perpetrator was male. "What man dared do this?" And yet if we are, as Irigaray proposes, to read the sexuate difference between male and female in this play, it is the question of the mark and the impression in relation to the earth that we cannot ignore. This is a difference that borders on unreadable indifference, between Creon and the force of woman he most fears, in the figure of Antigone who operates with the courage, it seems, if not in the manner of, a man.

If Antigone, in the passage above, a passage which is never adequately explained, leaves no traces in the earth, what of man? For just after Creon dismisses the guard with threatening instructions to find the man who has done these things, and just after the sentry mocks the possibility of finding him, the chorus offers its famous song concerning man.

> Wonders are many, and none more wonderful than man. This being goes with the storm-wind across the foamy sea, moving deep amid cavernous waves. And the oldest of the gods, Earth the immortal, the untiring, he wears away, turning the soil with the brood of horses, as year after year the ploughs move to and fro. (332ff.)

A song of humankind in general (*anthrôpos*), it seems; and yet how can one fail to see here that which differentiates Antigone (and with her, as we shall see, woman) from the apparently universal description of mankind?

> Respecting the laws of the land and the right of oaths sworn by the gods, he is a man of a lofty city; cityless is he who recklessly devotes himself to evil. (368ff.)

The progression of the choral ode culminates in a celebration of the state, the polis and its laws, precisely the male force bound to rational language that Creon counters to Antigone's loyalty to blood-relation. Man, for all its apparent neutrality[22] (unlike Antigone who, Creon reminds us repeatedly, is the incarnation of woman), does not leave the earth unbroken and unmarked (250ff.), as year after year he turns the soil of the earth with his plow. Universal man leaves his mark.[23]

Still, as the passage goes on to insist, although man can tame the sea, the earth, the birds of the air, and other beasts, although he has taught himself speech and he practices statecraft, what he cannot tame is death: "From death alone he will procure no refuge" (361ff.) And yet death, one could claim, is precisely what Antigone has—if not tamed (as Hegel would have it)—then at least broached: Antigone, who from the beginning speaks of death as no loss to her but gain, nor solely gain but also grief (462 ff.), a trivial grief and therefore neither grief nor gain precisely. Death, for Antigone, falls to the side of that simple concept of possession and exchange to which Creon obsessively returns. Antigone's non-marks on the earth tell the story of another economy: precisely not one that lives in relation to that outside herself as a property to be tamed and acquired, as in the chorus's description of mankind (or as Hegel's tale of womanly possession would have it—with woman as a perversion to the universal property of the state).

And, it is made clear elsewhere, the outside that man wills the possession of includes, of course, womankind: thus when Ismene expresses horror at Creon's will to destroy his son's bride, Creon replies: There are "others [who] have furrows that can be ploughed" (569). The others here are women: the image of forceful, visible, and readable digging in the earth is thus recast as sexual possession. Recast in retrospect, then, is the entire choral ode to man (why should it surprise us, since universal "man" is always recast as male?) which in the preceding scene differentiates itself from Antigone in particular and from all of womankind in Creon's crass metaphorization.

Thus when Antigone works the earth, or fails to, she does it differently from this universal man turned male, plowing for possession neither of the earth nor of the other. She leaves the ground unmarked, unbroken:

> And when the first day-watchman showed us this, it came as an unpleasant shock for us all. For the body was out of sight—not entombed, but lightly covered with dust, as if by one who was avoiding pollution. And there was no visible sign that any wild beast or dog had come near or had torn it. (253 ff.)

The body bears evidence, it would seem, of violating the sovereign's decree. But the "unpleasant shock" in what is brought to light is not simply that the body, contrary to law, now evades pollution. The shock is that it has taken those on watch quite unawares. No sign of delving in the earth—and now the body, it too "out of sight," escapes their gaze.

Out of sight and yet not out of sight, out of sight and yet "not entombed, but lightly covered with dust." The body is buried and yet not buried, actually, with just the thinnest veil of dust upon it. Antigone's gesture does not really make the child above the ground belong to those below, as Tiresias might have put it. Is this then the gesture that will make Polynices complete, that will concentrate him into a single completed shape (¶ 451, 270), that will save him from Nature and a natural death and deliver him to the universal as Hegel had described it? Or is something so unfathomable happening here that the chorus attributes it to the supernatural (278f.)? Is Antigone a threat to the intelligibility of the entire system that a male state implies (to an earth well plowed, for example); is she the eternal irony of the community, not because she buries the man or because she fails to, but because she makes a mark that cannot be properly located, because this woman at least, Hegel notwithstanding, neither buries nor fails to bury,[24] leaves her brother neither above nor below, neither universalizes nor fails to universalize the male, because what she performs is not intelligible to those around her and, perhaps, not even to herself?

The guards take up their watch again. Antigone returns, only to be arrested. For the sentinels, determined not to be caught off guard again, have remained vigilantly awake. And yet, when the same figure of a fool brings Antigone to Creon and improves his last tale of what he did not see with a report of what he did, the issues of seeing, knowing, speaking, and signifying are difficult to miss.

> CREON: This girl you are bringing—how and where did you arrest her?
>
> GUARD: She was burying the man. You know all.
>
> CREON: Do you know what you are saying? Do you mean it?
>
> GUARD: Yes, I saw this girl burying the corpse which you had said must not be buried. Am I speaking plainly and clearly?
>
> CREON: And how was she seen? Was she really caught in the act? (401ff.)

The precariousness of what takes place is difficult to miss because the guard unfolds a testimony that leaves his listeners at least as uncertain as before. Creon does well to ask the sentinel if he knows what he is saying, if he really means it; does well to question precisely how she was seen and whether that perception might really be called "catching her in the act."[25]

> GUARD: It happened in this way. When we arrived there, with those dreadful threats of yours in our ears, we wiped away all the dust that covered the corpse, stripped the damp body well, and sat on top of a hill to windward, taking care that the smell from the body should not reach us. Each man vigilantly kept his neighbour awake with a torrent of threats, in case anyone should neglect the task. This continued until the sun's bright disc stood in mid-heaven and it was blazing hot. And then suddenly a whirl-

wind raised from the earth a dust-storm, a trouble in the sky, and filled the plain, spoiling all the foliage of its woodland; and the wide air was choked with it. We shut our eyes[26] to keep out the god-sent plague. And when, after a long time, this had cleared, the girl was seen. . . . And at once she brought thirsty dust in her hands, and lifting up a fine bronze ewer she paid her respects to the corpse with a threefold libation. On seeing this, we rushed forward and captured her at once . . . (407ff.)

Can we speak plainly and clearly about what happens here? Can we answer Creon's question of how she was seen and whether she was really caught in the act? The sentries brush the dust from the body. Before they know it Antigone has come and found what the guard will call the bare corpse, and all her work gone to waste; before they know it, because something has intervened between the brushing away of dust and the advent of Antigone or at least the recognition of Antigone by the sentries. That same earth which Antigone had left without a trace, that same matter so dear to Antigone and to Irigaray as belonging to woman, has been raised by a whirlwind to trouble the sky. The whirlwind (dare we call it a force of Nature?)[27] fills the plain with dust so thick the sentries are forced to close their eyes. This is a dust so overwhelming it covers all the foliage and surely, therefore, although the sentry has nothing to say in this regard, perhaps because he doesn't see it, also the damp corpse of Polynices. It is difficult to conceive it happening otherwise: the body just mounded over with light dust, again, though not buried really.[28] If so, it is difficult to distinguish the work of Nature and that of the sister, despite Hegel's assertion that she supplements the natural process and interrupts it. No way to distinguish Nature and Antigone, both arriving, it seems, coincidentally and performing the same rite of scattering the dust that neither buries nor leaves unburied the decomposing figure of the male. The whirlwind comes more or less at the moment that Antigone arrives so that force of Nature, rather than being at odds with woman, enters into complicity with her crime. Like woman, Nature puts out reason and blinds the sentries, culminating a series of scenes that insist on the impossibility of witnessing with one's own eyes.

But this is not the whole story, plainly and clearly. For when the dust, after a long interval, has finally settled, when Antigone is finally open to view, she too has something to say of the matter. It is here, no doubt, that we should, in the words of Irigaray, "listen to what [Antigone] has to say"

(*Difference*, 84F, 70E) or if not what she has to say, then how she says it, "the conditions of [its] production" (*Ethics*, 17F, 10E).

> And when, after a long time, this had cleared, the girl was seen; and she ut-
> tered a piercing cry, the shrill note of a bird, as it cries when it sees, in its
> empty nest, the bed bereft of nestlings. So she, when she saw the corpse bare,
> broke out in lamentation, and called down curses on those who had carried
> out the deed. (422ff.)

Has the plague which troubles the sky and closes the eye really cleared? For what the sentinel finally sees can be offered only in a figural language that troubles the intelligibility of the scene. Antigone, as Hegel would have it, there to interrupt the work of Nature, to rescue her blood-relation from destruction, to keep from Polynices the dishonoring, unconscious appetites of carrion birds and dogs, nevertheless appears as one of these. She has, indeed, in Hegel's words, "put [her] own action in their place" (*Phenomenology*, ¶ 452, 271). How to come to terms with the fact that Antigone becomes once again interchangeable with a force of Nature, and specifically the bird which threatens the integrity of the body and threatens pollution, she who was to guarantee the completeness of shape, and universality?

The figure of the sentinel brings this transformation of Antigone about, a transformation that other blind seer will come to elaborate. When Tiresias comes before Creon he tells a tale, as he describes it, of the signs that belong to the power of the augur: a tale that teaches one, once again, to see double, a tale preceded, once again, by the question of meaning and words. One might have missed it as the sentinel spoke, yet Tiresias makes it all too clear, that it is to the birds that we must turn if we are to understand.[29]

> CREON: What do you mean? How I shudder at your words!
> TIRESIAS: You will learn when you hear the tokens that belong to my craft.
> As I took my place in the ancient seat of augury, where I had a gathering-
> place for every kind of bird, I heard the unfamiliar noise of birds shrieking
> in evil and unintelligible frenzy. And I realized that they were tearing each
> other with murderous talons; for the whirring of their wings was all too
> expressive. At once in fear I made trial of burnt offerings at a blazing altar.
> But Hephaestus did not shine forth from the sacrifice; instead wet slime
> oozed from the thigh-bones onto the embers, and smoked and sputtered,
> and the gall was sprayed high in the air, and the dripping thighs lay bare of

their covering of fat. I learned from this boy of these abortive prophecies from unrevealing rites; for he is my guide, as I am other men's. And it is your counsel that has brought this sickness on the city. For our altars and hearths have been defiled, every one, by birds and dogs, with carrion from the son of Oedipus who lies in miserable death. And hence the gods no longer accept sacrificial prayers from us, nor blazing thigh-bones, nor does any bird scream out intelligible cries, for they have consumed a stream of dead man's blood. (997ff.)

The "tokens" or signs (*sêmeia*) of the seer's craft are barely readable—as "abortive prophecies from unrevealing rites." For the birds who should offer "intelligible cries" shriek only in "unintelligible frenzy." Prophecy which, like the proper shape-giving burial of the dead, functions as a defining moment, even as a moment of interpretation, can no longer take place. How are we to comprehend that the birds of augury become unintelligible, that those who configure readable signs, a completed shape of what is to come, scream out the incomprehensible? Moreover, the unthinkable conflation takes place in which it is precisely these birds of (non)interpretation that consume the body and the blood of Polynices, as carrion birds.

In this play, where nothing seems to find its proper place, how can we fail to see as well that the place of the thighs offered as burnt sacrifice is now shared by the carrion of Oedipus's son, at every altar and at every hearth? And do they not also have this in common: that they have both, so to speak, blown their cover, the cover that was to guarantee meaning, cover of dust and cover of fat?[30] For just as Polynices' corpse appears at least once again to have lost the dust that pretended to complete its form, so the thighs have lost their covering of fat, necessary for the proper burning of the offering and thus for the proper revelation of meaning.

How are we to understand, at the same time, that this threat to understanding, the unintelligible shriek of frenzy which Tiresias hears, also resonates with those piercing cries of Antigone, described by the sentinel as the shrill note of a bird?[31] That then again, in the sentinel's figure in which Antigone returns to an empty nest, she assumes the shape, not only of a bird, but also of a mother? And if she is not precisely mother, then, as Robert Graves puts it in his etymology of "Antigone," she operates "in place of a mother."[32]

To be sure, this image that puts a mother in place (while displacing her traditional role) was not originally that of Sophocles. The filiation of the

guard's simile can be traced to Homer's *Odyssey*, the scene in which the
son comes to recognize the father. Surely no family could be farther from
that of *Antigone*. If nothing can set Antigone's kinships aright, if it is all
but incomprehensible that Hegel should choose the daughter of Oedipus
as the exemplary defender of the family, the return of Odysseus is nothing if not a reaffirmation of its nuclear form, its proper shape. The hero
of the Trojan War returns to the shores of Ithaca, prelude to his complete
return where the two generations of men will reclaim by violence the
proper configuration of the family: return of the father, dispossession of
the suitors, repossession of wife and the all but orphaned son. In unintelligible form, Odysseus appears to Telemachus who is made to understand
that this is indeed his father in disguise. Thereupon Homer clothes the
embrace of father and son in the image of the mother bird that Sophocles
will borrow: "and they cried shrill in a pulsing voice, even more than
the outcry of birds, ospreys or vultures with hooked claws, whose children were stolen away by the men of the fields" (*Odyssey*, XVI, 216–19).[33]
In this uncanny image Homer disguises the clasp of recuperation as one
of mourning, the gain of the father as the mother's loss.[34] To this loss
Sophocles returns, perhaps like a bird of prey stealing the image of his
forefather, or like a mother bird to her plundered nest. That is to say,
Sophocles indeed takes over the image of Homer, but the figure both tells
of and performs the loss of that which it pretends to grasp and generate.
Like the dust on Polynice's corpse.

How, then, are we to size up the place of the mother in *Antigone*?[35] Irigaray reads Antigone's relation to her mother first as a loyalty to the male,
for Antigone speaks of her crime as service to her mother's son:[36] "But if I
had allowed . . . my own mother's son . . . to remain an unburied corpse,
I should have grieved at that" (466ff.).

> Whatever her current arguments with the laws of the city may have been, an-
> other law is still drawing her along her path: identification with her mother. . . .
> Thus the sister will strangle herself in order to save at least the mother's son. She
> will cut off her breath—her voice, her air, blood, life—with the veil of her belt,
> returning into the shadow (of a) tomb, the night (of) death, so that her brother,
> her *mother's desire*, may have eternal life. (*Speculum*, 272F, 219E)

Something is out of order here in the eternal irony of the community.
Can we be as certain as Irigaray that Antigone strangles herself *in order
to* serve the mother's son? If Creon, head of state, takes upon himself

woman's work, the proper care of Polynices' corpse, the forming of the burial mound,[37] nothing in Sophocles suggests that the sister's suicide bears causal relation to that act.[38] To be sure, Antigone hangs herself precisely as her mother did, repeats Jocasta's murderous deed. This is Antigone's second performance of motherhood;[39] and just as before it fails to function in the service of . . . As she once again takes on the figure of the mother, Antigone defies the logic by which Tiresias, Creon, and even she herself had argued, the logic that marks the distinctions between the nether world and the world above. Suspended below ground, but above, she hangs from a noose, the Greek of which signals the return of the mother bird. (*Brokhos* is a noose for hanging and, in Sophocles, a snare for birds.)[40]

As it did for her mother before her, the bloody offspring of Antigone's deed, assumes the shape of lover.[41]

> The wretched boy, enraged with himself, pressed his body down upon the sword, just as he was, plunging half its length into his side. While still conscious, he clasped the maiden in a feeble embrace, and coughed up a fast stream of flowing blood which sprinkled her white cheek. And he lay, corpse enfolding corpse, achieving his marriage rites, poor boy, in the house of Hades. . . . (1234ff.)

Haemon, like Antigone, comes into the promise of his name (bloody). Could we say that Antigone conceived him thus, and, if so, according to whose sense of conception? As epigraph to "The Eternal Irony of the Community" Irigaray chooses a passage from Hegel's *Philosophy of Nature*:

> The male is, as a result of this differentiation, the active principle whereas the female is the passive principle because she remains in her undeveloped unity. One does not have to reduce generation to the ovary and to the semen/seed (*semence*) of the male, as though the product were nothing but a reunion of the forms or of the parts of the two. But it is certainly in the woman that the material element is and in the male subjectivity. Conception is the concentration of the entire individual in the simple unity which abandons itself there, in its representation: *the semen/seed* (semence) *is this simple representation itself—a point like the name and the self in its totality.*[42]

At issue here is how to conceive conception, not only in Hegel, but also in Irigaray, in Sophocles' *Antigone*, and even in Aeschylus. In Aeschylus's

Eumenides (produced some sixteen years before *Antigone*), as in Hegel, the seed of man is parent, not the "dark womb" of woman.

> The mother is no parent of that which is called
> her child, but only nurse of the new-planted seed
> that grows. The parent is he who mounts. (658ff.)[43]

Irigaray returns to the *Oresteia* in her 1980 lecture "Le Corps-à-corps avec la mère," in an essay implicitly critical of Hegel's position above (in the *Philosophy of Nature*). She bemoans that "the womb is never thought of as the primal place in which we become body" (*Sexes*, 28F, 16E). Antigone, it would seem, shares this position with Irigaray, for she argues repeatedly for the priority of "sameness of womb," and therefore, as Charles Segal specifies, "against the male-oriented, civic ethic of the polis."[44]

And yet, if Antigone takes Haemon into "*the womb of the earth*" (*Speculum*, 267F, 215E), if womb and tomb must be thought as dug out in the same unthinkable space, it may be neither the "primal place" of Irigaray's maternal production,[45] nor conception of the "entire individual in simple [male] unity" as Hegel insists in the *Philosophy of Nature*. As corpse enfolds corpse, we might say that Antigone, however silently now, however unconsciously, has conceived or produced Haemon thus. If Haemon becomes true to his name, we cannot quite attribute this representation, as Hegel would have it, to semen alone, nor is this Haemon's self in its totality. Hardly in its totality, because Haemon, as he lies side by side with Antigone, like Polynices before him, is rent, produces a stream of blood, what Tiresias tells us the carrion birds of augury feed on (1022). Haemon is not conceived there in simple representation or in wholeness; nor can one ignore the obvious, that in this bridal bed it is he who gives bloody signs of having been something of a virgin, fulfilling Creon's fear of Antigone's power to unman. A nontraditional fecundity indeed.

Antigone, no less than Irigaray, uses the fragmentation of the body, a transgression of enclosures, a corporeality that threatens simple intelligibility, that makes the Hegelian eye of the observer run for cover. Hegel says of woman that she "perverts" the universal property of the state and the verb he uses (*verkehrt*) smacks of the sexual. Antigone, in her unseemly act of sexuality, does indeed destroy the most important property of the state, the patrilineal heir. In Irigaray's words she takes man into her own place and places him in the womb of the earth (*Speculum*, 267F, 215E), "her womb" (*Speculum*, 271F, 218E), in an encounter that hardly leaves the male whole. She is there, perhaps then, less as the anti-woman that Irigaray suggests than as the etymologies her name whispers: what we call the kernels or seeds of her name, in all due irony. She is there on the one hand "before or against the production of seed," "against generation," and "in place of a mother"—not because she saves her mother's son, but because she is able to produce both the male and herself as incomplete and in suspension.

In the first scene of Antigone's motherhood, the embodiment of the male is no less at risk.

> And when, after a long time, this had cleared, the girl was seen; and she uttered a piercing cry, the shrill note of a bird, as it cries when it sees, in its empty nest, the bed bereft of nestlings. (422ff.)

In the figure of the bird, Antigone shrieks, echoing in advance the birds of augury, shrieks of a kinship that leaves obscure the difference between foretelling and predation, intelligibility and frenzy, and these with motherhood. In the family of Oedipus where the son is husband and the mother wife, why should it take us by surprise that the sister is mother? If, as sister, Antigone feels called upon to complete the shape of Polynices, to make him whole and deliver him to the universal, in the role of mother something quite other takes place. It is not a matter of conscious intention, as Antigone's resolve to bury her brother may have seemed. What takes place does so in the utterance of a sentinel whose trouble fixing his eyes, even keeping them open, is well-documented, whose ability to know what he is saying and to speak plainly and clearly is questioned at every turn. What takes place in the utterance of the sentinel is a figure that, unbeknownst to Antigone, makes her into a mother. Mother of Polynices, more or less. Mother of what remains. Mother of those remains—perpetually threatened by the carrion birds, which she, by analogy, might also figure as. Mother of that which cannot maintain its shape. Or, perhaps, mother of that which has not and cannot maintain its figure. Mother of that which in its multiplicity (nestlings) is not there. Mother, if one regards the passage more rigorously, only of what is gone, the dust which she had originally scattered, though everything in the sentinel's report of the storm suggests that it is there once more. Mother of the dust. Ashes to ashes and . . .

To be sure, the figure of Antigone as mother bird has so fleeting and obscure a place in Sophocles' tragedy that to unearth it in this manner

may seem to violate the laws of criticism. And yet, *Antigone* is punctuated by the image of the mother as mother of the dead: as when Antigone
compares her fate to that of Niobe, condemned to perpetual mourning
(823ff.)[46] or when she calls Polynices "the dead [male] one [born] from my
mother" (466f.), or when Eurydice, on the death of Haemon, becomes
the very mother or "true mother of [a] corpse" (1282). In the most trans-
gressive of these already horrific refigurations of motherhood, Tiresias
speaks of Creon's child as "one of those from your own *splankhna*." Segal
points out that "this word . . . generally denotes the womb and not the
loins."[47] Thus as Tiresias threatens that Creon will "render up an offspring
from his womb, a corpse in exchange for corpses" (1066f.), Creon, too, no
less than Antigone, becomes mother of the dead.

Antigone arrives in place of a mother, in the figure of a mother, an image, barely hidden, then, throughout the tragedy. That figure shocks us
into reimagining maternity and, therefore, mankind. And it cannot be
insignificant that the turn of phrase of Antigone's captor (as well as its
sources in Homer and Aeschylus) unsettle the relationship between the
terms of ostensible similarity in figural language. The menace to intelligibility, the threat to the interpretation of signs of which Tiresias speaks,
was surely already at play in the guard's figural production of motherhood, which, in turn, had signaled and performed the impropriety of language. For Antigone, as she assumes the place of destructive Nature, does
not give birth precisely, but rather death—and if not quite death then
the dispersal of the corpse's (Hegelian) claim to completeness of shape,
to universality, and to what Irigaray calls its "final figuration."[48] Antigone
is mother of the dead in its brokenness or perhaps mother of the film
that might have stopped, at least veiled the disruption that Nature, Hegel
tells us, brings about. Mother of that which is irrecuperably unwhole or
mother of an irretrievable attempt to supplement and rescue from destruction.

This startling transformation of maternal filiation in which genealogy
as identity proves unthinkable is of a piece with Antigone's redefinition
of the brother. When ordered to her burial by Creon, Antigone responds
with an apostrophe to Polynices.

> But now, Polynices, for shrouding *your* body, this is my reward.
> And yet, to right-thinking people, I did right to honour you. For never, if
> I had been the mother of children, or if my husband had been mouldering in

death, would I have taken on this task in defiance of the citizens. To what law do I defer in saying this? My husband being dead, I could have another, and a child by another man if I had lost a child; but as my mother and father are hidden in the house of Hades, no brother could ever be born again. Such was the law by which I singled you out for honour. (902ff.)

Antigone owes no honor to her husband or child but only to the child of the dead, those hidden out of view, owes honor only to that which cannot be reproduced.

This is not to say that Antigone identifies with Jocasta and gives birth to Polynices, who, because mother and father are in the house of the dead, cannot otherwise be replaced. If she takes the place of the mother, it is an act neither of production nor of identification; she occupies the place of the mother only by doing so differently. Antigone is in the place of a mother whose engendering can only be conceived as already in the past and whose offspring is, necessarily, the unreproducible. She becomes mother in the figure of the bird who, assuming the place of the carrion eaters, returns to a nest already bereft of nestlings. As mother, Antigone undefines the human as either origin or product. There is no reproduction before irreproducibility, before the fragmentation and dispersal which, as we have seen, is bound as well to both interpretation and unintelligibility.

Antigone's motherhood, far more than her sisterhood, would be, then, understandably, an unconscionable menace to the patriarchal state that Hegel foresees. Antigone engenders her offspring as bereft of all that might have held him (or them) together in a tradition to which Hegel is certainly no exception. And, no doubt, she is an unconscionable menace to the family as well: this is a motherhood that should never be mistaken for matri-archy. It is neither a conventional re-production of repetition, nor a labor of the negative, a production through dialectical negation. Antigone operates here as the other of the male, perhaps, though neither in Irigaray's sense nor in Creon's sense. To cannibalize the former: "the issue is not one of elaborating a new theory of which woman would be the *subject* or the *object*, but of jamming the theoretical machinery itself, of suspending its pretension to the production of truth. . . . "[49]

In her role as mother, once again, she *neither* preserves the family *nor* serves the state—the "two highest ethical powers" posited by Hegel:[50] and it is precisely in this neither/nor that another mode of ethics is, if not conceivable, then staged as an unrevealing rite of unintelligible frenzy.

The forms that have enabled Hegel and Irigaray, and so many others in between, to organize *Antigone*—call them if you will family and state, matriarchy and patriarchy, woman and man, Antigone and Creon—become dis-engendered. Antigone's unimaginable place as mother leaves no room for a clear oppositional struggle, for she who would bury Polynices and give him meaning and form also produces or rather has already produced the dispersal of that form-giving, as mother of the dust, as carrion-feeding bird, as prefiguration of intelligible interpretability gone awry. No one can gather these together into a single completed shape either of opposition or of resolution.

Ungatherable as well are the voices of the form-givers *Antigone* requires us to read together. The sentinel speaks to report the past, a (mockery of the) language of sensible certitude followed by perception, naive mimetic language put forth by the fearful servant of the king, sent out to catch Antigone as he catches her in the act. Tiresias too reports events, but, unlike the sentinel, is bound to catch precisely nothing. What he tells of (through the mediation of the boy who sees for him) is the failure to perceive or understand the meaning of what he hears and (fails to) see. His is a language of commentary, commentary on the consequences of catching Antigone in the act, but also, more powerfully, the language of pre-diction, a reversal of the relation of language to a seemingly objective reality in which the linguistic now precedes that which will take place. It is tempting to gather here, in the relation of the two seers, a sense of progression similar to that of speculative philosophy.

And yet, in reading them together as we have done, we might, with Philippe Lacoue-Labarthe, speak rather of a "caesura of the speculative."[51] At risk is not only the specific production of the negative that Hegel describes in passing from family to state but also the speculative movement of *Antigone as work*, its promise of mimesis, catharsis, and resolution.[52] And, if speaking of the exemplum of tragedy were truly conceivable, at risk as well would be the speculative movement of tragedy in general. Lacoue-Labarthe, after all, speaks of *Antigone* in relation to Hölderlin as an eccentric center, "a kind of pivot . . . which is impossible to center around," "the incarnation of the very essence of tragedy, if it be true that tragedy is for ever and ever a specifically Greek genre and, in this way is 'incapable of being reconstituted.'"[53]

This interruption of the speculative, inevitable, perhaps, where intelligibility and reproduction are so bitterly called into question, implicates as well our ability to think the ethical. It is to this we must fitfully return again and again. What Antigone performs is no supplement to a natural process, no addition of the movement of consciousness (*Phenomenology*, ¶ 452, 271) no "positive *ethical* action" (*Phenomenology*, ¶ 453, 271), rather an eternally possible irony that is bound to cover over the text ever so lightly and yet remain out of sight. An inconceivable ethical performance in which, Hegel notwithstanding, what is *ethical* need not be *actual* (*Phenomenology*, ¶ 470, 284).

Antigone, indeed, changes and transforms the concept of ethics; it perverts the universal and its promise of property: it perverts as well any fixed concept of revolution against patriarchy.⁵⁴ The "ornament" that is salvaged is that which the sentinel, figurally speaking, offers Creon, as interruption, in place of clear and plain narration. As Irigaray writes of Antigone, although, no doubt, she meant it otherwise: "No metaphor completes her" (*Speculum*, 284F, 229E). "Thus it was a matter of saying, quite simply, that which was said (but) *as that which has not been said.*"⁵⁵ One has to be vigilant when searching through works produced by the other, "searching through what is in them—for what is not there" (*Ethics*, 17F, 9E).

§ 2 Virtue Inside Out: Plato's *Symposium*

We arrive at the *Symposium* last, and with all the intoxications of a much later era, though with a belatedness that is no doubt inevitable for interpreters and historians alike. One comes to the dialogue, then, not unlike Alcibiades, whose speech seems superfluous after Socrates, with all the "eloquence [and] beauty of [his] words and phrases" (198b), has brought the discussion to its high point.[1] Arriving after Alcibiades who, uninvited, has himself broken in upon the scene at Agathon's house, can only increase the sense of our anticlimactic intrusion. And let us remember that the dialogue's opening lines suggest the necessity of this sense of aftermath: for it is narrated by Apollodorus who retells it with the admonition that he was not present, that he may not remember everything, that many years have since elapsed.

The crux of the situation, if one goes to the very heart of it, is that the symposium is purportedly about love. And Socrates will declare himself from the outset "to understand nothing but love-matters" (177b). Nevertheless, what matters in love will ultimately be love of the good. "What men love," he says, "is simply and solely the good" (206a). At the halfway point of the dialogue, then, at dead center, Agathon completes his speech on Eros and passes the word to Socrates. After not a little back and forth, perhaps more precisely up and down, after assuring us, albeit indirectly, that we cannot follow (210a), Socrates will take us on an ultimate ascent to divine beauty in its unique form (212a), which is more or less to say, to "virtue in general" (209a). If this has often been regarded as the crucial point of the dialogue, it is because, here as elsewhere, one tends to listen to the voice of Socrates, and to it alone, as one with, and purely that of

Plato. It is as though what precedes and what follows Socrates were mere semblance, just the outer casing, two halves that must be pulled open to reveal the truth within. To borrow the words and phrases of Alcibiades (221e), whose entrance on the scene marks the closure of Socrates' speech, Socrates' words alone, "so rich in images of virtue, so largely—nay so completely—intent on all things proper for the study of such as would attain both grace and worth" (222a) seem "the only speeches which have any sense in them" (222a). To be sure, what encases Socrates' monologue, what cloaks it round, is "on the outside . . . absurd words and phrases." Still it is only "anyone inexpert and thoughtless [who] might laugh [such] speeches to scorn" (222a).

Perhaps I have rushed all too precipitously to the heart of things. As it begins, the symposium is a drinking party at which, however, those present had "consented not to make their . . . meeting a tipsy affair" (176e). Other precautions have also been taken to ensure that it will be a sober gathering. Eriximachus proposes: "that the flute-girl who came in just now be dismissed: let her pipe to herself or, if she likes, to the women-folk within, but let us seek our entertainment to-day in conversation" (176e). The flute girl has been sent to the womenfolk where she belongs; music has been chased from the space of serious exchange, discourse, words.

Six men, one after another, have each made the "finest speech [they] could upon Love" (214b). Socrates, the last in line, has just completed his famous monologue which repeats the teachings of his mentor Diotima. The gathering has all but reached its state of closure when Alcibiades, thoroughly inebriated and unmistakably decked out as Dionysus,[2] suddenly knocks at the outer door and brings rushing back in with him—the flute-girl, music, women, and wine.

> So he was brought into the company by the flute-girl and some others of his people supporting him: he stood at the door, crowned with a bushy wreath of ivy and violets, and wearing a great array of ribands on his head. (212d–e)

From the moment Socrates began to speak we should have known that this would happen. For despite the seductive and orderly ascent to the pure and golden harvest of philosophy in which his speech culminates, that is not the way it begins. It is a question of a crisis postponed, but not of a crisis averted.

And now I shall . . . proceed with the discourse upon Love which I heard

> . . . from a Mantinean woman named Diotima: in this subject she was skilled, and in many others too; for once, by bidding the Athenians offer sacrifices ten years before the plague, she procured them [ten years] . . . delay in the advent of the sickness and she taught me of love-matters. (201d)

Diotima postpones the plague of Athens and in the same breath, in the same breath as Socrates speaks it, also teaches Socrates of Love. Postponing a plague through an economy of sacrifice—What's Love got to do with it? How does Diotima's profession of Love relate to a plague one can defer but not prevent: in what sense is Alcibiades the repressed in Diotima's speech, a speech that is bound to return and out itself? And to turn things inside out. Most notably Socrates.

Socrates' speech fails to offer teleological closure, but this is not only because Alcibiades rushes in upon the scene. Socrates' encomium, after all, is not his final word. In the last lines of the narrative that Aristodemus tells (through Apollodorus), we hear of yet another exchange long after the formal speeches:

> [Aristodemus] awoke toward dawn, as the cocks were crowing; and immediately he saw that all the company were either sleeping or gone, except Agathon, Aristophanes, and Socrates, who alone remained awake and were drinking out of a large vessel, from left to right; and Socrates was arguing with them. (223c)

Agathon who has just won the prize for his tragedies and Aristophanes, the writer of comedies, argue with Socrates.

> The substance of it was . . . that Socrates was driving them to the admission (*homologein*) that the same man could have the knowledge required for writing comedy and tragedy—that the fully skilled tragedian could be a comedian as well. (223d)[3]

These are the final words uttered by Socrates at the symposium, that the tragedian and comedian are forced to speak the same language. So, however staggering an enterprise it may be, let us not hesitate to listen to Alcibiades when he declares that Socrates' place is with the humorists, nor hesitate to read the serious where one would least expect it, within the speech of Alcibiades and even that of Aristophanes.

Alcibiades staggers in upon the scene and shares his Dionysian headdress with those serious and sober men, Agathon on one side, Socrates on the other. He agrees to add his eulogy to those that came before. But whereas his predecessors have all praised Eros, Alcibiades will insist on praising Socrates instead: Socrates in place of Eros—Socrates as the figure of Love. To be sure Socrates will embody the attributes Diotima has assigned to Eros. This is one of the commonplaces of the readings of the dialogue.

But as Socrates becomes a figure standing in for Love, more is at stake than even Socrates anticipated. In a sense we might have seen it coming. At least Socrates has already warned of the danger of such rhetorical moves. When Agathon concludes his speech to tumultuous applause, Socrates explains his reluctance to eulogize in turn. He compares Agathon's language to the rhetoric of Gorgias, the sophist. Just as Odysseus feared the Gorgon's head on his descent to Hades, so Socrates fears the eloquence of Gorgias that he hears in Agathon's speech.

> For [Agathon's] speech so reminded me of Gorgias that I was exactly in the plight described by Homer: I feared that Agathon in his final phrases would confront me with the eloquent Gorgias' head, and by opposing his speech to mine would turn me thus dumbfounded into stone. (198c)

No chance of this. Socrates goes on to speak at twice the length of anyone before him. The rhetorical figure that Socrates pretends to fear in the guise of Gorgias proliferates speech rather than deterring it: in the lines just read it is the rhetorical play on Gorgias and Gorgon that generates the passage.[4] Still, Socrates might well fear the transformation into statuary, he might well fear, as he puts it, being turned "dumbfounded into stone." For Alcibiades' similes will indeed leave Socrates something of a victim of Medusa's power after all, something of a figure in stone.

But let us not forget that Alcibiades is driven to his mode of speaking out of Love, both to his substitution of Socrates for Love and his substitution of other figures for that of Socrates. Love has everything to do with figuration in the *Symposium*. The opening line of Alcibiades' eulogy reads: "The way I shall take, gentlemen, in my praise of Socrates, is by similitudes [*eikonôn*, likenesses, images, similes]" (215a).[5] Alcibiades will speak of Socrates by generating images of him, and, as we shall see, by putting Socrates in a state to beget some images of his own.

If Alcibiades' love of Socrates engenders similes, if its point of departure is by way of images, there were already moments in Diotima's teachings that conceive the act of Love rather similarly. Love, she says, is a great spirit that, moving between the mortal and immortal, interprets (*hermêneuon*), puts into words, carries over messages, translates (202e). And Diotima calls the behavior of those that love a begetting: "All humans are pregnant," she tells Socrates (206c). "The pregnant approaches the beautiful [and] flows over with begetting and bringing forth" (206d). Love is not *of* the beautiful but an "engendering and begetting upon the beautiful" (206e). What Alcibiades in his love engenders are images of Socrates.

How shall we understand these similes? What can we in turn generate upon reading them? In what way is reading always a giving birth, a generation, if not quite reproduction? Love operates as an interpretation or translation and also an engendering. Before we read Alcibiades' particular delivery, we might dwell a bit longer with the more sober words of Socrates' mentor. They anticipate what we will find in the final speech.

> The mortal nature ever seeks, as best it can, to be immortal. In one way only can it succeed, and that is by generation; since so it can always leave behind it a new creature in place of the old. (207d)

This thrust toward immortality (which leaves behind the new in place of the old), this is what astonishes, at least until the close of Diotima's speech, promises incessant change rather than fixed "singularity of form" (211b). This is so on the one hand of the body of man, but no less of his soul and also of his knowledge. (207e)

> And here is a yet stranger fact: with regard to the possessions of knowledge, not merely do some of them grow and others perish in us, so that neither in what we know are we ever the same persons; but a like fate attends each single sort of knowledge. What we call *conning* [*meletan* from *meletaô*—to care for, attend to, study, practice speaking, declaim] implies that our knowledge is departing; since forgetfulness is an egress of knowledge, while conning substitutes a fresh one in place of that which departs, and so preserves our knowledge enough to make it seem the same. Every mortal thing is preserved in this way; not by keeping it exactly the same forever, like the divine, but by replacing what goes off or is antiquated with something fresh, in the semblance of the original. Through this device, Socrates, a mortal thing partakes of immortality, both in its body and in all other respects; *by no other means can it be done.* (207e–208b, emphasis added)

By no other means can the mortal partake of the immortal but by leaving behind something else, replacing that which goes off with something different, though similar to the original.

Love, according to Socrates' Diotima, then, functions as interpretation and a putting into words; also as an engendering or begetting, an engendering, however, that leaves the new in place of the old, "not only in the body but [also] in the soul" (207e) of man, and not only in these, but also in his knowledge and in "each single sort of knowledge," substituting the new, while forgetfulness befalls the old.

And have we not here an uncanny prefiguration of Alcibiades' declaration of love for Socrates, which substitutes Socrates for Eros, and then, in turn, similes for Socrates—a generation of images in which Alcibiades' declaiming leaves the original behind, a perpetual loss and moving beyond the object of love? By no other means can love take place, even if body, soul, knowledge, and Socrates are at stake.

Still, we are assured, Alcibiades speaks the truth. "I shall speak the truth," he proclaims. "If I say anything that is false, have the goodness to take me up short and say that there I am lying" (214e–215a). Socrates never breaks in upon Alcibiades' speech, although Alcibiades often repeats his invitation to contradict.

This speech of love, this speech of truth, then, begins, once again, for I have delayed it long enough, as follows:

> "The way I shall take, gentlemen, in my praise of Socrates, is by similitudes (*di' eikonôn*). Probably he will think I do this for derision; but I choose my similitude for the sake of truth, not of ridicule. For I say he is likest to the Silenus-figures that sit in the statuaries' shops (*en tois hermoglupheiois*); those, I mean, which our craftsmen make with pipes or flutes in their hands: when their two halves are pulled open, they are found to contain images of gods. And I further suggest that he resembles the satyr Marsyas." (215a–b)

The rhetorician, it seems, has indeed reared his gorgon head, turning Socrates, as the philosopher feared, "dumbfounded into stone" (198c). For Socrates from now on falls strangely silent, as well a statue might.[6]

And yet in the hand of these figures is the threat of an unwelcome sound, the pipes and flutes banished earlier in the dialogue, which have a certain history not only in the biography of Alcibiades but also in myth, indeed in a long tradition of Greek culture.[7] In Alcibiades' simile Socrates is transformed into something of a flute-girl, and a pregnant one at that, for when the two halves of the figure are pulled open, Alcibiades tells us,

we find them teeming with smaller statues within. The image begets images. Not just any images, however, but those that do honor to the gods.

Let us pause for a moment to say the obvious, to mark the similarity between the close of Diotima's speech and Alcibiades' figure that follows it.
Diotima, in her final words, embarks on a path that no longer simply replaces the old haphazardly with the new.[8] In an orderly hierarchical ascent
she leaves behind pregnancy of body for pregnancy of soul (208e–209a),
and the particular for the general, in the economy of sacrifice we read of
earlier that was temporarily able to defer the plague of Athens and perhaps
the plague of Love, till the "fair fruits of discourse and meditation [are
brought forth] in a plenteous crop of philosophy" (210d). Her ascending
ladder culminates in "a wondrous vision" (210e) of "divine beauty" (211e)
"existing ever in singularity of form" (211b) that "neither comes to be nor
perishes" (211a).[9] He who "behold[s] . . . divine beauty itself" (211e–212a),
she tells Socrates, becomes "dear to the gods" (212a).

Diotima marks out a "right and regular ascent" (210e) that valorizes
a fixed telos of the divine, which is also to say, the good:[10] Alcibiades
parodies this vertical ascent in a relation of outside to in. The "outward
casing"[11] (216d) of Socrates is like that of an ugly satyr, a creature usually
sunk in lust for another's bodily exterior; but inside is the serious, images
that are "divine and golden . . . perfectly fair and wondrous" (217a). Like
the speech of Diotima which culminates in the heights of divine beauty,
in becoming dear to the gods, Alcibiades' speech, then, will favor the
godly and inward over the exterior body. For Socrates, he will go on to
make clear, has no desire for the sensual body.

To be sure, Alcibiades is going nowhere with all this. His entrance on
the scene disrupts the regular and unilinear ascent of the speeches. From
the very beginning, moreover, he has claimed the right to recall what he
has to say haphazardly, to tell his reminiscences "one from one place another from another" (215a). For his intoxication makes it impossible to give
"a fluent and regular enumeration, one after another" (215a) of Socrates'
oddities (*atopian*, 215a, also 221d). At issue, however, is not merely the fact
that Alcibiades jumps from one eccentricity to another, that he seems to
speak in no special order, to compare Socrates to the Silenus figure and
Marsyas, to speak of Socrates' disinterest in physical love, his obliviousness
to hardship, his prolonged states of philosophical contemplation, his immense valor at war, and the apparent senselessness of his language. Such
jumping about disorders merely the external subject matter of Alcibiades'

line of argument. Let us open up and get inside his speech if only to see this first disorder pale in comparison. And so again . . .

> "The way I shall take . . . in my praise of Socrates, is by similitudes. Probably he will think I do this for derision; but I choose my similitude for the sake of truth, not of ridicule. For I say he is likest to the Silenus-figures that sit in the statuaries' shops . . . : when their two halves are pulled open, they are found to contain images of gods. And I further suggest that he resembles the satyr Marsyas." (215a–b)

The order the first simile imposes is unmistakable, as unmistakable, say, as the difference between ridicule and truth. On the outside Socrates may be ridiculous as Silenus, but within the statue we are sure to find the divine. This figure may seem deceptively laughable; but within, it is suggested, lies the truth. This is what Alcibiades' simile tells us, not only of Socrates, but implicitly of figures in general, as long as we are certain we can distinguish the outside from the inside, the figure's casing from its core. But are we certain we can do this when within the one, figural, statue we find, not something more intelligible or knowable, but rather a proliferation of statues? The images within the Silenic figure of Socrates are *agalmata*, a term with all the atopic[12] eccentricity of Socrates himself. *Agalma* means glory, delight, honor, and also a pleasing gift, especially for the gods, for that matter any statue or portrait, but also more specifically a statue in honor of a god, and then again an image that functions as an object of worship, taking the place of the god. You get the picture. The statue of Silenus gives birth to a multitudinous, if glorious, disruption of the structure necessary to make the simile meaningful, because the distinction between image and imaged is impossible to reify here.

In this manner also, Socrates, pictured by Alcibiades as pregnant with *agalmata*—glory, honor, and images of the gods—is about to give birth to *Diotima*. For the name *Diotima* suggests, it too, honor of the gods. But then we knew that Socrates had Diotima in his belly, he who ventriloquized her teaching, who spoke for her as he let her speak for him, as Plato, in turn, speaks for all concerned, although our knowledge of this is continually in egress. Belly-talk of the feminized, pregnant Socrates: it speaks honor to the gods by generating figures that speak honor to the gods, but never reaches them.

Moreover, no sooner does Alcibiades compare Socrates to a statue of the satyr Silenus than he compares him as well to the satyr Marsyas himself. "And I further suggest that he resembles the satyr Marsyas." How can Socrates resemble both a figural satyr and a satyr *tout court*? How can Socrates be both like the image and the thing imaged, given that what critically determines the figure, as Alcibiades would have it, is the difference between its deceptive exterior on the one hand and the something else and something elsewhere that it really figures? Can we ascribe this slide from the figure to the figured simply to Alcibiades' intoxication that breeds his tendency of taking his images "one from one place, another from another" (215a)? The moment he cons Socrates, the moment he practices speaking him, the knowledge gained by the first image seems to depart in that egress of knowledge that Diotima declares intrinsic to generation.

This is not merely the slide from the statue of Silenus to the satyr Marsyas himself. If Marsyas is introduced, apparently to corroborate the lesson of Silenus, nothing in Marsyas's tale produces quite the same effect as the split statue; for he is one of those unfortunates of Greek myth who chooses to challenge rather than to honor the gods, a threat to heaven and the good, rather than its celebration.[13]

Marsyas, as the myth goes, picked up the flute that Athene first cursed and then tossed aside.

> No sooner [had he] put [it] to his lips than it played of itself, inspired by the memory of Athene's music. . . . Apollo himself could not have made better music [his audience cried] and Marsyas was foolish enough not to contradict them. This, of course, provoked the anger of Apollo, who invited him to a contest.[14]

There Apollo calls upon Marsyas to do with his flute what Apollo does with his lyre, to turn the instrument upside down and play and sing at the same time. (Two versions of the same piece, perhaps not unlike the two similes that Alcibiades offers.) Marsyas, having failed the test, is turned, not upside down but inside out. For Apollo repays his victim for vying with heaven by flaying him alive and tacking his satyr's hide to a tree. Getting under the skin of the Silenus statues, Alcibiades' first simile, promises beauty and godliness, a ladder of ascent to the immortals: inversely, getting under the skin of Marsyas, Alcibiades' second simile, brings no golden interior, but proves, rather, that he who dares approach the realm of the gods, and by analogy Socrates, cannot, after all hope to be their equal. This is the lesson as well of Aristophanes' circle men.

The two similes are clearly at odds with one another. If from the perspective of myth the double figuring of Socrates is impossible to figure out, no doubt we should leave tradition behind and listen rather to Alcibiades' explanation of the comparison.

> Are you not a piper? Why, yes, and a far more marvelous one than the satyr. His lips indeed had power to entrance mankind by means of instruments. . . . You differ from him in one point only—that you produce the same effect with simple prose unaided by instruments. (215b–c)

We must forget then what myth teaches us, that the logics of inside and out in the two comparisons between the Silenus statue and Marsyas are hardly similar, that the doubling of the figures for Socrates engenders lessons in which figuring cannot get it straight. But Alcibiades, it seems, had in mind to insist, rather, on Socrates' superiority to Marsyas, Socrates who made his music unaided by any instrument, or rather Socrates who speaks prose rather than playing music. At least Alcibiades makes no claim for Socrates that, like Apollo, he can perform both.

But Socrates' words, we read, do have something in common with Marsyas's tunes after all. Athene's pipes, once put to the lips, seem to play themselves, making the paltry flute-girl interchangeable with Marsyas, and Marsyas, as we know, interchangeable with Socrates.

> [Marsyas's] lips indeed had power to entrance mankind . . . a thing still possible to-day for anyone who can pipe his tunes: . . . So that if anyone, whether a fine flute-player or paltry flute-girl, can but flute his tunes, they have no equal for exciting a ravishment. . . . (215c)

And so it is with Socrates. The power to entrance mankind lies not in the man, but in the words which, like the tunes that Marsyas plays, take on a life independent of their source.

> You produce the same effect with simple prose unaided by instruments. . . . So soon as we hear you, or your discourses in the mouth of another,—though such person be ever so poor a speaker . . . we are all astounded and entranced. (215c–d)

Socrates is a "far more marvelous" piper than the satyr, producing his effect unaided by instruments, a superiority attributable, then, to his independence from anything outside him. And yet if Socrates can do without an instrument to produce his discourses, his words, in turn, are able to do without him, wandering off to other speakers, using the instruments of other voices with no loss in power. Not unlike the manner in which Diotima's discourse has used the voice of Socrates, a discourse of honor to the gods that speaks from the belly of the philosopher and also of the Silenus figure. Socrates' words astound and entrance even in the mouths of those no better than the paltry flute players who were banished from the scene of the symposium and of serious philosophy. They return again and again, not least where we least expect them, in the place of Socrates.

But then again, if Socrates' words can be effectively uttered by any speaker, if he can be replaced by just about anyone, still, Alcibiades continues, he is un-comparable to any human, living or dead.[15]

> There are many more quite wonderful things that one could find to praise in Socrates: but although there would probably be as much to say about any other one of his habits, I select his unlikeness to anybody else, whether in the ancient or in the modern world, as calling for our greatest wonder. . . . With the odd (*tên atopian*) qualities of this person, both in himself and in his conversation, you would not come anywhere near finding a comparison if you searched either among men of our day or among those of the past, unless perhaps you borrowed my words and matched him, not with any human being, but with the Silenuses and satyrs, in his person and his speech. (221c–d)

The eccentricity of Socrates is such, his a-topicality (out-of-placeness), the inability to find a place for him, that he cannot be compared to or imaged by any other human being, despite the earlier conclusion of Socrates' infinite interchangeability with everyone to which the simile of Marsyas leads us. If you wish to find a simile for him, a medium in which to con Socrates, best to borrow Alcibiades' words—evidently as lendable as those of his beloved—and compare him both to the Silenus-statues and to satyrs, with all the incompatibility between the two that we have seen those double similes to generate; with all the disruption of the power of both figuring and naming that the mutual exclusiveness of those figures brings about.

Still, it is not only Socrates' person but also his speech that resembles the statues of Silenus.

> For there is a point I omitted when I began—how his talk most of all resembles the Silenuses that are made to open. If you chose to listen to Socrates' discourses you would feel them at first to be quite ridiculous; on the outside

they are clothed with such absurd words and phrases—all, of course, the hide of a mocking satyr. (221d–e)

Getting under the skin of Alcibiades' speech has been no easy experience. Here Alcibiades invites us to get under the skin of Socrates' words, just as we opened up the statues of Silenus to find the golden images of the gods within.

> When these are opened, and you obtain a fresh view of them by getting inside, first of all you will discover that they are the only speeches which have any sense in them; and secondly, that none are so divine, so rich in images of virtue, so largely—nay, so completely—intent on all things proper for the study of such as would attain both grace and worth. (222a)

Divine images of virtue are no surprise here—only, perhaps, in Alcibiades' description, how these discourses are clothed, covered over, and hidden.[16]

> If you chose to listen to Socrates' discourses you would feel them at first to be quite ridiculous; on the outside they are clothed with such absurd words and phrases—all, of course, the hide of a mocking satyr. His talk is of pack-asses, smiths, cobblers, and tanners, and he seems always to be using the same terms for the same things; so that anyone inexpert and thoughtless might laugh his speeches to scorn. (221e–222a)

What is Socrates talking about? What is Alcibiades, as he takes Socrates' images, talking about in turn? What are they trying to hide with their "absurd words and phrases" as if under the "hide of a mocking satyr"? Alcibiades implies that though what meets the eye or ear in Socrates' speeches seems senseless, if we get under the skin of this discourse, what lies underneath is totally different—rich in divinity, virtue, and sense, like those golden figures within the Silenuses.[17] But let us not go for the gold quite so precipitously.

Pack-asses, smiths, cobblers, and tanners. This is the non-sense one might laugh to scorn or which one might even disregard, searching for something utterly different within. But asses, smiths, cobblers and tanners hang together, though the relation of smiths to asses is one thing, that of tanners and shoemakers to asses quite another. If the smith, practicing the profession of Hephaestus, shoes animals similar to the ass, the ass, by way of tanner and cobbler, shoes or clothes others, in this strangest of dialogues, where being shod and unshod, covered and uncovered, is a recurrent topos.[18] It is simply a question of getting under the ass's hide, not unlike Apollo at his contest with Marsyas. These "absurd words and phrases" that clothe the discourses of Socrates and Alcibiades lead us less to wondrous golden images of the gods, less to "images of virtue" (222a) than to an ironic reverberation of the structure of similes (skin on the outside, something else, or perhaps violent deformation, within) whose contradictions and repetition we seem unable to escape.

A reverberation as well of that other, earlier speech one tends to laugh to scorn, the myth that Aristophanes relates. The Silenuses of Alcibiades propagate a multitude of golden images within: forever being opened, their breaking in two promises access to the divine toward which Diotima's ladder to the harvest of philosophy also led. But in Aristophanes' narration, the slicing, first of the circle men to produce two-legged creatures, and then of the two-legged creatures into figures like statuary on tombs, is of another order.

For the *Symposium*, like the statues of Silenus, propagates within itself a multitude of images, clothed not unlike the speeches of Socrates in apparently "absurd words and phrases." Returning to Aristophanes, similarities strike us at every turn. Still the connections are uneasy ones. And Aristophanes' speech is about uneasy connections, about disconnections, about wounds potentially as incurable as those of Marsyas. Punctuated as it is with a vocabulary of cutting, slicing, cleaving, the comedian's speech tells a rather tragic tale.

Aristophanes' famous myth of the circle men speaks of an originary doubled human figure hacked in two by Zeus for "scheming to assault the gods in fight" and attempting "to mount high heaven" (190c).

> Then Zeus . . . spake at length and said: . . . I propose now to slice every one of them in two, so that while making them weaker we shall find them more useful by reason of their multiplication; and they shall walk erect upon two legs. (190c–d)

Aristophanes goes on to say:

> We may well be afraid that if we are disorderly toward Heaven we may once more be cloven asunder and may go about in the shape of those outline-carvings on the tombs, with our noses sawn down the middle, and may thus become like tokens of split dice. (193a)

Zeus's standing threat (193a), should humans attempt the ascent to heaven once more,[19] is to cut us asunder yet again, like the bas-reliefs on tombs.

Aristophanes' myth, like Alcibiades' first simile and like the gorgon of whom Socrates spoke, turns the human to statues of stone. But whereas the cracking open of the Silenus figure generates images in honor of the gods, apparently, at least, connecting him to the divine, promising immortality, the double slicing of the circle men results from a failure to give the gods their due and reminds us of our mortality. Alcibiades, like Socrates and Diotima before him, spoke of pregnancy in relation to production and plenitude, a generation of excess from the belly—as voice, as image, as image of the image—but the Silenus figures that break open in the middle are not without an ominous resonance. Aristophanes' mythical figures, at the site of their wound, above all experience loss, lack.[20] As in the language of Socrates, here too the cobbler has his place, but he fashions a center that marks disconnection from the locus of birth, a wound one is forced to contemplate.

> So saying, [Zeus] sliced each human being in two . . . and at the cleaving of each he bade Apollo turn its face and half-neck to the section side, in order that every one might be made more orderly by the sight of the knife's work upon him; this done, the god was to heal them up. Then Apollo turned their faces about, and pulled their skin together from the edges over what is now called the belly . . . ; the little opening he tied up in the middle of the belly, so making what we know as the navel. For the rest, he smoothed away most of the puckers and figured out the breast with some such instrument as shoemakers use in smoothing the wrinkles of leather on the last; though he left here a few [wrinkles] which we have just about the belly and navel, to remind us of our early fall. (190d–191a)

This cobbler reminds us that, cut open as we are, we resemble the Silenus figures far less than Marsyas. For Marsyas too challenged the heavens, and more specifically Apollo, the very god who works equally well, it seems, both in techniques of flaying and de-flaying, in cobbling the human back together, so that by a turn of the face we might remember the wound.

～

But perhaps there is an out, an outside at least, a realm beyond this. Perhaps it is there we must seek the sobriety so threatened by the figurations of Alcibiades and their echoes in the speech of Aristophanes. If one wants, as Alcibiades puts it, to make "speeches which have any sense in them" (222a) I see now in which direction one is bound to go. For rather than whirling around in any direction one pleases, like Aristophanes' circle men before they are sliced in two, and like Alcibiades who follows images here and their reverberations there as I have been doing, doesn't making sense depend on a proper sense of direction, on knowing where one should go and where one shouldn't? Surely this is the lesson of Aristophanes' myth that warns about the error of attempting the ascent to heaven. As surely as it is also the lesson of Diotima's finale that, perhaps paradoxically, recommends that very route.

This is a tale of another student, Stanley Rosen, and his mentor, Leo Strauss, one that shuts the Silenus figures, one that closes the door on Alcibiades, keeping him and his cronies behind closed doors, a reading in which the intoxication of figure is replaced by the rigid designations of historical fact.[21] For what, if not history, at least in its most naïve linguistic emanation, could claim to stand outside the complexities of figuration we have encountered. No doubt "history" makes sense, depending as it does on a proper sense of direction, on knowing which way one is going. It gives one directions as clearly as the herms referred to in Plato's *Hipparchus*.

And isn't there a fixed or fixable truth also to be located with respect to the *Symposium*, if only we know where to seek it? On the streets of historical Athens, Socrates, as he began his speech, gave us some guidelines when he spoke of a truth uttered, it seems, unproblematically "in whatsoever style of terms and phrases [that] may chance to occur by the way" (199b). And if Diotima's first teachings had us moving rather endlessly back and forth *between*—"between understanding and ignorance" (202a)—in acts of interpretation and translation, did she not ultimately promise unidirectionality, "a certain single knowledge" (210d)?[22] As in the *Republic* at the close of Book VI, the culmination of Socrates' speech points, we saw, to a realm beyond figuration. To be sure, Diotima's sense of a knowledge gained through sacrifice of the particular couldn't be farther from the turn to history, that other way to escape figuration that I am here proposing. Conventional history, rather than moving from the particular to the general, to the eternal singularity of form, guarantees the particular, adequate re-presentation. You will understand what might compel a literary theorist nowadays to turn to historical fact. If the purely serious, what really counts, lies outside the confines of the *Symposium*, it is perhaps in history that we can find it. Moreover, in this manner, finally, we might leave those images behind that set limits at every juncture, these statues with their ominous threats of being opened up and cut in two, those mutilations performed by angry gods on satyrs and humans alike.

The long opening passage situates the symposium a decade and a half after the 430 plague of Athens. Its events are narrated a decade and a half later by Apollodorus, and written by Plato yet another decade and a half later, shortly after 385, inevitably with all the hindsight of the intervening years. Readers of the *Symposium* often, but usually in passing, place the dialogue in its historical setting, for it takes place, they remind us, at a critical crossroads of Athenian history, at which another plague of Athens cannot be deferred. The banquet is usually situated by classical scholars in 416 BC, or perhaps a year later. A year later the city of Athens is in turmoil. The year 416, almost all agree, is the date dictated by Agathon's triumph at the dramatic competition[23] repeatedly referred to in the dialogue. Alcibiades is also at the height of his political power, but a height from which he is shortly destined to fall.[24] A year from now he will become the embodiment of a threat to the gods and a threat to the state, a staggering burlesque of betrayal on betrayal. It is this proximity to crisis that Plato's readers sense, but dare not read.

Or did the symposium, fictional or actual, take place just a bit later in 415? It makes all the difference from Alcibiades' point of view. Leo Strauss, in unpublished lectures,[25] as Stanley Rosen writes, places it on a night that no Athenian could forget, on the eve of the Sicilian expedition, the night of the "mutilation of the Herms." Alcibiades was subsequently charged with this sacrilege and with others as well, and, in absentia, condemned to death. Strauss, naming that fateful night as the date of the symposium, claims that Plato's intention is to prove Alcibiades' innocence. The symposium within or rather Alcibiades' encomium becomes an alibi for the monstrous crime without.

Our turn to history surrounds the tale of Plato's dialogue with crime.[26] It is an answer of sorts to the preoccupation with the good in Socrates' discourse and to the question of honor and dishonor to the gods, especially in those of Alcibiades and Aristophanes.[27] In 415, then, an ethical crisis takes place as radical threat to the state and as a religious transgression of the most critical kind that rends Athenian society. Mutilation of the Herms.

But what are Herms whose disfigurement brought on this second plague of Athens, a plague of accusation, lies, false testimony, banishment, execution, chaos? The Herms were sacred figures, "so common in the doorways of private houses and temples."[28] Used in earliest times as boundary marks,[29] they were set up at crossroads as guides to direction along the road, pointing the traveler toward an ultimate destination. They were marked in the fifth century, as Socrates in the *Hipparchus* reminds us, with an inscription in the stone.[30] Nowhere were they more abundant or more venerated than in Athens, not only at all entrance ways but in the agora, on the Acropolis, virtually everywhere.[31] And "so great was the demand for these works [in Athens] that the words *hermogluphos* . . . and *hermoglupheion* [became generic terms] for a sculptor."[32] This is a variation of the term Alcibiades uses when he speaks of the makers of the Sileni: "he is likest to the Silenus-figures that sit in the statuaries' shops (*en tois hermoglupheiois*)"[33] (215b). Socrates in his relation to figuration, therefore, is not untouched by the question of the Herms.

The Herms consisted of four-sided pillars which in the fifth century terminated, generally, in a head of Hermes. The most rudimentary representation, one might say, of the male form, all the more so since its only distinguishing feature, other than its inscription, was what one source in polite Victorian language calls "the significant mark of the male sex."[34] Figuration of the human, then, as a simple quadrangular pillar[35] topped by a head and adorned by an erect phallus. These reappear in Aristophanes' myth as the parts of the anatomy, head and genitals, that Zeus, in his anger, on the one hand, and in his pity on the other, has Apollo turn to the front of the sliced circle-men.

On the night before the Sicilian expedition, proposed and co-led by Alcibiades, almost every Herm in Athens is attacked. The state is violently threatened by this act of iconoclasm. The perpetrators are never definitively named. Thucydides, in his, the most famous, account of this outrageous act of impiety, writes: "In the midst of these preparations all the stone Hermae in the city of Athens, that is to say the customary square figures, so common in the doorways of private houses and temples, had in one night most of them their faces mutilated."[36] Perhaps the crime was actually castration of the Herms.[37] Thucydides speaks of mutilation of the face, but modern interpreters wish to understand that face as a figure for the phallus. Face and phallus. Interchangeability of the only two distinguishing features on the otherwise simple pillars of stone: mutilation of the face, which in Aristophanes' speech takes cognizance of the cut, mutilation of the genitals, source of generation, which Zeus had brought round to the front in compensation for the loss man suffers in his split state.

The Herms are the simplest of monuments, monuments in a sense to the possibility of figuration in general, as the generalization of the term "herm" to mean "statuary" suggests. Monuments as well to the honor of the gods. In 415 great violence is done to unproblematic figuration, as in Alcibiades' similes: great violence is done as well to the honor of the gods. Therein lies the sacrilege. The *Symposium*, too, turns around these issues, for the entire topic for the evening's conversation as proposed by Eriximachus and Phaedrus, is to do proper honor to the god of Love. That honor to the god has been disrupted, at least complicated, in the byways that inscripted figurations take in the discourse of the participants.[38] The sacrilege on the streets of Athens is rehearsed at Agathon's symposium in a theatrical performance far more threatening than the actual iconoclasm of 415.[39]

The turn to history promises a move beyond the confines and involutions of figuration, but history gives us, it too, a slice of life that returns us abruptly to all the issues we have seen the dialogue to raise. The story history tells is not an escape from, but of a piece with the dialogue. On the night of violence, as Plutarch puts it, "The Hermae [were found] in a single night [to have] had their faces and forms disfigured"[40]—just as figuration, as we have read it in the *Symposium*, attacked in its logic, becomes at odds with itself.

Truth to tell, Hermes must haunt any reading of the *Symposium* from beginning to end.[41] For the Herm was erected not only to honor the god, but also as a marker of boundaries, and the definer of the difference between exterior and interior, so important in Alcibiades' monologue. How can we forget that whereas Socrates, at least at the beginning of the dialogue, had to be coaxed repeatedly over Agathon's threshold, Alcibiades' contaminating entry is quite another matter. He first appears, just outside the door of the house, in the place of the Herm, a force of invasion. Nor can we limit the name of this danger to Alcibiades alone. For after Alcibiades completes his speech, the disruption of the household border, perhaps no longer marked by a Herm, takes place once again.

> Suddenly a great crowd of revelers arrived at the door, which they found just opened for someone who was going out. They marched straight into the party

and seated themselves: the whole place was in an uproar and, losing all order, they were forced to drink a vast amount of wine. (223b)

It is here that Socrates himself will come to insist on the almost indifference of what seems mutually exclusive, comedy and tragedy.

The symposium, then, is a parallel world to the seemingly historical, factual world located just outside it. Contra Leo Strauss, Agathon's house, his name notwithstanding, is no privileged space of innocence. If Alcibiades' monologue, with all its reverberations, performs anything, it is the inevitable overlap of those disparate realms we tend to call Platonic dialectic, figure, and history. This may be the same as saying that Hermes need not be mutilated to pose the threat that Thucydides, the historian, describes. For Hermes is at play in Plato, and especially in the *Symposium*, as a linguistic force that need not be embodied in stone. Such are the disclosures when one labors to get under the skin of a Platonic dialogue, opening it up here and there to show the figures inside, while at the same time producing others.

§ 3 Subversions of the Political: Plato's *Republic*

> We shall always keep to the upper road. . . . (621c)
>
> In order to get the finest possible look at these things another and longer road around would be required. (504b)
>
> Don't you call this journey dialectic? (532b)

The Underground

It is a commonplace—one with which we will endlessly have to come to terms—that when Plato opens the *Republic* Socrates is out of bounds.[1] Leaving the city behind, Socrates goes down to the Piraeus, the port of Athens, for the festival of a Thracian deity (327a). Bendis, goddess of the underworld, native of Hades, appears on the shores of the Athenian port, miles outside the city. Socrates *"goes down"* to offer prayers to the foreign invader.[2] We read of this departure in the opening line of the dialogue, a dialogue and yet a narrative after all, told exclusively in the voice of Socrates. This is as it should be, for in Book III Socrates will dramatically rail against the dangers of assuming the voice of another, which can only result in turning thought elsewhere, leading it astray (393a–b).[3] Socrates narrates, or does he? "I went down" (*katebên* [327a]).[4] Socrates, citing Homer, speaks surreptitiously in the voice of Odysseus as the hero recites his descent into hell. Odysseus has come here, perhaps Socrates too, to seek advice for the homeward journey.[5] Tiresias warns him not to offend Helios, god of the sun. This is "all the truth" (*Odyssey,* XI, 107) the blind seer has to offer.[6] Inevitably Odysseus, nonetheless, will do so. Inevitably Socrates will do so too; for who can avoid crossing paths with the sun, however wrong a turn this may be?

Socrates has gone underground, joined the underground we might claim, violating the rules of state at the very moment he sets out to constitute it.[7] Socrates creates a new polis in speech, in which strict, if not totalitarian hierarchy of the classes will mirror that of the individual soul, governed by calculation, reason, speech. Along the way of its creation, which is also the way of analogy, Socrates sets up the revolutionary underground, an underground as the counterforce to the not so secret policing on which the polis is founded. His return to the upper world, which is and is not that of Athens,[8] is interrupted. Like Orpheus, the prototypical poet, whom the philosopher would surely have banned from the city, willingly or not Socrates is seduced into turning around. And turning around—this cannot escape the reader, nor can the reader escape it[9]—has everything to do with the *Republic*.

Perhaps Plato stands behind us as we read Socrates' narrative, whispering to us to picture, or so we imagine we hear, Socrates' subterranean stories. It is a call to get our fill of the shades and shadows he casts. No doubt we should be disgusted and turn away. Socrates may fail to notice, but the desire inevitably overwhelms us to make common cause with what reason and speech declare must *not* be done. Perhaps there is something down below of which Socrates too cannot get his fill. Perhaps a part of him desires; would that be too strong to say? Perhaps a certain spiritedness, which Socrates will sometimes speak of as the seat of rage (375a–e), perhaps a certain *thumos* on his part, does not serve his reason well.[10] In any case, Socrates interrupts his ascent. This is where the dialogue takes place between Socrates and his interlocutors. The in-between, between the Piraeus and Athens, between Hades and the upper realm, becomes the locus of the dialogue.[11]

And who could not see that the underground and its sub-versive activities are all the rage in the *Republic*? Not only because it opens beneath Athens with reverence offered to the goddess of the underworld; not only because its central passage, the one that captivates every reader, is the allegory of the cave; not only because it closes, or fails to, with the myth of Er and his enigmatic tour of the world of shades.[12] Plato punctuates the dialogue with these and other subterranean moments, storied passages which we will have to explore, storied, because the underground is inevitably bound to telling tales. But this simplistic, because thematic, preoccupation with the underground, the image of the underground, cannot begin to account for the declivities of Socrates' narrative.

Power, Persuasion, Eristic

"Legend has it that Plato rewrote the opening section of the *Republic* ten times."[13] Whereas Socrates pretends to let the argument go wherever it might,[14] Plato, it seems, was determined to control its direction, an indication that we too, as readers, must follow every turn of phrase. Caught in a space between city and not city, in a nether world that equivocates as well at the boundary of individual human life, Socrates is stopped dead in his tracks.

> Catching sight of us from afar as we were pressing homewards, Polemarchus, son of Cephalus, ordered his slave boy to run after us and order us to wait for him. The boy took hold of my cloak from behind and said, "Polemarchus orders you to wait."
>
> And I turned around and asked him where his master was. . . .
>
> A moment later Polemarchus came along. . . . Polemarchus said, "Socrates, I guess you two are hurrying to get away to town."
>
> "That's not a bad guess," I said.
>
> "Well, . . . do you see how many of us there are?"
>
> "Of course."
>
> "Well, then," he said, "either prove stronger than these men or stay here." (327b–c)

For the moment it is an issue of master and slave, of who is stronger, of power. But it is also an issue of the force of language: it is these that will preoccupy Socrates and keep him below.

> "Isn't there still one other possibility . . . ," I said, "our persuading you that you must let us go?"
>
> "Could you really persuade," he said, "if we don't listen?" (327c)

Irrefutably, Allan Bloom has gotten it right: "the first fact is brute force," he writes, a brute force, we might add, that is calculable, measurable as number ("do you see how many of us there are?"). "There is a confrontation here between wisdom, as represented by Socrates, and power, as represented by Polemarchus," Bloom continues,[15] as though wisdom and power in the *Republic* were incompatible. And yet, it will soon go without saying that the so-called philosophical voice (as though Plato might have spoken with a single tongue!), what Bloom terms "wisdom," is not necessarily devoid of power. It is not coincidental that this passage, seemingly about an incidental state of relative strength among its characters, should introduce a treatise about state power in its relation to philosophy. These cannot be separated out into discrete forms.

Cephalus, father of Polemarchus, welcomes Socrates to his home. Here the road to Hades, up till now metaphorical, becomes the more literal topic of discussion.

> "For my part, Cephalus, I am really delighted to discuss with the very old," I said. "Since they are like men who have proceeded on a certain road that perhaps we too will have to take, one ought . . . to learn from them what sort of road it is. . . . From you in particular I should like to learn how it looks to you, for you are now at just the time of life the poets call 'the threshold of old age.'" (328d–e)[16]

Still, Socrates refuses to go where Cephalus hopes to lead him. "Pleasures . . . connected with the body," the old man says, "wither away in me" and "the desires and pleasures that have to do with speeches grow the more" (328d). Thus for those who "are orderly and content with themselves" "it is possible to be rid of very many mad masters" (329d). Cephalus speaks, almost, in the voice of that other master, this one by no means mad; for is this not the lesson that Socrates teaches, a mastering of desire in the name of order, a rejection of desire and pleasure in the name of speeches (*logous*)?[17]

And yet Socrates, preferring disputation, it seems, will link Cephalus's bearing in old age, rather, to his wealth. How are we to understand this willful shift away from potential and seemingly inevitable agreement to the question of money, possession, accounting? For Plato has Socrates' interlocutor, now pressed to it, redefine his relation to death in a manner calculated to bring on Socrates' disapproval—in terms of reckonings, both moral and monetary, the moral as monetary:

> "The tales told about what is in Hades—that the one who has done unjust deeds here must pay the penalty there—at which he laughed up to then, now make his soul twist and turn because he fears they might be true. . . . [He] reckons up his accounts and considers whether he has done anything unjust to anyone." (330d–e)

This begins the long discussion of justice that will occupy several books of the dialogue. If injustice in this world, according to Cephalus's reformulation, is assessed unproblematically by a reckoning of accounts, a payback in the next,[18] the system seems summed up in Simonides' proposal "That it is just to give to each what is owed" (331e).

Socrates refutes this definition with the following example: "everyone would surely say that if a man takes weapons from a friend when the latter is of sound mind, and the friend demands them back when he is mad . . . the man who gave them back would not be just" (331c). The argument meanders where it will, but its point of departure, the lurking possibility of madness at every turn, the threat of violence, and the argument's continual return to the deposit and counting of gold and money, its culmination in the admission of Polemarchus (who has taken over the argument from his father) that he no longer knows what he means (334b), its final truth that "it is never just to harm anyone" (335e), all these are not coincidental.

In Cephalus's concept of injustice, in Polemarchus's concept of justice, what is it, however surreptitiously, that falls victim to Socrates' future argument? To be sure, silver and gold, currency of a material kind, will be pollution for the guardians of the idealized polis to come (416e, 417a). But it is not only the fall into desire for wealth that is on the line here, even before the city is envisioned, but also seductive concepts of reckoning and adequation: justice as depositing and paying back in equal measure. What seems comparable and according to measure is threatened with a madness that may alter the nature of what is deposited. Nothing is, necessarily, equivalent to itself.

The potential for violence is in the hands of the madman but Socrates shifts it to the population at large: the discussion of justice, Socrates goes on to say, requires a control of all violence to the other, requires that harm be done to no one, not even one's enemies in order to pay back injury.

> "Then it is not the work of the just man to harm either a friend or anyone else. . . . Then if someone asserts that it's just to give what is owed to each man—and he understands by this that harm is owed to enemies by the just man and help to friends—the man who said it was not wise. For he wasn't telling the truth. For it has become apparent to us that it is never just to harm anyone."
>
> "I agree," he said.

How are we to reconcile this conclusion with the lines that immediately follow?

"We shall do battle then as partners, you and I," I said, "if someone asserts that
Simonides, or Bias, or Pittacus or any other wise and blessed man said it."

"I, for one," he said, "am ready to be your partner in the battle." (335d–e)

The disparity between the physical and the philosophical is not a slip of
the stylus. Contradiction of this sort is never, simply, unwilling. It is this
disparity that opened the dialogue in the confrontation between Socrates
and Polemarchus (327c). Polemarchus and Socrates, somewhat fatuously,
declare their eagerness for philosophical battle. With heavy-handed irony
the aggression that is banned in the physical world finds a welcome place
in philosophical discussion. This is a call to battle, to do harm to one's
enemies, Bloom's commentary on the difference between wisdom and the
power of brute force notwithstanding.

The rest of Book I, the beginning of Book II, perhaps all of the *Republic*, speaks about justice and the polis, but also speaks to the issue of how
the dialogue is to be conducted. The relation between the two is always
challenging, unpredictable, and cannot be ignored. If Socrates declares
the argument a state of war ("we shall do battle then . . . "), in retrospect,
we are forced to note that the mode of Socrates' arguments until now has
already been a series of battles, of ever-renewed eristic attack.

This is a mode of argumentation soon to be set aside. A number of stories are told of this shift away from eristic. Plato is rumored to have written the first book of the *Republic* as a dialogue entitled the *Thrasymachus*,
which he then chose to abandon.[19] The *Republic*, it is said, marks a turning point, mid-dialogue, for just here Plato moves from his first period
to his middle period and this entails a shift from eristic to the dialectical
form of argument.[20] What are we to make then of the early eristic encounters? Are we to imagine that Plato, writing in the name of that thinker
who declares only the examined life worth living,[21] having engaged in
eristic and subsequently seen the error of his ways, found himself unable,
somehow, to return and expunge his earlier text? Is it a question of a false
start? Did he casually step into his "middle period," too oblivious, too
lazy, too busy to rewrite Book I? In the *Republic*, hardly timid in its many
calls to expunge, repress, and expel offensive texts,[22] the opening pages
remain as Plato's monument to a mode of struggle we ignore at our peril.
Thrasymachus's accusations notwithstanding, this abrupt switch from eristic to dialectic is something Socrates does and does not talk about, never
openly, and only belatedly, condemning eristic in the name of dialectic,

as though the first never had a part to play earlier in the dialogue. For just four books later, he is contemptuous of such face-offs.

Book V of the dialogue has this to say of eristic. It is at a critical moment when Socrates all but surrenders the hierarchical position of men in Greek society, wishing to argue that women are the equal of men in the polis, almost.[23] (It is this "almost" to which we will have to return.)

> "Oh, Glaucon, I said, "the power of the contradicting art is grand."
>
> "Why so?"
>
> "Because," I said, "in my opinion, many fall into it even unwillingly and suppose they are not quarreling but discussing (*ouk erizein alla dialegesthai*), because they are unable to consider what's said by separating it out into its forms (*kat' eidê diairoumenoi*). They pursue contradiction in the mere name (*auto to onoma*) of what's spoken about, using eristic, not dialectic, (*eridi, ou dialektôi*) with one another."
>
> "This is surely what happens to many," he said. "But this doesn't apply to us too at present, does it?"
>
> "It most certainly does," I said. "At least we run the risk of unwillingly dealing in contradiction (*antilogias*)."
>
> "How?"
>
> "Following the name alone, we courageously, and eristically, insist. . . ."
>
> (454a–b)

The exchanges of Book I (which tellingly begin with Polemarchus's posturing as the stronger) are eristic, celebrations of the art of confutation, of *elenkhos*, a testing for the purpose of disproof[24] (LS). Socrates forces first Cephalus, then Polemarchus, then Thrasymachus into a state of contradiction: he wins each round by attacking both the opponent and his position, marking these as exterior to himself and the realm of truth.[25] To be sure, it is not here, in the course of eristic argument, but only later that the nature of justice is actually brought to light. As a gesture of refutation, of proving what is *not* the case, eristic battle leads exclusively to dead ends of non-knowledge (331d, 335d).[26] It remains forever incapable of producing what *is*. Polemarchus admits he did not know what he meant (334b); Thrasymachus's argument about the just is "turned around in the opposite direction" (343a). Eristic goes by way of doing harm to one's friends, as though they were enemies.[27]

The act of contra-diction leaves one side of the argument abandoned and irrecuperably dishonored. Eristic, rather brutally, produces winners and losers; and yet it somewhat paradoxically maintains both the loser's

identity and what is refuted as positional differences precisely in the moment of rebuttal. Dialectic will be something else altogether. A discussing,
rather than quarrelling and quibbling, dialectic is a "separating . . . out
into . . . forms" (454a) in which the integrity of the object contemplated
nevertheless remains, remarkably, unthreatened. It takes in all otherness
of the interlocutors, a seemingly benign movement of assimilation to the
same, in the name of the ever so slightly different.[28] This discourse, dialectic, moreover produces the gentle, if saccharin agreement of Socrates'
often indistinguishable disciples, who, in the words of Thrasymachus, act
something like fools, making way for him—whose voices give forth the
embarrassing choruses of "Most certainly," "Plainly," "Right," "Quite so"
(464–65)[29] that echo throughout the *Republic*. It is these forms, eristic and
dialectic, and perhaps one or two more, which we must separate out, if
not quite dialectically, then as best we can.

But dialectic is not yet the mode of discussion, and never less so, it
would seem, than when Thrasymachus disrupts the discussion, toward
the end of Book I, threatening to strike Socrates dumb: "I think if I had
not seen him before he saw me, I would have been speechless" (336d).[30]
Just when Polemarchus and Socrates agree to do battle against anyone
who asserts "it is . . . just to harm anyone," Thrasymachus goes on the
attack. His intervention may be violent, a simulacrum of eristic, but his
insistence, nevertheless, is that Socrates give up refutation and say outright what justice is:

> Now Thrasymachus had many times started out to take over the argument
> in the midst of our discussion, but he had been restrained by the men sitting
> near him. . . . But when we paused and I said this, he could no longer keep
> quiet; hunched up like a wild beast, he flung himself at us as if to tear us to
> pieces (*diarpasomenos*). Then both Polemarchus and I got all in a flutter from
> fright. And he shouted out into our midst and said, "What is this nonsense
> that has possessed you for so long, Socrates? And why do you act like fools
> making way for one another? If you truly want to know what the just is, don't
> only ask and gratify your love of honor by refuting whatever someone an-
> swers—you know that it is easier to ask than to answer—but answer yourself
> and say what you assert the just to be." (336b–c)

Socrates does not do this, at least not here, not now. His love of honor in
battle is matched only by his lust for dishonoring. He will not give up eristic. He is sidetracked from the question of what justice is, as he himself

will finally admit: getting a hold of the arguments, pulling and tearing at them one after another like a puppy, misusing them always to contradict Thrasymachus, who called on him, precisely, not to refute.[31]

> Before finding out what we were considering at first—what the just is—I let go of that and pursued the consideration of whether it is vice and lack of learning, or wisdom and virtue. . . . I could not restrain myself from leaving the other one and going after this one, so that now as a result of the discussion I know nothing. (354b–c)

Socrates' confession closes Book I: still, what precedes it is hardly beside the point. Whereas Socrates declines a definition of justice, Thrasymachus all too willingly offers one: "The just is nothing other than the advantage of the stronger" (338c), by which he suggests that the just is whatever the stronger deems it to be. "The ruler, insofar as he is a ruler . . . sets down what is best for himself" (340e–341a). We might put it another way and say: "the stronger" controls "the mere name of what's spoken about" (454a), which, according to Socrates, is the key weapon of eristic struggle.

Perhaps this is clearest in a critical reversal in Thrasymachus's language. He has lost a significant round to his opponent. Socrates' narrative retelling declares that he has "turned [his opponent's argument] in the opposite direction" (343a). At this point Thrasymachus becomes particularly belligerent:

> "And you are so far off about the just and justice, and the unjust and injustice, that you are unaware that justice and the just are really someone else's good, the advantage of the man who is stronger and rules, and a personal harm to the man who obeys and serves. Injustice is the opposite, and it rules the truly simple and just; and those who are ruled do what is advantageous for him who is stronger . . . " (343c–d)

What astonishes in Thrasymachus's original argument is the use of the term "just" just where common parlance would have placed its opposite. Yet in the passage cited above his language slips, giving the "truly simple and just" man his due, as victim to the *injustice* of the stronger. As he continues, over a long and cynical passage (343d–344c), he maintains his position that the strong control the weak, but uses a terminology in which the "just" are the wronged while the stronger are the "unjust," thus abdicating the power he had earlier usurped to redefine the meaning of the name "justice." It is only at the end of his long harangue that the controlled reversal of the terms returns, moving as his rhetoric does from conventional concepts of just and unjust and tumbling thereafter into a confusion of the two. Thrasymachus is no longer master of his language: "'So Socrates, injustice, when it comes into being on a sufficient scale, is mightier, freer, and more masterful than justice; and, as I have said from the beginning, the just is the advantage of the stronger, and the unjust is what is profitable and advantageous for oneself'" (344c).

Socrates has indeed taken "hold of [Thrasymachus's] argument in the way [he] can work it the most harm" (338d, also 341a), has pounced on this argument, torn it to shreds, challenged the role Thrasymachus ascribes to "the stronger." Paradoxically, his attack proves Socrates more powerful as the latter takes control of what is spoken about.

The Socratic method here is one of persuasion which, from the first encounter with Polemarchus, he posed as the counter-force to bodily strength (327c). It does not bring truth to light so much as bring to darkness what is *not* true: "Then do you want to persuade [Thrasymachus] . . . that what he says *isn't true*?" (348a, emphasis mine). "The stronger" (338c) in the definition of Thrasymachus fares no better than it had in the threat of Polemarchus ("prove stronger than these men or stay here" 327c). Polemarchus's name may suggest a "leader in battle," and Thrasymachus's a boldness in battle (LS), but, if our argument were to "[follow] the name alone" (454b), we would have to remember that the name Socrates suggests an assurance of power, and this he achieves through eristic attacks that impose his will.[32] Socrates' argument is a matter of power. Justice in Book I, then, is, after all, what the stronger insists it is. Or, more correctly: justice is *not*, what Socrates, as the stronger in the eristic argument, insists it is not. Socrates may not openly voice the truth of Thrasymachus's argument, but he performs it: the nature of "justice" is determined by the stronger. Still, he leaves himself and his interlocutors without definition and without form. His practice of eristic is effective but nonproductive, or rather nonproductive because effective.

What is it then that dialectic will produce, and how? For is the *Republic* not a showcase for the power of dialectic as Socrates repeatedly reminds us, or, perhaps more precisely, for a shift from eristic to dialectic as Plato more subtly reminds us?[33] Still, if dialectic becomes the path of the discussion only in the middle of Book II (368), how are we to account for what leads up to it at the end of Book I and the beginning of Book II, passages that lay the groundwork for dialectic with an irony we dare not miss? How do Thrasymachus and Socrates finally come to terms? How do they come to agree?

> "Now," I said, "if we should speak at length against him, setting speech against speech, telling how many good things belong to being just, and then he should speak in return, and we again, there'll be need of *counting* the good things and *measuring* how many each of us has in each speech, and then we'll be in need of some sort of judges who will decide. But if we consider just as we did a moment ago, coming to *agreement* with one another, (*anomologoumenoi pros allêlous*) we'll ourselves be both judges and pleaders at once." (348a–b, emphases mine)

Once again Socrates wishes to leave the counting and measuring out of the mix. The reckoning and accounting in Cephalus's view of Hades (330d–e), the deposit and payback of that early definition of justice (331c) are all of a piece with a mode of argument that Socrates will avoid at all costs. Agreement is what he is after, a becoming-one of judges and pleaders, a sameness of saying.

Socrates returns to getting the better of Thrasymachus, to beating him out in eristic exchange. They may come to agreement, say the same thing, but the process, as Socrates gets a hold of Thrasymachus in his resistant difference, is something of a struggle. The more overwhelming agreement that will come with dialectic is not yet openly on the scene. Still this is something of a dress rehearsal. It is a question of who will get the better of whom, and not only Socrates and Thrasymachus. The parallels between the conditions of discussion and "what's spoken about" (454a) are again what we need to keep in mind. They mark the difference between the just and unjust man, whom the just and unjust man will get the better of, and who, in turn, each then resembles.

> "Let us say it, then, as follows," I said, "the just man does not get the better of what is like but of what is unlike, while the unjust man gets the better of like and unlike?"
> "What you said is very good," he said.
> "Then the man who is both good and wise will not want to get the better of the like, but of the unlike and opposite?"
> "It seems so," he said.
> "But the bad and unlearned will want to get the better of both the like and the opposite?"

"It looks like it."

"Then," I said, "the just man is like the wise and good, but the unjust man like the bad and unlearned."

"I'm afraid so."

"But we were also agreed that each is such as the one he is like."

"We were."

"Then the just man has revealed himself to us as good and wise, and the unjust man unlearned and bad." (349c–d, 350b–c)

In this dizzying eristic argument, itself an attempt to get the better of the unlike, Socrates of Thrasymachus and vice versa, at stake is the act of struggle to get the better of . . . At stake is also who one is, as determined by who one is like. The just man, who wishes to get the better only of those who are unlike him, is thus wise and good because he is like the wise and good in this endeavor. Similarity evolves into identity. And if we do not see here the scene of agreement which Socrates had proposed (348a–b, quoted above), if Socrates vanquishes his unlike and reluctant adversary, Thrasymachus, while declaring that like and like (the just and the wise and good) come together as one, a milder scene of agreement, of saying the same thing, is nevertheless about to be prepared by Socrates.

> Now, Thrasymachus did not agree to all of this so easily as I tell it now, but he dragged his feet and resisted, and he produced a wonderful quantity of sweat, for it was summer. And then I saw what I had not yet seen before—Thrasymachus blushing. At all events, when we had come to complete agreement (*diômologêsametha*) about justice being virtue and wisdom, and injustice both vice and lack of learning. . . . (350c–d)

Thrasymachus replies:

> "But even what you're saying now doesn't satisfy me, and I have something to say about it. But if I should speak, I know well that you would say that I am making a public harangue. So then, either let me say as much as I want; or, if you want to keep on questioning, go ahead and question, and, just as with old wives who tell tales, I shall say to you, 'All right,' and I shall nod and shake my head." (350d–e)

Thrasymachus nods and shakes his head like a charmed snake (358b). He agrees with Socrates, as with an old wife, "to satisfy [him]," "since [Socrates] won't let [Thrasymachus] speak" (350e). This is not quite the "saying the same" that the Socratic dream of agreement might have promised, but it allows what Socrates terms an "orderly" and "thorough consideration of the argument about the character of justice" (350e–351a). Thrasymachus "[grows] gentle with [Socrates] and [has] left off being hard on [him]" (354a).

Let us forget this is just a pose, one performed with bitter irony, that in this Thrasymachus tries to mimic his interlocutor: "'Here is that habitual irony of Socrates. I knew it, and I predicted to these fellows . . . that you would be ironic and do anything rather than answer if someone asked you something'" (337a). Let us forget that *eirôneia* in Greek implies a dissimulation, an assumed ignorance, a saying less than one thinks (LS). What Thrasymachus has agreed to agree about, it turns out, is faction and difference—in their relation to injustice.

> "For surely, Thrasymachus, it's injustice that produces factions (*staseis*), . . . and justice that produces unanimity and friendship. Isn't it so?"
> "Let it be so, so as not to differ with you (*soi mê diapherômai*)."
> "And it's good of you to do so, you best of men. . . ."
> "And what about when injustice comes into being between two? Will they not differ (*ou dioisontai*) and hate and be enemies to each other and to just men?" . . .
> "Then does [injustice] come to light as possessing a power such that, wherever it comes into being . . . it first of all makes that thing unable to accomplish anything together with itself due to faction and difference (*dia to stasiazein kai diapheresthai*), and then it makes that thing an enemy both to itself and to everything opposite and to the just? Isn't that so?"
> "Certainly." (351d–352a)

Injustice produces factions (351d), an oppositional setting over and against, which is to say a differing from one another, the differing that Thrasymachus abdicates under the terms of his truce with Socrates ("so as not to differ with you" [*soi mê diapherômai* (351d)]). Justice, then, is not just what the dialogue speaks about here. However forced and however ironically, justice, with its banning of faction, is the mode of the discussion between Socrates and Thrasymachus. Thus, the "Certainly"s, "Let it be"s, and "Yes"s of Thrasymachus, however farcically, stage the theater of justice: that which is spoken about (justice) and the nonfractious speaking about it mirror one another in docile agreement. This will be all the more dramatically the case once dialectic takes its effective hold. The practice of dialectic is to endlessly dissolve the follower into the univocity of the

Socratic narrative that vigilantly guards against the factions of multiple voices—just as its content (as foreshadowed in the talk of factions) is ever a movement from the multiple to the one.

Dissimulations

Book II: and the simulated agreement of Thrasymachus gives way to simulated faction. This is the necessary prelude, it seems, to falling in with Socrates in unquestioning and genuine thrall. Why this ineluctable passing by way of arguments of pure seeming, a speaking that covers over the actual position of the speaker? First Glaucon and then Adeimantus "restore" the arguments of Thrasymachus (358c) but do so in the hopes of being truly persuaded that "it is better to be just than unjust" (357b), that justice is "a kind of good that we would choose to have . . . for its own sake" and "not because we desire its consequences" (357b). The quest is "to hear . . . what power (*dunamin*) it has all alone by itself" (358b), to understand what the just *is* and not just its seeming. To this end Glaucon proposes contemplating the life of the perfectly unjust man, whose extreme of injustice provides him "with the *greatest reputation* for justice" (361a), makes him "*seem* to be just when [he] is not" (361a, emphases mine). In contrast he proposes the just man whose "seeming [to be just] must be taken away" (361b), having "the greatest reputation for injustice" (361c), that is, who must seem, he too, like Glaucon, to be what he is not. For Glaucon himself also operates in a space of seeming, taking on a persona, claiming it is not he who speaks but rather a shadow form of "those who praise injustice ahead of justice" (361e). He chooses to argue that "one shouldn't wish to be, but [rather] to seem to be, just" (362a), that reputation, opinion, and exterior seeming are all that counts.

The most baffling example he gives is the famous story of the ring of Gyges (359c–360d). Glaucon speaks of an ancestor of Gyges rather than Gyges himself, but both Glaucon and Herodotus in his *Histories* tell the story of a man who murders the king of Lydia, marries his wife. and usurps the rule.[34] Herodotus writes of a king obsessed with proving the beauty of his wife. He forces a royal guardian to view his master's wife in all her nakedness, bereft, then, of the covers that Glaucon and his brother are so wont to draw. "Near the door there's a chair," the king instructs Gyges, "she will put her clothes on it as she takes them off, one by one. You will be able to watch her with perfect ease." As the king puts it "a man always believes his eyes better than his ears."[35] Gyges does this against his will, and takes the life of the king only when the queen gives him no choice.

Glaucon's tale does not speak of a guardian, a figure so key to the political tale that Socrates is about to tell, understandably he cannot be tainted in the *Republic*; Glaucon speaks rather of a shepherd of the king.[36] A man may believe his eyes in Herodotus, but that will not be the case in Plato. For the nakedness of the queen who sheds her seeming with her garments one by one, making available to the eye what the façade of clothing had covered over, Glaucon substitutes the invisibility of the ancestor of Gyges.

Once again, it is an underground affair. For, like Socrates before him in the opening line of the dialogue (*katebên* [327a]), the ancestor of Gyges also "goes down."[37]

> They say he was a shepherd toiling in the service of the man who was then ruling Lydia. There came to pass a great thunderstorm and an earthquake; the earth cracked and a chasm opened at the place where he was pasturing. He saw it, wondered at it, and went down (*katabênai*). He saw, along with other quite wonderful things about which they tell tales, a hollow bronze horse. It had windows; peeping in, he saw there was a corpse inside that looked larger than human size. It had nothing on except a gold ring on its hand; he slipped it off and went out. (359d–e)

The earthquake makes visible what was previously closed to view. Let us put aside the hollow horse, the echo of Homer's vehicle of camouflage, surprise, and reversal. In the underground, on a naked corpse, the shepherd discovers a gold ring[38] that will render him invisible, allowing him to carry out injustice, not by veiling himself over, but by disappearing from the scope of human vision. There are two ways, it seems, to carry out injustice: the first, so insisted upon by Glaucon and his brother, takes place behind the cloak of deceit, the second almost lost in this moment of myth in which it is suggested, taking place outside the realm of the senses. One dare not remain blind to the cloak of invisibility as one listens to Socrates in the books to come. He wears it often.

Adeimantus comes to the aid of his brother and "out of [what is also his] desire to hear the opposite from [Socrates]" (367b) speaks against justice as vehemently as he can. "There is no advantage in my being just, if I don't also seem to be," for, he adds, "'the seeming overpowers even the

truth'" (365b–c). Thus, Adeimantus tells us, a man might choose to surround his life with deceit as with an architectural structure:

> "In all likelihood he would say to himself, after Pindar, will I 'with justice
> or with crooked deceits scale the higher wall' where I can fortify myself all
> around and live out my life?" (365b)

And he repeats that gesture as he invokes Archilochus. "As façade and
exterior I must draw a shadow painting of virtue all around me, while behind it I must trail the wily and subtle fox of the most wise Archilochus"
(365c). This wall, the "counterfeited seemly exterior" (366b), this seeming,
behind which one might pass one's unjust life, is, structurally at least, like
the façades the brothers set up as they argue in praise of injustice, while
claiming, all the while behind it, to "[remain] unpersuaded that injustice
is better than justice" (368a).

Overwhelmed as he must be by the theatrics of Glaucon and Adeimantus, Socrates does not counter these arguments so much as admit that he
doesn't "see very sharply" (368c). They are at their most articulate saying
what they do *not* mean, circling themselves round, drawing in front of
themselves a façade, praising the advantage of injustice, and describing a
world in which dissimulation and appearance are all we encounter. Here
seeming overpowers truth—overpowers it to the point that no one knows
anymore, and perhaps never has, what justice is and what "power" (358b)
it wields. Their flurry of assertions insists on "[taking away] the true reputation" while "[attaching] the false one" (367b) to both the speakers and
that which is spoken about (justice and injustice). And if Socrates does
not, like Thrasymachus, Glaucon, and Adeimantus before him, take on a
role that betrays his beliefs, if he does not draw round him a false façade,
nevertheless the path which he proposes is hardly direct. In the coming
books of the *Republic,* although Socrates' disciples are determined to dog
his footsteps and one thing seems inevitably to follow from another, the
direction and indirections of the discourse are nevertheless not easy to
fathom.[39]

This is made clear in Book IV, with the culmination of the search for
justice. Three of the forms to which the city will owe its virtue have been
"spied out" (432b). Only justice remains to be found.

> "We must . . . pay attention so that justice doesn't slip through somewhere

and disappear into obscurity. . . . Look to it and make every effort to catch sight of it; you might somehow see it before me and could tell me."

"If only I could," he said. "However if you use me as a follower and a man able to see what's shown him, you'll be making quite sensible use of me."

"Follow," I said, "and pray with me."

"I'll do that," he said, "just lead."

"The place really appears to be hard going and steeped in shadows," I said. "At least it's dark and hard to search out. But, all the same, we've got to go on."

"Yes," he said, "We've got to go on."

And I caught sight of it and said, "Here! Here! Glaucon. Maybe we've come upon a track; and, in my opinion, it will hardly get away from us."

"That's good news you report," he said.

"My, my," I said, "that was a stupid state we were in."

"How's that?"

"It appears, you blessed man, that it's been rolling around at our feet from the beginning and we couldn't see it after all, but were quite ridiculous." (432b–d)

What intervenes, then, once Socrates takes over from Adeimantus in Book II, is quite ridiculous, "steeped in shadows," "dark and hard to search out," unavailable to the human eye, especially for one who does not see very sharply, which is not to say completely invisible. We need to make every effort to catch sight of the tracks of Socrates as he leads and Glaucon follows. Because all along in Books II–IV, and even from the beginning, much rolls around at our feet that threatens to trip us up.

The Turn to Analogy

Thrasymachus, Glaucon, and Adeimantus have each had his say. They have left eristic well behind, with its language of faction and differing, the openly oppositional positioning of one speaker over and against another. First Thrasymachus feigns agreement, and offers ironic docility in relation to each of Socrates' arguments. Glaucon and Adeimantus then feign disagreement. Like Thrasymachus, they draw before them a shadow painting at odds with the person trailing behind, an image, one might say, oppositionally distinct from but determined by the intentions of its puppeteer, a differentiation soon to be blurred.

As Socrates sets up the process to come, no one poses and no one opposes. Socrates doesn't pretend to be one thing and mean another. Dis-simulation is cast aside. He "makes . . . in speech" (369c) a new mode of agreement to which his followers readily agree. What is the role of analogy and on what kind of path does it take us? In what sense does the shift away from disputation, debate, refutation to the point of contradiction, the shift away from all the properties of what is conventionally understood as the early, Socratic method, also imply the shift to another mode of argumentation which is based on the "like"? His search sets up a relation of similarity and likeness unmenaced, or so it seems, by the faction of eristic or the difference of simulation.[40]

> "It looks to me as though the investigation we are undertaking is no ordinary thing, but one for a man who sees sharply. Since we're not clever men," I said, "in my opinion we should make this kind of investigation of it: if someone had, for example, ordered men who don't see very sharply to read little letters from afar and then someone had the thought that the same letters were somewhere else also, but bigger and in a bigger place, I suppose it would look like a godsend (*hermaion*) to be able to consider the littler ones after having read these first, if, of course, they do happen to be the same."
>
> "Most certainly," said Adeimantus. "But Socrates, what do you notice in the investigation of the just that's like this (*ti toiouton*)?"
>
> "I'll tell you," I said. "There is, we say, justice of one man; and there is, surely, justice of a whole city too?"
>
> "Certainly," he said.
>
> "Is a city bigger than one man?"
>
> "Yes, it is bigger," he said.
>
> "So then, perhaps there would be more justice in the bigger and it would be easier to observe closely. If you want, first we'll investigate what justice is like (*poion* [of what sort]) in the cities. Then, we'll also go on to consider it in individuals, considering the likeness (*tên . . . homoiotêta*) of the bigger in the *idea* of the littler?" (368c–369a)

The differential of power in the concepts of stronger and weaker, so critical to what preceded this moment, now gives way to the likeness of bigger and littler.[41]

The struggle for supremacy seems to disappear here, both in the argument as analogy and in the relation of the speakers: still it will be the *republic* of the dialogue's title that replaces the topic at hand. We all but forget that the goal is justice—more precisely justice as it is found in the individual. Analogy, unlike the façades and shadow paintings of Thrasymachus, Adeimantus, and Glaucon, does not, ostensibly, present a false front, diametrically opposed, to what it covers over. The analogy is based on similitude and comes into play as the means to what it simulates. Nevertheless, the one part of the analogy, the city, at least for a while, and perhaps, as its title suggests, throughout much of the dialogue, covers over, surreptitiously, what it imaged after all. No wonder it would look like a "godsend" (*hermaion*), as Socrates tells us, a gift from Hermes, that trickster messenger of the gods, if we were able to consider the smaller letters after reading the larger letters of the polis, writ at a distance from one another, but ultimately side-by-side and comparable.

Still, yet smaller than the letters of justice in the individual there might be another text, even more difficult to decipher. What if writ large in the city about to come into being are not only the little letters of justice in the individual—but also the considerably smaller letters of philosophy? These would be, not simply philosophy in terms of what the *Republic* might have to say about the role of the philosopher in that polis, but also the practice, the Platonic practice, of philosophical discussion as it comes into being in speech.

Socrates proposes, not simply reading the larger letters in the contemplation of a city already at hand nor, less simply, "[making] a city in speech"(369c) as he will put it shortly, but the composite act of creating the city while all the while watching oneself making it—"[watching] a city coming into being in speech" (369a). Socrates turns to analogy and in doing so he sets up the analogy of analogy, thus offering a signal of sorts about the ineluctable relation between analogy and reading. What does the similarity of analogy now proposed by Socrates have to do with the political agenda to come? How is this to be distinguished from dialectic, which also has far-reaching political implications?[42]

The Path of Dialectic

Let us recapitulate. The goal is *justice* in the individual. *Eristic* confrontation (Cephalus, Polemarchus, and Thrasymachus's engagements with Socrates) has been cast aside. So has the *differential dissimulation* of speaking contrary to intention along with its semiological parallel, those façades of seeming that veil injustice (in the speeches of Glaucon and Adeimantus). The provisional means, the necessary steppingstone to the goal of justice in the individual, is the *analogy* between city and man.

The method they will come to practice while making a city in speech, Socrates will later claim to have been *dialectic*. The path that Socrates lays out for himself (and implicitly sets out as well for his would-be readers) is not the observation of something already at hand. It is, rather, a consideration of "what's said by separating [the city] out into its forms" (454a), alongside an observation of the way in which the detours he takes, create a city in speech, which will ultimately lead him to the city's analogon, the individual, and the parallel justice therein. These are the signposts so far (in Plato's day they would have been called "Herms," with all the complications we have seen that term to take on in the previous chapter): *eristic, simulation, dis-simulation, analogy,* and *dialectic*, at least some of the byways the dialogue takes. There is a progression here that will attempt to leave difference behind. Socrates turns to analogy and in doing so he offers a signal of sorts about the ineluctable relationship between analogy and reading.

Thereafter he moves by way of dialectic on a nonfractious path in search of justice. What does justice, which, as we have already read, "produces unanimity and friendship" (351d), have to do with dialectic? What does it have to do with the almost imperceptible movement of self-differentiation that drives the narrative, a form never recognized as difference or distinction?

We must take into account, on the one hand, the way in which similarity and difference will function in the city, how it will function, for example, as the relationship among the classes. And we must take into account on the other the way it functions as the relationship of Socrates to his chorus of interlocutors who so often fade into the in-difference of fatuous approval which also, surely, has to do with the political structures he proposes. They give us the sense for hundreds of pages that the idiosyncratic path of dialectic could never have gone in any other direction. Either that or the reader misses something. What we miss once dialectic sets in is any sense of the other. Where quarreling and wrangling and the interruptions of contradiction now fear to tread, dialectic takes their place in an uncanny flow of agreement. And from this perspective Socrates' insistence in his exchange with Thrasymachus (350b–c) that the unjust man will "get the better of both like and unlike" (that the unjust man will be at odds, that is, with everyone) while "the just man will not get the better of the like but of the unlike," also takes on political significance. This, after all, is the pattern laid out for a polis whose classes are in harmony with one another but which, driven by necessity, will be at war with those un-like itself and outside its borders.

Overstepping the Boundaries

The city is formed, we read, because of need (369b) and as the city is made in speech it is, in turn, "our need, as it seems [that] will make it" (369c). How are we to understand this? Is ignorance, a lack of knowledge of what a city is, to be satisfied by way of analogy, or is it another force? Is analogy, as Socrates sets up his famous first argument, itself a structure of lack of sorts? We lack knowledge of justice in the individual and therefore move by way of its analogon to justice in the city.

The city comes into being "because each of us isn't self-sufficient but is in need of much" (369b): not self-sufficient because "each of us . . . differs in his nature (*diapherôn tên phusin*); different men are apt for the accom-plishment of different jobs" (370a–b): each man practices one skill, "One man, one art" (370b). The difference among men enables each to perform different jobs, but that difference, we shall see, will blur in the service of the wholeness and wholesomeness of the state. Glaucon and Socrates cre-ate a first city of modest needs mutually satisfied by its inhabitants, the healthy and "true city" (372e). Its only relation to the outside is an import and export of goods and a wary eye toward the possibility of war (372c).

All this will change in the luxurious city that follows, the feverish city they go on to create. It is a question of borders, of multiple boundar-ies that must be overstepped: the boundaries of the original needs, the boundaries of the original range of "jobs" (370b)[43] required to meet the needs of the first city, and the geographical boundaries of the state.

"Then must we cut off a piece of our neighbors' land, if we are going to have sufficient for pasture and tillage, and they in turn from ours, if they let them-selves go to the unlimited acquisition of money, *overstepping the boundary of the necessary?*"

"Quite necessarily, Socrates," he said.

"After that won't we go to war as a consequence, Glaucon? Or how will it be?"

"Like that," he said.

"And let's not yet say whether war works evil or good," I said, "but only this much, that we have in its turn found the *origin of war*—in those things whose presence in cities most of all produces evils both private and public."

"Most certainly."

"Now, my friend, the city must be still bigger, and not by a small number but *by a whole army*. . . . " (373d–374a, emphases mine)

The city is constituted in the necessity of war, the crossing of borders, perhaps not unrelated to the invasion by the goddess Bendis. The violent struggle with the other that we have seen embodied in the form of eristic is expulsed outside or rather to the borders of the city.[44] This is the repeated gesture of the *Republic*, marking out the distinction between Greek and barbarian in acts of hostility, while maintaining an insistence on harmony within.[45]

And the human at the border of that distinction between what is and what is not the state is, of course, the guardian, who becomes necessary only with the advent of war and to whose education so much of the early part of the dialogue is devoted. In the first city, the healthy city, guardians do not appear on the scene. "Many men gather in one settlement as partners and helpers" (369c): farmers, house builders, weavers, shoemakers (369d), carpenters, smiths, cowherds, shepherds (370d), merchants (371c), tradesmen (371d), and wage earners (371e)—but no soldiers, no guardians. In fact, all those who make up the healthy city will occupy only the lowest class in the second. Guardians, auxiliaries, rulers, and even philosophers, it seems,[46] come into being only in the luxurious "feverish city" (372e).

The guardian comes into being by way of yet another analogy. He will be like a "noble puppy" (375a): first, because, as warrior, he must be courageous.

"Then, will horse or dog—or any other animal whatsoever—be willing to be courageous if it's not spirited (*thumoeidês*)? Haven't you noticed how irresistible and unbeatable spirit (*thumos*) is, so that its presence makes every soul fearless and invincible in the face of everything?" (375a–b)

At the heart of courage is *thumos*, both spirit and the seat of rage. "Yet, they must be gentle to their own and cruel to enemies" (375c),[47] Socrates adds, and *thumos*, apparently, enables only the second. If they have lost their way for the moment, this is because they have "abandoned the image (*eikonos*) [they] proposed" (375d). Little takes place in the *Republic* that does not go by way of the image: they lose track of it here, just as Socrates, having taken up the image of the polis, will later lose track of the definition of justice that was all the while rolling around at his feet. "By nature the disposition of noble dogs is to be as gentle as can be with their familiars and people they know (*tous sunêtheis te kai gnôrimous*) and the opposite with those they don't know" (*tous agnôtas* [375e]). With the coming into being of the guardians, made possible by a return to the image (of the noble puppy), philosophy will first come to light. It is a strange light, however, although not explicitly marked as such. We need to remember that philosophy appears on the scene at the moment of the founding of the second city, at the moment of defining its borders along with its pivotal warrior class, without which the city cannot exist.

> "In your opinion, then, does the man who will be a fit guardian need, in addi-tion to spiritedness (*thumoeidei*), also to be a philosopher in his nature?"
>
> "How's that?" he said. "I don't understand."
>
> "This, too, you'll observe in dogs," I said, "and it's a thing in the beast worthy of our wonder."
>
> "What?"
>
> "When it sees someone it doesn't know (*agnôta*), it's angry, although it never had any bad experience with him. And when it sees someone it knows, it greets him warmly, even if it never had a good experience with him." . . .
>
> "Well, this does look like an attractive affection of its nature and truly philosophic."
>
> "In what way?"
>
> "In that it distinguishes friendly from hostile looks by nothing other than by having learned the one and being ignorant of the other," I said. "And so, how can it be anything other than a lover of learning since it defines (*horizomenon*) what's its own and what's alien by knowledge and ignorance?" . . .
>
> "Well, I said, "but aren't love of learning (*philomathes*) and love of wisdom (*philosophon*) the same?" . . .
>
> "So shall we be bold and assert that a human being too, if he is going to be gentle to his own and those known to him, must by nature be a philosopher and a lover of learning?" (375e–376c)[48]

The guardians must be spirited, enraged toward the enemy and yet they must not be "savage to one another and the rest of the citizens" (375b): they must not destroy "their own" (375c). The philosophical is what makes gentleness to one's own possible.

Once again, the tacit, the unspoken, the repressed analogy that is al-ways at work in the *Republic*, which remains fundamentally unspoken even at the moment that it is openly pronounced, is the relation between the structure of the state and the movement of philosophy.[49] We need to come to terms with the political implications of the gestures of philosophy and vice versa. Philosophy here is love of one's own and has to be thought in its relation to *thumos*, spirit, as the force of raging against the enemy. Socrates declares the latter necessary, because, as a result of overstepping "the boundary of the necessary" one has to "cut off a piece of our neighbor's land" (373d). The act of war has the potential to make that which is foreign one's own, to colonize it, which has a great deal to do with the recent history of the Athens in which Plato wrote, both its grandeur and its fall. But colonization, it is hard to miss here, would also be analogous to the gesture that makes knowledge possible: knowledge results from having come to know, making the unknown into one's own, into that which is familiar. Philosophy, then, is not simply the flip side of rage in war, as a being gentle to one's own; it is also very like the process by means of which war's successes are assimilated, in a movement of ever expanding borders. The dog "defines what's its own and what's alien by knowledge and ignorance" (376b). The word that Socrates uses for "defining" is *horizomenon*. It suggests both a taking possession of for oneself (LS) and a marking out of boundaries, boundaries expanded and redefined each time that one takes something new into one's sphere of knowledge, just as boundaries are redefined each time the state cuts off a piece of its neighbor's land.

"Telling Tales in a Tale"

Analogy and dialectic are the declared paths of the argument. Their implications are far-reaching as we have already begun to see. Analogy sets out a structure of similarity and difference between its apparently distinct elements that allows the relatively unproblematic shift from one to the other. It seems to cast aside hierarchical difference, the inevitable upshot of eristic debate. In the analogy of city to individual, the city seems the path to the individual because they are bound together in their similarity. Still we have only begun to explore dialectic. Under its aegis the polis obliterates the individual, all but makes one forget the purpose of analogy, substitutes justice in the one for justice in the other for several books. In the course of the discussion as well as in the description of the polis, the individual is subservient to the state. Alongside these are somewhat erratic detours not so easily offered up to the reader's grasp. And yet it is also these that produce, one way or another, the polis.

The city is constituted by a lack that leads to the necessity of exceeding its own borders and the need for a warrior class. Similarly, the city is also constituted by another lack, the need to know what the polis will be. Weak of sight, Socrates sets out to create a city, because "easier to observe" (368e), analogous to, but larger than, the individual man. He creates the city in speech while demanding they watch themselves create (369a). Here, too, he may not see very sharply or make explicit what slips all too often into the shadows of invisibility. Paradoxically he turns to creating the guardian, something of an individual after all. The education of the guardians preoccupies the discussion through the end of Book III and on and off at least through Book VII. "Like men telling tales in a tale," Socrates proposes that they "educate the men in speech" (376d). As they themselves tell this tale within the tale of creating the city, tale-telling is also, coincidentally, the first stage of education. "Don't you understand . . . that first we tell tales to children? And surely they are, as a whole, false, though there are true things in them too. We make use of tales with children . . . " (377a). From the beginning it is not strictly a question of truth; rather "What ought to be blamed first and foremost [is] if the lie a man tells isn't a fine one" (377d). The stories currently told, such as those of Hesiod and Homer, must be purged of the dangers they pose to the new state, especially those that speak of the origin and attacks on the origin, acts of castration, gods killed by their sons.

> "First," I said, "the man who told the biggest lie about the biggest things didn't tell a fine lie—how Uranus did what Hesiod says he did, and how Cronos in his turn took revenge on him. And Cronos' deeds and his sufferings at the hands of his son, not even if they were true would I suppose they should so easily be told . . . " (377e–378a)

Such "unspeakable secrets" (378a) in which "gods make war on gods, and plot against them and have battles with them" (378b–c) must not be uttered; they make it difficult "to persuade [the young] that no citizen was ever angry with another and that to be so is not holy" (378c), make it difficult if "its laws are going to be well observed" (380b) and if the city is to be regarded as one.

It is not, as in the famous passage that opens Book X, a matter of the poet failing to make "what *is*" (597a). It is not an issue of creating soldiers

who are godlike, but rather of creating a model of what we might wish
the guardians to be, compelling the poets (378d–379a) to form the image
of the gods accordingly, and offering this up in turn for imitation by the
guardian class (378d). The dizzying logic of this creation is not man made
in god's image, but the image of the god made according to the guardian we wish to create, so that the young may emulate gods whose actual
existence is irrelevant. These gods, we read, are really good and cause only
the good, never deceive and never pass into other shapes (381b–e), never
depart from their own idea (380d). "About gods, then, . . . such, it seems,
are the things that should and should not be heard, from childhood on,
by men who would honor gods and ancestors and not take lightly their
friendship with each other" (386a).

If the gods are "altogether simple and true in deed and speech" (382e),
if they do not "want to lie, either in speech or deed" (382a), for humans,
the lie in speeches is "useful" (382c), and especially for founders, as we begin to fathom: "And, in the telling of the tales we were just now speaking
about—those told because we don't know where the truth about ancient
things lies—likening the lie to the truth as best we can, don't we also
make it useful?" (382c–d). Lies, likened to the truth, play a part in what
we have just witnessed: the founders decide just what they wish, out of
which they create in speech, *ex nihilo*, the guardian class.

But, as we enter Book III, Socrates no longer finds a clean slate on
which to inscribe, unobstructed, his political will. This absence of an
arena of pure foundations will periodically compromise the possibility of
the polis they create. The *Republic* alternates between a project of utterly
new construction and the struggle against a feverish city (372e) in need
of vigilant purging. Not all human lies, it seems, are as useful as those of
the founders. "If [the guardians] are to be courageous" they must "also
be told things that will make them fear death least" (386a). Socrates illustrates this by page upon page of what they must *not* be told, lies that are
not "fine," in a realm (his project of founding notwithstanding) already
overrun by the work of such poets as Homer. Hoping to "find some limit
to wrongdoing" he cuts "off the heads of [the] Hydra" (426e) of cowardli-
ness "in the face of death" (386b). As he strikes wildly at example after
example, we read verse after verse, dozens of such passages, that must not
be seen or heard. This uncontrollable production by "expunging" (386c)
is underscored by a vocabulary of madness and language run wild: "no

mind" or "understanding," "wailing," "gibbering," "roaming distraught," "unquenchable laughter" (386c–389a).[50]

In a frenzy of cited passages (his method is deletion [387c] by citation), many of them descriptions of Hades, Socrates seems to produce precisely what he attacks, the excess he means to curb. He needs to expunge the fear of death, which is also the threat of a nether world, what lies beyond the border of this one. Much of the *Republic* might be conceived in terms of a series of borders, between life and death, the polis and the barbarians, "enemies from without and friends from within" (414b), the intelligible and the visible, the upper world and the cave in Socrates' famous allegory, truth and lie.[51] And yet none of the above can completely account for what takes place in the *Republic*. Although Socrates leaves eristic behind, a practice of drawing a line in the sand if ever there was one, and chooses dialectic instead, which instantiates a practice of inclusion, he nevertheless oscillates between exclusionary gestures[52] and those that eradicate the borders he himself sets up in the name of the polis.

No more clearly articulated example of this than the close of Book III. In Book II, Adeimantus had asked Socrates to tell "which tales we mean" when we speak of ensuring that children hear "the finest told tales" (378e–379a).

> And I said, "Adeimantus, you and I aren't poets right now but founders of the city. It's appropriate for founders to know the models according to which the poets must tell their tales. If what the poets produce goes counter to these models, founders must not give way; however, they must not themselves make up tales." (378e–379a)

Socrates refuses the role of poet here, only to assume it with relish later, both proposing the model and telling the tale. It is time to lie outright, to produce a fine lie and fine line if ever there was one. As they educate the guardians in Book III we witness a diatribe against, almost a fixation about, change, multiplicity, and disharmony. This extends to our perception of the gods, to poetry, the relations between citizens, the jobs they undertake, the instruments they play. Correlative to the fear of the manifold are the repeated warnings against illusion and deception, although there is a place for these. "Further, truth must be taken seriously too. For if what we were just saying is correct, and a lie is really useless to gods and useful to human beings as a form of remedy, it's plain that anything of the sort must be assigned to doctors. . . . Then, it's appropriate for the rulers, if for anyone at all, to lie. . . . " (389b).

In a polis that will have three classes of citizens, the craftsmen or moneymakers, the guardians, soldiers, or auxiliaries, and the rulers, it is now the moment of choosing the guardians, and, from among these, the elite class of rulers. Here the evils of deception will once again come to the fore. Socrates chooses a story that "would be good for making [the guardians and rulers] care more for the city and one another" (415d). In these, the penultimate pages before finding justice in the city, we find a passage that defines the ruling class. Socrates, pondering how to select the rulers, tells us they will be those least vulnerable to persuasion (413), those "who [have] a memory and [are] hard to deceive" (413c) and are therefore least "likely [to] forget and be deceived out of" their convictions "that one must do what is best for the city" (412e), all of which Socrates more or less equates with "[having] the truth" (413a).

Having just declared the perils of lies (or isn't "being deceived about the truth bad, and to have the truth good?" [413a]), Socrates suddenly seems devoid of memory, when, though hesitating, he dares to speak. No wonder that it is only by way of persuasion that Glaucon convinces him to speak. "'Could we,' I said, 'somehow contrive one of those lies that come into being in case of need, of which we were just now speaking, some one noble lie?'" (414b–c). Socrates plans "to persuade first the rulers and the soldiers, then the rest of the city" (414d) to make them forget, and "charmed by pleasure" (413c) to bewitch and deceive them of the truth. It is an abrupt turnaround, determined, precisely to charm, persuade,[53] and make one forget his recent words that "to opine the things that are, is to have the truth" (413a), and that one suffers being "deprived of true opinion" only when "robbed, bewitched by wizards, or forced" (413a–b).

> "I shall speak—and yet, I don't know what I'll use for daring or speeches in telling it—and I'll attempt to persuade first the rulers and the soldiers, then the rest of the city, that the rearing and education we gave them were like dreams; they only thought they were undergoing all that was happening to them, while, in truth, at that time they were under the earth within, being fashioned and reared themselves, and their arms and other tools being crafted. When the job had been completely finished, then the earth, which is their mother, sent them up. And now, as though the land they are in were a mother and nurse, they must plan for and defend it, if anyone attacks, and they must think of the other citizens as brothers and born of the earth."

"It wasn't," [Glaucon] said, "for nothing that you were for so long ashamed to tell the lie." (414d–e)

Indeed Socrates should be ashamed, given his definition of the rulers as those most resistant to parting with the truth: and yet a tale within a tale, the nobly born lie, serves a noble purpose, one that is no stranger to the overall strategy. One might even say that it is precisely this strategy, the strategy of a differentiation repeatedly established in order to be subsumed by the one, which constitutes the republic.[54] An insistence on the *one* that stands in contrast to the *many* and always with the power to encompass them, here a multiplicity of brothers, nevertheless born of the same earth, offspring of the same mother. The differences among men, which Socrates now goes on to mark, must be differences held in check by a harmony in service to the original unity of the regime, for Socrates is not "looking to the exceptional happiness of any one group among us but . . . of the city as a whole" (420b).[55]

"'All of you in the city are certainly brothers,' we shall say to them in telling the tale, 'but the god, in fashioning those of you who are competent to rule, mixed gold in at their birth; this is why they are most honored; in auxiliaries, silver; and iron and bronze in the farmers and the other craftsmen. . . . And, if a child of [the rulers] should be born with an admixture of bronze or iron, by no manner of means are they to take pity on it . . . ; and, again, if from these men one should naturally grow who has an admixture of gold or silver, they will honor such ones . . . , believing that there is an oracle that the city will be destroyed when an iron or bronze man is its guardian.'" (415a–c)

Each knows his place here, for difference takes place only in the name of unchallengeable hierarchy and under the aegis of a unified polis.[56] Yet how are we to come to terms, then, with the opening lines of the passage (414d–e) in which reality as "dream" is declared subservient to "truth"? The noble lie (414c) fabricates a logic of its own, and thus laying it out side by side with the allegory of the cave, it is difficult to know which image has the upper hand. Prefiguration of the allegory of the cave, no doubt, the noble lie, abyss in abyss, nevertheless inverts the values of that famous topography of knowledge, the centerpiece of the dialogue by which all readers, including Socrates, measure the power of the philosopher. In the allegory we will learn that everything we think to be real actually has its locus in a cave of shadows and misconceptions beneath the ground. This is a gesture, it might seem, identical to the shift from above to below in the noble lie. What one imagined to have taken place above has really taken place "under the earth" (414d). The not insignificant difference is that reality, according to the noble lie, lies below rather than above. Moreover, this tale of subterranean origins, the noble lie, inverts the real and the dream, misnames them, thus committing precisely the same error as the cave dwellers, for Socrates convinces his audience that what in actuality took place above ground, their "rearing and education," was "like dreams" and that his mythic tale buried in the depths of mother earth is "truth."[57] An open and cynical subversion takes place, then, in the name not of truth, but rather of establishing the power structure of the polis and insisting on its unity.[58]

Justice in the City

A perfect prelude to the song of justice itself, not that justice comes forth in the guise of a lie, but where Socrates hunts it is "hard going and steeped in shadows. . . . dark and hard to search out" (432c). This is a seeking in the dark, in an obscurity that smacks of the underground.

> "That rule we set down at the beginning as to what must be done in everything when we were founding the city—this, or a certain form of it, is, in my opinion, justice. Surely we set down and often said, if you remember, that each one must practice one of the functions in the city, that one for which his nature made him naturally most fit."
>
> "Yes, we were saying that."
>
> "And further, that justice is the minding of one's own business. . . . "
>
> "This—the practice of minding one's own business—when it comes into being in a certain way, is probably justice. . . . " (433a–b)
>
> "The money-making, auxiliary, and guardian classes doing what's appropriate, each of them minding its own business in a city—would be justice and would make the city just." (434c)

Justice, so Socrates' ultimate definition prescribes, demands that each practice those things which are his own, yet the discoverers of this maxim come as unlikely messengers of this call to self-recognition, having themselves been all but blind to that which is at hand and nearly deaf to their own voices as they spoke.

> "As men holding something in their hand sometimes seek what they're hold-

ing, we too didn't look at it but turned our gaze somewhere far off, which is also perhaps just the reason it escaped our notice. . . . In my opinion, we have been saying and hearing it all along without learning from ourselves that we were in a way saying it." (432d–e)

The noble lie stresses that all the men of the city, division into classes notwithstanding, are brothers, children of the same mother, born of the earth, and bound to the same land. But ruling by the men of gold, soldiering by those of silver, crafting by those of bronze or iron, in the definition of justice offered outside the medium of this founding myth, brings greater anxiety to the fore with respect to contamination among the divisions. The potential if highly exceptional movement across class lines, as described in the noble lie, seemed a formula crafted to assure cohesion and acceptance and in this respect might be associated with the form of moderation as unanimity and assent. However, in the definition of justice, the telos of the discussion, such movement threatens destructuring and destruction of the polis.

> "When one who is a craftsman . . . tries to get into the class (*eidos*) of the warrior, or one of the warriors who's unworthy into that of the adviser and guardian, and these men exchange tools and honors with one another; or when the same man tries to do all these things at once—then I suppose it's also your opinion that this change in them and this meddling are the destruction of the city."
> "That's entirely certain."
> "Meddling (*polupragmosunê*) among the classes . . . is the greatest harm for the city and would most correctly be called extreme evil-doing." (434a–c)

Balance is never reached between the desire for mythic union in the polis and the obsessive marking of differences among the citizens underscored by a fear of meddling and melding.

When Socrates turns to justice in the individual we encounter the same uncertainties. Let us reiterate: in the stylistically striking moment, the theatrically staged final hunt for justice, the strange conditions of its hunt and capture have everything to do with the exemplary story of justice in the individual that follows. While looking for justice we've been stupidly blinded "[turning] our gaze somewhere far off" (432e), deaf to our own speech and unable to learn from it, unable, then, to watch and hear justice coming into being in speech. Justice, originally hit upon by chance, or through some god, rather than through the agency of philosophy (443b), comes forth as a breakdown in the projected discussion.

Justice in the Individual: The Example of Leontius

Justice in the individual, as Socrates explains it, can be every bit as difficult to pin down as the justice implicit in the noble lie. In the analogy upon which the whole investigation has been built, a similar economy of hierarchical harmony and obedience is at stake, no longer among three classes of citizens, but this time among the three forms of the individual soul: the highest form, the power of calculation or reason; the lowest form, the irrational that hungers after or desires; and a third which Socrates, once again, calls *thumos* or spiritedness. Socrates envisions an interrelation of moderation in which spirit serves calculation by angrily reining in desires. To illustrate the exemplary interworking of the three, he tells the story of Leontius in whom the rational and irrational are at odds.[59]

For those who have a memory, this is an unlikely scenario for justice in the individual. Earlier Socrates asserts that "injustice . . . produces factions . . . and justice . . . unanimity" (351d). And shortly after his story he speaks of injustice as "a certain faction among those three—a meddling, interference, and rebellion of a part of the soul against the whole" (444b). How, then, can justice in the soul take place "as though there were two parties [the rational and irrational] at faction" (440b)? Far more is at faction here than reason and desire. Socrates' stance of rationality notwithstanding ("So we won't be irrational," he says [439d]) the irrational still has its role to play, and not simply by luring the soul with desire.

At issue is whether spirit, *thumos*, will ally itself with the calculating (*logistikon*) part or with the irrational (*alogiston* [439d]). To decide this question Socrates tells a story that he "trusts"—although "trust" is a term Socrates teaches us to mistrust later in the *Republic* (509d, 511d–e). To believe this tale, perhaps it's best to forget how it's told. One must close one's eyes to the Greek letters writ small, and rather read the passage in a translation that erases the similarities of its terms. In order to trust this tale one needs to cover over the Greek, for the vocabulary that marks Leontius's desire (*epithumêtikon, tôi epithumêtikôi, epithumoi, epithumias*) echoes *thumos* at its core, the very spiritedness that is called to do battle with desire. So which side is spirit on? Socrates: "'But,' I said, 'I once heard something that I trust. Leontius, the son of Aglaion, was going up from the Piraeus under the outside of the North Wall when he noticed corpses lying by the public executioner'" (439e).

Leontius, son of Aglaion, of whom scholars find no historical trace, doubles the path of Socrates between the Piraeus and Athens, in an underworld beneath the polis populated with the dead, victims of the public executioner. Not only Leontius, he who gazes on the bodies, but also the corpses themselves, have much in common with Socrates, for Socrates, like those who lie here condemned by the people (*nekrous para tôi dêmiôi keimenous*), is soon to be condemned by the state, and will face his own death. Plato writes nothing without this death in view.[60] And is this not what philosophy teaches us to do, to come to terms with death, even in this strangest of texts that begins education by suppressing all fearful mention of the end (Book III), and closes with the myth of Er who travels to and returns from the land beyond?

But the call here, it seems, is to *not* look upon death, to rather struggle against the desire to confront this realm of shades, to turn away.

> "[Leontius] desired to look, but at the same time he was disgusted and made himself turn away (*apotrepoi*); and for a while he struggled and covered his face. But finally, overpowered by the desire, he opened his eyes wide, ran toward the corpses and said: 'Look, you damned wretches, take your fill of the fair sight.'" . . .
>
> "This speech," I said, "certainly indicates that anger sometimes makes war against the desires as one thing against something else." . . .
>
> "And in many other places, don't we," I said, "notice that, when desires force someone contrary to calculation (*logismon*), he reproaches himself and his spirit is roused against that in him which is doing the forcing; and, just as though there were two parties at faction, such a man's spirit becomes the ally of speech [or reason] (*tôi logôi*)? But as for its making common cause with the desires to do what speech has declared must not be done, I suppose you'd say you had never noticed anything of the kind happening in yourself, nor, I suppose, in anyone else." (439e–440b)

This is *not* compelling speech to prove that anger or spiritedness wars against desire, that in the individual, as in the ideal state, the three forms work together under the aegis of a moderation that guarantees the mythic and untroubled union of the whole. It does not demonstrate that "the ruling part and the two ruled parts are of the single opinion that the calculating part ought to rule and don't raise faction against it" (442c–d). We do not witness the "parts of the soul in a relation of mastering, and being mastered by, one another" that Socrates tells us "is according to nature" (444d).[61]

Leontius's *thumos* doesn't know what it desires or what it says, whether it lies on the side of speech (as calculation and reason) or on that of desire. "Overpowered by the desire [to see]" (440a), a slave to the senses if every there was one, Leontius opens his eyes and runs toward the dead. The *thumos* of Leontius speaks a language that does battle with itself more clearly than with desire. Hardly a command to turn away, Leontius's words are a call to "take [one's] fill of the fair sight." Thus Socrates' exemplary citation of Leontius has him saying precisely what he does not or at least should not mean when it bids him to indulge his scopic desires: it depends, in the blind anger of its sarcasm, on the duplicity of an irony that does and does not serve reason. He may hear himself speak, but he doesn't learn from it.

Nor is the pupil of this lesson in desire any more certain than its utterance. Leontius "opened his eyes wide" and "ran toward the corpses and said: 'Look, you damned wretches, take your fill of the fair sight'" (440a). These desire-inflected words are directed, it seems, to Leontius's eyes in their excessive lust, but just as easily directed to the corpses. Perhaps Leontius calls for the dead to look upon him: he who, with the gesture of having "covered his face," was already like one of them. Indeed there are times when *thumos*, as anger, listening to the speech of reason, makes war against desire and also times when it does not. And sometimes it is the same time, when speech doubles itself and doesn't know which way it is looking, whether it is looking near at hand or far off, whom it is speaking to, and what it is saying.

Remainders

That justice in the individual should come to such a pass and in such an out-of-the-way place in Socrates' story should perhaps not surprise us. Justice is marked by Plato as at once critical to the republic and yet an add-on. That is, when Socrates finally sets his sights on justice, its position is that of a difficult to account for remainder.

> "So then, son of Ariston," I said, "your city would now be founded. In the next place, get yourself an adequate light somewhere; and look yourself—and

call in your brother and Polemarchus and the others—whether we can somehow see where justice might be." . . .

"Now, then," I said, "I hope I'll find it in this way. I suppose our city—if,
that is, it has been correctly founded—is perfectly good."

"Necessarily," he said.

"Plainly, then, it's wise, courageous, moderate and just."

"Plainly."

"Isn't it the case that whichever of them we happen to find will leave as the
remainder (*to hupoloipon*) what hasn't been found?" . . .

"If we recognized the other three first, this would also suffice for the recognition of the thing looked for. For plainly it couldn't be anything but what's
left over (*to hupoleiphthen*)." (427c–428a)

Justice is found in the shadows of a space dark and hard to search out, as a
remnant,[62] as what was "left over" after wisdom, courage, and moderation
have come "plainly to light" (428a and b). For the third time (and there
are other instances as well) in this text so concerned with accounting for
and taking all multiplicity into the oneness of its political machine, the
left-over and left-out threatens. The culminating search for justice follows
immediately upon another trajectory that also dead-ends in a remainder,
and so we must read them side by side.

"Then what," [Adeimantus] said, "might still remain (*loipon*) for our legislation?"

And I said, "For us, nothing. However for the Apollo at Delphi there remain the greatest, fairest, and first of the laws which are given."

"What are they about?" he said.

"Founding of temples, sacrifices, and whatever else belongs to the care of
gods, demons, and heroes; and further, burial of the dead and all the services
needed to keep those in that other place gracious. For such things as these we
neither know ourselves, nor in founding a city shall we be persuaded by any
other man, if we are intelligent, nor shall we make use of any interpreter other
than the ancestral one. Now this god is doubtless the ancestral interpreter of
such things for all humans, and he sits in the middle of the earth at its navel
and delivers his interpretations." (427b–c)

This is the scene that immediately precedes the search for justice, it too
in inadequate light. It brings us once again underneath the earth, to the
question of the dead, to a realm invoked precisely when Socrates is at a
loss, when he must admit there are such things we cannot know ourselves.
All this takes place in an uncertainty about the powers of human interpre-

tation, as a deferral of interpretation, and in the name of Apollo at Delphi as the only and ancestral interpreter. This is the same god who famously declared no one wiser than Socrates (*Apology* 20e), which Socrates attributed to the fact that he alone did not think he knew what he did not know (*Apology* 21d). Thus there is much that resonates with the enigmatic tale of Leontius beneath the city of Athens.

The Weaker Sex

The discussion arrives at its original goal, a definition of justice in the individual. What Socrates seeks, after all, is less the external business of the polis, a mere phantom this, he says (443c), than justice "with respect to what is within, with respect to what truly concerns him and his own," a setting of the individual's "house in good order" (443c–d). What remains, then? He is finished, he believes, with the creation of the ideal polis in speech ("Good, then, and right, is what I call such a city and regime and such a man . . . " [449a]) and sets out to describe the rest, the four bad regimes possible in city and soul. "And I was going to speak of them in the order that each appeared to me to pass from one to the other. But Polemarchus—. . . . " (449a–b). Socrates is nevertheless wrenched back to his political regime because of something left out and something left over, the small matter of women and children that, in an aside, he had decided to leave aside.

> "If by being well educated they become sensible men, they'll easily see to all this and everything else we are now leaving out (*paraleipomen*)—that the possession (*ktêsin*) of women, marriage, and procreation of children must as far as possible be arranged according to the proverb that friends have all things in common." (423e–424a; in 449c: "the things of friends will be in common.")

That elision had allowed both argument and regime to continue in undisturbed progression: "And hence," I said, "the regime, once well started, will roll on like a circle in its growth" (424a).

Book V opens with an interruption, however, the repetition of the interruption that opened the *Republic*, the pull on the himation, the insistence on new arguments and discussion, the forced intrusion on progression.[63] Socrates has been arrested in his ordered movement that rolled on like a circle in its chosen path. He thought he had brought to completion the creation of the good regime so that he could go on to distinguish it

from the bad. But like Arion in Herodotus's *Histories*, the greatest musi-
cian of his time, whose songs earn him a fortune which he prepares to
bring home, something conspires to rob Socrates of his glory, something
that smacks of a democratic resolution on the part of his interlocutors.[64]

> And I was going to speak of [the four bad regimes] in the order that each ap-
> peared to me to pass from one to the other. But Polemarchus—he was sitting
> at a little distance from Adeimantus—stretched out his hand and took hold
> of his cloak from above by the shoulder . . . and said some things in his ear
> . . . : "Shall we let it go or what shall we do?"
>
>   "Not in the least," said Adeimantus, now speaking aloud.
>
>   And I said, "What in particular aren't you letting go?"
>
>   "You," he said.
>
>   "Because of what in particular?" I said.
>
>   "In our opinion you're taking it easy," he said, "and robbing us of a whole
> section of the argument, and that not the least, so you won't have to go
> through it. And you supposed you'd get away with it by saying, as though it
> were something quite ordinary, that after all it's plain to everyone that, as for
> women and children, the things of friends will be in common." (449a–c)
>
>   "In fact," said Thrasymachus, "you can take this as a resolution approved
> by all of us, Socrates." (450a)

Let us leave aside for the moment our spirited rage, misplaced, perhaps,
looking far off from the perspective of the twenty-first century, that the
relation to women and the children they produce is one of acquisition
and use (*ktêsis te kai khreia* [451c]). What surprises the disciples, of course,
is not the fact that women are possessions, but that, like most other property of the guardians, they will be held in common ("no one will possess
any private property except for what's entirely necessary" [416d]). Much is
at stake in this interruption, but not only the question of women.

Setting out to speak of the bad regimes, Socrates is halted in his tracks
and turned into something of a drama queen. Whatever certainty the
dialectical pondering of the nature of justice has brought, "women" will
throw it all into disarray.

> "What a thing you've done in arresting me," I said. "How much discussion
> you've set in motion, from the beginning again as it were, about the regime I
> was delighted to think I had already described, content if one were to leave it
> at accepting these things as they were stated then. You don't know how great

a swarm of arguments you're stirring up with what you are now summoning to the bar." (450a–b)

Let us take Socrates at his word and ask: Why should the issue of woman demand starting all over? Why do the arguments in whose order Socrates took such pride threaten to swarm, returning to sting their master? And why is the very possibility of the polis suddenly on the line?

> "It's not easy to go through, you happy man," I said. "Even more than what we went through before, it admits of many doubts. For, it could be doubted that the things said are possible; and, even if, in the best possible conditions, they could come into being, that they would be what is best will also be doubted. So that is why there's a certain hesitation about getting involved in it, for fear that the argument might seem to be a prayer. . . . " (450c–d)

Housekeeper to the state, Socrates needs to return it to good order. Binding together the recalcitrant parts, making it one from many, he must harmonize any deleted form of the argument, which now includes the formerly omitted form of the populace, women (443d). He goes back to "what perhaps should have been said then in its turn" (451b–c) and "having completely finished the male drama [goes on] to complete the female" (451c). It is quite a theatrical performance, as we've already begun to see. He foresees, not only a threat to the possibility of the city he creates, but also jeering laughter, overwhelming waves, bodies of water that seem unswimmable, possible losses at sea. In doubt as he is, the danger, he declares, is "slipping from the truth" (451a). However much he fears falling himself and dragging his friends with him (451a), however threatened he is by the terrain below, the place at which he wishes to arrive is clear. It is a city that experiences pleasure and pain communally, in which "all the citizens alike rejoice and are pained at the same comings into being and perishings" (462b), in relation to which everyone will regard everything as "my own" (462c), a city "most like a single human being" (462c), a city that is one (462b).

Socrates proposes achieving this unity through a control of reproduction in which sacred marriages, those most beneficial to the city, replace "irregular intercourse" (458d). The breeding of hunting dogs, noble cocks, horses, and other animals serves as a model for the reproduction of the "guardians' herd" (459e). Socrates calls for rulers who will "use many drugs" (459c), "a throng of lies and deceptions for the benefit of the ruled" (459c), a lottery of permissions for intercourse with "subtle lots . . . fabricated so that the ordinary man will blame chance rather than the rulers for each union" (460a).

> "There is a need for the best men to have intercourse as often as possible with the best women, and the reverse for the most ordinary men with the most ordinary women; and the offspring of the former must be reared but not that of the others, if the flock is going to be of the most eminent quality And all this must come to pass without being noticed by anyone except the rulers themselves if the guardians' herd is to be as free as possible from faction." (459d–e)
>
> "All these women are to belong to all these men in common. . . . And the children, in their turn, will be in common, and neither will a parent know his own offspring, nor a child his parent." (457c–d)

The holding in common of women and children binds each of the guardians to all the others, as brother, sister, father, mother, son, daughter, descendants, or ancestors (463c), and "Since they are free from faction among themselves, there won't ever be any danger that the rest of the city will split into factions against these guardians or one another" (465b).

Reproduction is deceptively regulated by the rulers, those to whom the distinction between good and bad is alone entrusted, and who nevertheless convince the guardians of an equality among one another as pure as simple chance. Something similar might be said of the position of woman, for in a gesture whose radicality must not be overlooked Socrates declares her the equal of her male counterpart, almost.[65]

> "Then," I said, "if either the class of men or that of women shows its superiority in some art or other practice, then we'll say that that art must be assigned to it. But if they look as though they differ in this alone, that the female bears and the male mounts, we'll assert that it has not thereby yet been proved that a woman differs from a man with respect to what we're talking about; rather, we'll still suppose that our guardians and their women must practice the same things." (454d–e)

Even though not *yet* proved that woman differs from man, even though it's only a *supposition* that she will practice the same things, even though she takes her place as a *possession* of the guardians here and elsewhere ("guardians and their women" [454e]), woman it seems is the equal of man.

Or if not quite the equal of the male guardian, she will, in any case, practice the same things, stand by her man, so to speak, doing the same things, even though always a little bit weaker.

> "Therefore, my friend, there is no practice of a city's governors which belongs to woman because she's woman, or to man because he's man; but the natures are scattered alike among both animals; and woman participates according to nature in all practices, and man in all, but in all of them woman is weaker than man." (455d–e)
>
> "Men and women, therefore, also have the same nature with respect to guarding a city, except insofar as the one is weaker and the other stronger." (456a)[66]

Weaker but seemingly equal, though elsewhere in the *Republic* frequently and repeatedly denigrated as a ludicrous or dangerous model for male behavior,[67] woman can practice all the pursuits of men. "There is no practice relevant to the government of a city that is peculiar" to man (455b), but also none "peculiar to woman" (454b). Of course "the female bears (*tiktein*) and the male mounts" (454d); over and against the fixity of the masculine role as Socrates describes it, is a hint of that proliferation, that multiplicity, so unsavory in the city. But in all other regards woman is the same, or almost the same, taken into the male fold, the "herd" (459e), originally left out of Socrates' argument, but only because he was hesitant to admit just how he planned to take her in.

No doubt this explains why the critical passage we cited on eristic (454a–c) as counter position and counterpart to dialectic appears precisely with respect to the question of woman. Socrates had been practicing dialectic, on the sly, long and hard, ever since setting up his comparison between city and man, for three of the dialogue's ten books without mention of his dialectical mode of argument. That eristic is openly and insistently cast aside just as woman gets taken in is a coincidence, no, a parallel, to which one needs to pay heed. The "contradicting art" of eristic, the staging of individuals over and against one another, just won't do for Socrates' polis where the possibility of faction must preemptively be eradicated, even at the price of assimilating women, a group of weaker outsider insiders who might otherwise maintain their difference and get out of hand. Thus banning eristic at the very moment that (shocking as it may be to fourth-century Athenians) woman is declared more or less the same, is of a piece with the desire for oneness of the city (454a). In the *Meno*, also, Socrates contrasts eristic to dialectic:

> "And if my questioner were a professor of the eristic and contentious sort, I should say to him: I have made my statement; if it is wrong, your business is to examine and refute it. But if, like you and me on this occasion, we were friends and chose to have a discussion (*dialegesthai*) together, I should have to reply in some milder tone more suited to dialectic (*dialektikôteron*). The more dialectical way (*dialektikôteron*), I suppose, is not merely to answer what is true, but also to make use of these points which the questioned person acknowledges he knows." (*Meno*, 75c–d)[68]

"The power of the [dialectic] art is grand" (454a), but above all it is mild and friendly, conducive to eradicating the difference between the interlocutors, as the questioner makes use of the ideas of the questioned to bring him or her into line.[69]

And yet, turning "our gaze somewhere far off" to women, as we have done, is only half the story. The other half, which "we have been saying and hearing . . . all along without learning from ourselves that we were in a way saying it" (432d–e) is the tale of guardians turned into "a throng of noble cocks" (459a) or a domesticated "herd" (459e). Thus from the beginning, for, as Socrates warned, it is necessary to begin again (450a), it is not only that women practice those things which seemed particular to men, but that, more or less, all of the guardians and all of the craftsmen are transformed into what one might tend to call (at best) "women"—or even domesticated animals. Unwillingly and unknowingly manipulated by those who control their procreation and everything else besides, in relation to the rulers, all of them, gender notwithstanding, will always remain the weaker sex.

The Pattern of Philosophy

We might interrupt the path of the argument here, if not to get an overview, at least to mark the interrelations of all the "remainders" we have been trying to account for, the leftovers that appear in somewhat rapid succession in Plato's text, or at least laid out side by side in considerable proximity to one another: the legislation that is left to Apollo at Delphi (427b); the remaining attribute of the city, the last to be found:

justice (432d); and the form that was left out just prior to these, and then subsequently called into question at the opening of Book V (449): woman. What remains for the god is the care of a hierarchically enumerated list of beings that moves from the gods above to demons to heroes and finally to the dead below. These are the exceptional ones who might escape the purview of what Socrates otherwise maps out for control by the republic. Justice, itself remaindered, is the force within the city, as we have seen, that gathers all other individuals, as groups, into the fold of its rule, a force of mastering. Women are, apparently, the threateningly large group that cannot be left out of the civil order and that Socrates' justice must find a way to assimilate. Three times (and these are not the only instances) the possibility of the left-out and left-over menaces and is accounted for in this dialogue so concerned with taking all multiplicity into the oneness of its political machine.

Socrates has survived the first two waves brought on by the interruption of the dialogue in the name of woman. Let us leave adrift for the moment the fact that *kuma* (457b) suggests anything swollen as if pregnant and might just as well suggest the foetus in the womb as a wave of the sea:[70] it is as though the fruits of women's reproductive capacities (that alone in which women differ from men [454d–e]), despite the system of elaborate strictures, might yet be a force to reckon with. It is these conventionally feminine capacities that become the model, in a sexually suggestive later passage, for the lover of learning, who seeks to grasp "what *is*":

> ". . . he grasps the nature itself of each thing which *is* with the part of the soul fit to grasp a thing of that sort; and it is the part akin to it that is fit. And once near it and coupled with what really is, having begotten intelligence and truth (*gennêsas noun kai alêtheian*), he knows and lives truly, is nourished and so ceases from his labor pains. . . . " (490b)

And yet, Socrates, at least here and now, is not woman enough to be able to grasp "what *is*": he is in precarious waters, threatened by the wave, the big one. Still, he is swimming—and, if not moving along swimmingly, nevertheless doing the crawl and not the dead man's float, and heading for home. He has escaped the first wave of the "woman's law" that lays down that men and women guardians "must share all pursuits in common" (457b–c) and the second law of women belonging "to all these men in common" (457c). "The third wave" will bring doubt of the possibility of the regime in general. Socrates had proposed the question earlier himself, tenuously, asking "whether after all it is possible, as it is among other animals, that this community come into being among human beings too, and in what way it is possible" (466d).

Between the waves, as it were, what seems a space of respite: between the two waves of woman and the third that questions the possibility of the regime in general, Socrates, postponing the answer to that question, launches a seemingly innocuous passage: "How," Socrates asks, "will our soldiers deal with enemies?" (469b). In contrasting the relation of Greek to Greek with that of Greek to barbarian, he puts the law of woman (457b) in perspective and mans a lifeboat in advance of the third wave to come.

"Now the name faction[71] is applied to the hatred of one's own, war to the hatred of the alien. . . . I assert that the Greek stock is with respect to itself its own and akin, with respect to the barbaric, foreign and alien."

"Yes," he said, "that is fine."

"Then when Greeks fight with barbarians and barbarians with Greeks, we'll assert they are at war and are enemies by nature, and this hatred must be called war; while when Greeks do any such thing to Greeks, we'll say that they are by nature friends . . . and this kind of hatred must be called faction." (470b–d)

"And they will have their differences like men who, after all, will be reconciled." (471a)

"Faction" is taken to name the strife of Greek with Greek and its horizon is always reconciliation: this makes explicit what we observed both in Socrates' move to take in women and in the shift from eristic to dialectic. Eristic on the sociological scale is the waging of war that defines the hatred between Greek and barbarian. The shift from "war" to "faction" here in the strife between Greek and Greek means the promise of reconciliation similar to that of dialectic: dialectic as the repression of difference—mildness in the name of a harmony that guarantees the oneness of the city.

The city is shored up against the third wave that will place its possibility in question. As in the opening discussion (373d–374a) in which the boundaries of the regime and war were the decisive elements of founding the city, so here, too, the city is defined, its limits marked, in relation to the enemy. And yet, the enemy, as it were, also challenges from within, for Glaucon, noting the ploy of Socrates' detour, has not forgotten the left-over, left-out question of the possibility of the regime and sees all too well that "if one were to allow [him] to speak about this sort of thing, [he] would never remember what [he] previously set aside in order to say all this. Is it possible for this regime to come into being, and how is it ever possible?" (471c).

Socrates responds:

"Perhaps you don't know that when I've hardly escaped the two waves, you're now bringing the biggest and most difficult, the third wave. When you see and hear it, you'll be quite sympathetic, recognizing that it was, after all, fitting for me to hesitate and be afraid to speak and undertake to consider so paradoxical an argument." (472a)

The ineluctable condition of possibility of the regime is the coincidence of political power and philosophy (473d). In retrospect, the parallels between the mode of Socratic philosophy and the regime he sets out to create go without saying. This coincidence is the inevitable conclusion, and precondition, in a text both political and philosophical, whose premises all depend on the possibility of a perfected hierarchy. This is what Socrates likens "to the biggest wave," likely "to drown [him] in laughter and ill repute" (473c). And yet, in insisting on the becoming-one of these two just men, philosopher and ruler, Socrates puts aside his earlier, first response to Glaucon's challenge, "how [is it] possible for this regime to come into being" (472b), a response better forgotten since it sets out explicitly the problematic nature of the like which has been at play since the search for justice began.

"Then," I said, "first it should be recalled that we got to this point while seeking what justice and injustice are like. . . . [If] we find out what justice is like, will we also insist that the just man must not differ at all from justice itself but in every way be such as it is?" . . .

"We'll be content with that," he said.

"It was therefore, for the sake of a pattern," I said, "that we were seeking both for what justice by itself is like, and for the perfectly just man, if he should come into being, and what he would be like once come into being; and, in their turns, for injustice and the most unjust man. Thus, looking off at what their relationships to happiness and its opposite appear to us to be, we would also be compelled to agree in our own cases that the man who is most like them will have the portion most like theirs. We were not seeking them for the sake of proving that it's possible for these things to come into being. . . .

Do you suppose a painter is any less good who draws a pattern (*paradeigma*)
of what the fairest human being would be like . . . but can't prove that it's also
possible that such a man come into being?" (472b–d)

This unsettling passage places the philosopher in the role of the painter,
that craftsman so famously attacked in Book 10 as the producer of an imitation of an imitation (596–597). Socrates tells us, at least here, at least for
the moment, that philosophy takes place "for the sake of a pattern" (*para-
deigmatos ara heneka*), a para-digm, literally an exhibiting side by side,[72] of
justice and the just man, of happiness, and so on. That what philosophy
seeks is not necessarily what *is,* but the production of the side-by-side,
something very akin to the structure of analogy that set the search for
justice in motion, is what one should not, but will inevitably, set aside
and forget.

This is all the more difficult to keep in mind, since, if a laying side by
side is the prelude to the third wave, the wave itself will be registered as
the celebratory and necessary coincidence, agreement, falling or coming
together, of the ultimate positions in the structure of human hierarchy,
philosopher and king (473c–d). It may be possible to imagine this coincidence; still Socrates also reminds Glaucon that, though a painter may
"[draw] a pattern of what the fairest human being would be *like,*" he cannot necessarily "prove that it's also possible that such a man come into being" (472d). By the same token, what they say is no "less good on account
of [their] not being able to prove that it is possible to found a city the
same as the one in speech" (472e). And so they must settle for "[finding]
that a city could be governed in a way *most closely approximating what has
been said*" (473a, emphases in the last several quotes mine).

What takes place here is not only the impossibility of the city as created
in speech, but also the impossibility of shedding the difference of comparison. Thus there is hardly a sentence in the long passage cited above
(472b–d) that eludes the "like." At least with regard to the city, this seems
to cast a pall on the quest for what *is.* Yet perhaps, after all, this is only
the disparity between form and what might inevitably take form in the
sensible world. For the philosopher will nevertheless be able to catch sight
of what is and to distinguish it from what merely "participates in it." As
difficult as it is to make out here, it is the double gesture of the side-by-
side, of the *paradeigma,* on the one hand and the transcendent move to
unity of political and philosophical power on other that will account for
much in the next two books.

The Great Divides: I. The Divided Line

With this Socrates has established the pattern for the larger, more articulated gestures in Books VI and VII: the divided line and the allegory of the cave, and more immediately for the distinction among knowledge, opinion, and ignorance at the close of Book V.

> "Is the man who holds that there are fair things but doesn't hold that there is beauty itself and who, if someone leads him to the knowledge of it, isn't able to follow—is he, *in your opinion*, living in a dream or is he awake? Consider it. Doesn't dreaming, whether one is asleep or awake, consist in believing a likeness (*to homoion*) of something to be not a likeness, but rather the thing itself to which it is like?"
>
> "I, at least," he said, "would say that a man who does that dreams."
>
> "And what about the man who, contrary to this, believes that there is something fair itself and is able to catch sight both of it and of what participates in it, and doesn't believe that what participates is it itself, nor that it itself is what participates—is he, *in your opinion*, living in a dream or is he awake?"
>
> "He's quite awake," he said.
>
> "Wouldn't we be right in saying that this man's thought, because he knows, is knowledge, while the other's is opinion because he opines?" (476c–d, emphases mine)[73]

Opinion results from experiencing the manifestation of a form in those things that participate in the form, the apparitional manys, without the experience or understanding of the form itself, the experience, say, of beautiful things but not of beauty itself (476a–b). One "opines neither that which *is* nor that which *is not*" (478c). That which *is not* is relegated to ignorance or nescience (478c). Knowledge, on the other hand, is dependent on what *is*. Thus knowledge would be the seeing of beauty itself as well as its individual apparitions in things while knowing the difference between the form and the appearance, the thing and its likeness.

And isn't this the kind of path on which dialectic advances, not only what we have emphasized up till now, the friendly and mild setting aside of the face-to-face hostilities of eristic contradiction, but also a "[consideration of] what's said by separating it out into its forms" (454a)? For dialectic has multiple aspects which we must try to think together: all the moves to draw both interlocutors and what's spoken about into a sphere of agreement, but also a separating out (400c, *dielesthai*, from *diaireô*) a taking one from another, dividing into parts, distinguishing, saying distinctly, defining (LS).[74] How do we think these two, agreement and separating out, together and how think them in relation to the other role set forth for dialectic in the *Republic*, the activity at the highest level in the realm of the intelligible?

> "Well, then, go on to understand that by the other segment of the intelligible I mean that which argument itself grasps with the power of dialectic, making the hypotheses not beginnings but really hypotheses—that is, steppingstones and springboards—in order to reach what is free from hypothesis at the beginning which is the whole."[75] (511b)

Freedom from suppositions, a grasp of the whole, this is what dialectic brings about as it "leads the soul powerfully upward and compels it to discuss (*dialegesthai*)" that which is in no way "attached to visible or tangible bodies" (525d), compelling "the soul to use the intellect itself on the truth itself" (526b), to try "by discussion—by means of argument without the use of any of the senses—to attain to each thing itself that is. . . . " (532a).[76] It "goes back down again to an end; making no use of anything sensed in any way, but using forms themselves, going through forms to forms, it ends in forms too" (511b–c).[77] In this way one comes "to the very end of the intelligible realm" in the "journey" that Socrates calls "dialectic" (532a–b).[78]

Dialectic separates out into the proper forms: it orders, organizes, while functioning itself as the very path through an upward-graded hierarchy, transcendence made possible by the activity of division. Dialectic as journey will present some stumbling blocks, but its purpose is clear: as the power of discerning divisions, of sorting out properly according to form, its effect is, nevertheless, to repress difference. It moves through the divisions it marks out, drawing them together and arranging them into a whole. Thus philosophic discussion lays out the three parts of the city, in turn like those of the soul, in which each part seems separate and yet is destined to serve in a mild and friendly manner the interests of the whole.[79]

The more elaborate path to intellection, of which the division into knowledge, opinion, and ignorance was the preamble, will be laid out in a similar way, this time according to "four affections arising in the soul" (511d) rather than three. The struggle between the high and the low (reason and desire), around a pivotal middle position (*thumos*), in the city and in the soul, which we observed earlier in the dialogue, now shifts to a pattern of four that allows structures of simile and analogy to govern the schema. As Book VI opens Socrates announces that he and Glaucon have, "through a somewhat lengthy argument," "brought to light" "who the philosophers are and who the nonphilosophers" (484a). At the close of that book he sets forth the pattern for understanding this distinction as the divided line, a line on which, to begin with, the "intelligible class and region" (509d) and the "visible" will be distinguished.

> "Then, take a line cut in two unequal segments, one for the class that is seen, the other for the class that is intellected—and go on and cut each segment in the same ratio. Now, in terms of relative clarity and obscurity, you'll have one segment in the visible part for images. I mean by images first shadows, then appearances produced in water and in all close-grained, smooth, bright things, and everything of the sort, if you understand."
>
> "I do understand."
>
> "Then in the other segment put that of which this first is the likeness—the animals around us, and everything that grows, and the whole class of artifacts."
>
> "I put them there," he said.
>
> "And would you also be willing," I said, "to say that with respect to truth or lack of it, as the opinable is distinguished from the knowable, so the likeness is distinguished from that of which it is the likeness?"
>
> "I would indeed," he said. (509d–510b)

The horizontal division in Fig. 3.1 makes the slice between the intelligible above and the opinable or visible below.[80] The under-the-line is populated with living things and artifacts and, below them, with their images. The relation between image and thing, we are told, is like that between the entire visible realm of the lower section of the schema and the entire upper section, the intelligible.

That is:

images (or imagination) : animals, plants and artifacts
::
opinable : intelligible (or knowable)

The opinable, then, functions as an image of the knowable. Indeed it is only through this imaging of the knowable world, its metaphorization in terms of "things," that we come to understand it here and elsewhere, most especially in the allegory of the cave. It is the side-by-side, the patterning

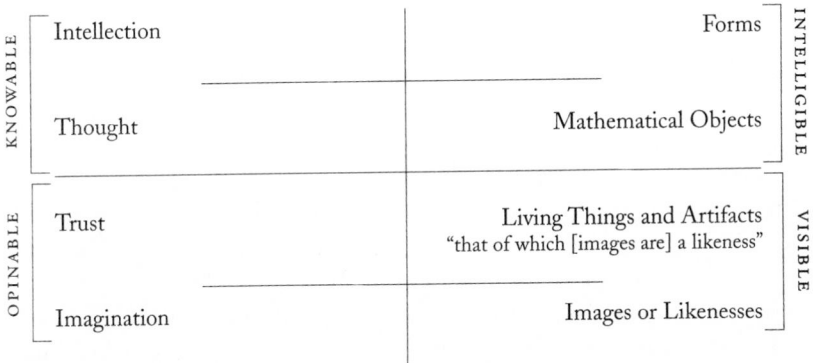

FIGURE 3.1.   The Divided Line: Book VI of Plato's Republic (509d–511e)

of the one section of the line on the other, which makes forms or intellection available to understanding.

A different, but not unrelated complication takes place as Socrates describes the cut in two of the intelligible. As an example of thought (the lower section of the intelligible realm) Socrates proposes the way in which the geometrician uses particular examples of a figure to reach an understanding of that figure in general and contrasts this with the other, higher, segment of the intelligible.

> "I suppose you know that the men who work in geometry, calculation, and the like treat as known the odd and the even, the figures, three forms of angles, and other things akin to these in each kind of inquiry. These things they make hypotheses and don't think it worthwhile to give any further account of them to themselves or others, as though they were clear to all. Beginning from them, they go ahead with their exposition of what remains and end consistently at the object toward which their investigation was directed."
>
> "Most certainly, I know that," he said.
>
> "Don't you also know that they use visible forms besides and make their arguments about them, not thinking about them but about those others that they are like? They make the arguments for the sake of the square itself and the diagonal itself, not for the sake of the diagonal they draw, and likewise with the rest. These things themselves that they mold and draw, of which there are shadows and images in water, they now use as images, seeking to see those things themselves, that one can see in no other way than with thought." . . .

> "Well, then, this is the form I said was intelligible. However, a soul in in-
> vestigating it is compelled to use hypotheses, and does not go to a beginning
> because it is unable to step out above the hypotheses." (510c–511a)

If the upper section of the intelligible, that of forms and intellection, uses
hypotheses merely as steppingstones to go beyond, if it is here that the
"argument itself grasps with the power of dialectic. . . . making no use
of anything sensed in any way" (511b–c), this is a mode of argument that
Socrates himself, and most clearly in his laying out of the divided line,
is unable to reach. "Then, take a line cut in two unequal segments . . .
—and go on and cut each segment in the same ratio" (509d): this is the
language of geometry, bound to the realm of thought. "It uses as images
those very things of which images are made by the things below. . . . "
(511a).[81]

This should not surprise us. If the divided line is prefaced by a discussion of "the *idea* of the good" as "the greatest study" (*hê tou agathou
idea megiston* [505a]), for which it may not "do to look at a sketch" (*hu-
pographên* [504d]), nevertheless it is of this that "we don't have sufficient
knowledge" (505a). And Socrates refuses "to speak about what [he] doesn't
know as though [he] knew" (506c).

> "Let's leave aside for the time being what the good itself is—for it looks to me
> as though it's out of the range of our present thrust to attain the opinions I
> now hold about it. But I'm willing to tell what looks like a child of the good
> and most similar to it, if you please, or if not, to let it go."
> "Do tell," he said. "Another time you'll pay us what's due on the father's
> narrative."
> "I could wish," I said, "that I were able to pay and you were able to receive
> it itself, and not just the interest, as is the case now. Anyhow, receive this
> interest and child of the good itself. But be careful that I don't in some way
> unwillingly deceive you in rendering the account of the interest fraudulent."
> (506d–507a)

The deception here is indeed unwilling, for it is not that Socrates, through
a sleight of hand, offers the child, the interest, the token, in place of the
father, the capital, the thing itself.[82] Socrates openly announces his inability to pay, along with Glaucon's inability to receive the good itself.
The fraud is not the substitution of the one for the other but the bogus
assumption that the good "itself" might be conceivable outside its relation to its image.

Socrates has the good come to light through its offspring: the sun. This, in turn, shines forth in an act of "yoking," the bringing together of two bodies, a marriage of sorts, between sight and the seen that will prove very productive.

> "Then the sense of sight and the power of being seen are yoked together with a yoke that, by measure of an *idea* by no means insignificant, is more honorable than the yokes uniting other teams, if light is not without honor." (507e–508a)

Socrates explains the good by way of the image of the sun's relationship to physical sight. As in the divided line we gain access to the intelligible world only by way of an analogy with the visible or opinable world. Just as sight shows itself to be in the eyes only when the things it engages are illumined by the sun: "think that the soul is also characterized in this way. When it fixes itself on that which is illumined by truth and that which *is*, it intellects, knows, and appears to possess intelligence" (508d).

> "Therefore, say that what provides the truth to the things known and gives the power to the one who knows, is the *idea* of the good. And, as the cause of the knowledge and truth (*epistêmês . . . kai alêtheias*), you can understand it to be a thing known; but, as fair as these two are—knowledge and truth—if you believe that it is something different from them and still fairer than they, your belief will be right. As for knowledge and truth, just as in the other region it is right to hold light and sight sunlike, but to believe them to be sun is not right; so, too, here, to hold these two [knowledge and truth] to be like the good is right, but to believe that either of them is the good is not right. The condition which characterizes the good must receive still greater honor." (508e–509a)

Doesn't this mark the progress of dialectic? The "lover of learning [striving] for what *is*" (490a), whose "passionate love" grasped its object of desire in a coupling, begetting, and production (*gennêsas*, 490b) of "intelligence and truth" through "labor pains," was earlier couched in terms of feminine sensuality (see above, p. 86). Here Socrates seems to fulfill the promise of dialectic, attempting to shed a discourse of the tangible body (525d), to produce "discussion—by means of argument without the use of any of the senses" (532a).

The entire passage, nevertheless, is framed as a question of generation. The sun provides not only the power of seeing and being seen but also "generation" (509b), and the relation between the sun and the good is that of offspring. "'Well, then,' I said, 'say that the sun is the offspring of the good . . . begot in a proportion with itself'" (*analogon heautôi* [508b]). What is it that the good produces in giving birth to the sun, if not an image of itself? The good not only provides power to the one who knows and truth to the things known but also generates images: on the one hand the sun, but also that which seems to escape the language of the senses: "intelligence and what is intellected" (508c). Knowledge and truth are "*like* the good" (509a, emphasis mine).

There is no getting around it. The *Republic*, its call to what *is* and its denigration of becoming notwithstanding, is a hotbed of reproduction.[83] This is that small matter which distinguished woman from man (454d) in a polis in which, we have suggested, just about everyone is more or less woman. Woman is no longer a mark for exclusion but rather definition of nearly the entire community and one definition as well of the mode of argument. No reader of the dialogue can overlook this. Thus, it is not only here where he speaks of the sun as image (*eikona* [509a]) and likeness (*homoiotêta* [509c]), but throughout that Socrates readily admits his passionate desire for images alongside his admonitions against them.

> "The question you are asking," I said, "needs an answer given through an image (*di' eikonos*)."
> "And you, in particular," he said, "I suppose, aren't used to speaking through images."
> "All right," I said. "Are you making fun of me after having involved me in an argument so hard to prove? At all events, listen to the image so that you may see still more how greedily I liken." (487e–488a, translation altered)

Images from beginning to end: still something has happened to the status of the "like" in the course of the dialogue. Even before the famous and pivotal analogy of city and man that sets the course for books to come, Socrates had been in love with "the like." In his "early period" (Book I) that is, Plato makes plentiful use of argument through comparison,[84] just as he does in the books that follow. But here in Book VI, just when dialectic should be freeing itself from that which it condemns, the realms of sense and imaging, and just when the intelligible is announced as analogous to its offspring, a rigorous hierarchy of their relationship is established. The good is the father and the sun its mere child (506e, 508b), "out of the range of our present thrust" (506e); the *idea* of the good is "the cause of the knowledge and truth" (508e) but "is something different from them and still fairer" (508e), "beyond them in beauty" (509a), "beyond being" and "exceeding [them] in dignity and power" (509b). "And Glaucon, quite ridiculously, said, "Apollo, what a demonic excess/hyperbole/casting beyond!" (*Apollon, ephê, daimonias huperbolês!* [509c, translation extended]). Sometimes it's the children who get it right. Futile as it inevitably may be, Socrates' repeated gesture is to separate out the goodly and the godly, casting them beyond, up to a realm untouched by its offspring and analogons.

Is this not what the divided line and ultimately dialectic is about, separating what *is*, the "real," from the imagined, the light from the shadows, and, as it will turn out, the men from the boys?

> "Let's proceed to the song itself and go through it just as we went through the prelude. So tell what the character of the power of dialectic is, and, then, into exactly what forms it is divided; and finally what are its ways (*hodoi*). For these, as it seems, would lead at last toward that place which is for the one who reaches it a haven from the road (*hodou*), as it were, and an end of his journey."
>
> "You will no longer be able to follow, my dear Glaucon," I said, "although there wouldn't be any lack of eagerness on my part. But you would no longer be seeing an image of what we are saying, but rather the truth itself, at least as it looks to me. Whether it is really so or not can no longer be properly insisted on. But that there is some such thing to see must be insisted on." . . .
>
> "And, also, that the power of dialectic alone could reveal it to a man experienced in the things we just went through, while it is in no other way possible?" (532d–533a)

It is hierarchization at every turn, in the classes of the polis, in the forms of the individual soul (435c), in the conceptualization of knowledge, all of which promise a resistance to the lure of the underground. And yet, in this critical movement of dialectic—that of separating out into forms, which is as political as it is philosophical, and as counterproductive as it is productive—the law of analogy inevitably holds a certain sway. Dialectic sets up the great divides, to salvage intellection from thought, trust from imagination, the intelligible from the visible, but can do so only by simultaneously generating the forms of the lower realms as images of the upper—unwanted by-products that cannot be expunged, hypotheses, those stepping stones and springboards Socrates was so eager to transcend: reproduction forever counterbalancing the ascent while making it possible.

The Great Divides: II. The Cave

Perhaps this explains the opening of Book VII. No sooner has Socrates reiterated the schema of the divided line in the most abstract of terms (511d–e) than we are pitched into the image and images of the cave. The cave is "next" (514a); it follows, but is also next to the divided line as its ineluctably generated image. Dialectic, analogy, the underground: these are conceivable only in the relation between the below and above, inextricably bound to one another. Socrates will describe the prison home of the cave and contrast it with a realm above, lit by the light of the sun. The *idea* of the good in the region of the intelligible, it seems, has once again begotten an offspring in proportion with itself and its relation to the visible.

> "Well, then, my dear Glaucon," I said, "this image as a whole must be connected with what was said before. Liken the domain revealed through sight to the prison home, and the light of the fire in it to the sun's power; and, in applying the going up and the seeing of what's above to the soul's journey up to the intelligible place, you'll not mistake my expectation, since you desire to hear it. A god doubtless knows if it happens to be true. At all events, this is the way the phenomena look to me: in the knowable the last thing to be seen, and that with considerable effort, is the *idea* of the good; but once seen, it must be concluded that this is in fact the cause of all that is right and fair in everything—in the visible it gave birth to light and its sovereign; in the intelligible, itself sovereign, it provided truth and intelligence. . . . " (517a–c)

This melancholy passage is, in a sense, the culmination of the description of the cave. It summarizes the image in all its gloom and seems to leave Socrates somewhat in the dark. For Socrates remains in the realm of "phenomena," with ultimate judgment once again left to the god: only the "god doubtless *knows* if it happens to be true" (emphasis mine). A few pages later, as we have seen, the problem shifts from Socrates to Glaucon, who "will no longer be able to follow," because it is "no longer [a matter of] . . . seeing an image of what we are saying, but rather the truth itself" (533a). Still, even there "whether it is really so or not" (533a) remains unresolved.

Nevertheless the allegory opens with Socrates very much in command.

"Next, then," I said, "make an image of our nature in its education and want of education, likening it to a condition of the following kind. See human beings as though they were in an underground cave-like dwelling with its entrance, a long one, open to the light across the whole width of the cave. They are in it from childhood with their legs and necks in bonds so that they are fixed, seeing only in front of them, unable because of the bond to turn their heads all the way around. Their light is from a fire burning far above and behind them. Between the fire and the prisoners there is a road (*hodon*) above, along which see a wall, built like the partitions puppet-handlers set in front of the human beings and over which they show the puppets."
"I see," he said. (514a–b)

Socrates is pulling the strings here, handling his puppet who, dutifully, when commanded to see, sees. Glaucon is called on to make and see "an image of our nature": the human beings with their necks and heads in bonds facing the inside of the cave; behind the prisoners the road along a wall over which the puppet-handlers carry the artifacts; behind the wall and puppeteers the fire that casts the shadows. Behind the fire Glaucon who, like the prisoners, stares, almost silently, into the depths of the cave, with Socrates, no doubt, standing behind him and uttering the sounds that tell him what to see and do.

"Then also see along this wall human beings carrying all sorts of artifacts, which project above the wall, and statues of men and other animals wrought from stone, wood, and every kind of material; as is to be expected, some of the carriers utter sounds while others are silent."
"It's a strange image," he said, "and strange prisoners you're telling of."
"They're like us," I said. "For in the first place, do you suppose such men would have seen anything of themselves and one another other than the shadows cast by the fire on the side of the cave facing them?" (514b–515a)

Just as the "*idea* of the good" "provides the truth to the things known and gives the power to the one who knows" (508e), just as the sun "provides what is seen with the power of being seen" (509b) and enables sight to show itself in the eyes (508d), just as the fire in the cave has similar properties in relation to the prisoners, so it is in Socrates' hands to have Glaucon both make an image with the power of being seen and to see it. Us too perhaps. Socrates, figure of the fire, or is it the sun? Or should we be seduced into thinking that he illuminates like the *idea* of the good? In any case, Socrates causes the image and images of the cave to be made and seen: and yet they are still "attached to visible or tangible bodies" (525d), and come into being only through an act, however cerebral, of imagination. Glaucon and we, perhaps Socrates as well, see ourselves as the shadows cast by Socrates, in the guise of prisoners.

Turning Compulsion

Why, when Socrates had made such headway in the region of knowledge, moving along the divided line, as he thought, in thought, up to intellection, does he turn back, fall back to the region of opinion, more particularly that of imagination in his allegory of the cave? Why must the relation between the intelligible and opinable be staged as though all in the visible? At the close of Book VI, in response to one of his rare moments of extended utterance (711c–d) Glaucon had won praise from the master for an exposition that seemed to confirm his understanding. Can it then be, as it seems, that Socrates spins the allegory of the cave for a pupil who could not otherwise follow? Where lies the necessity of this turning around from the heights of intellection into the depths of imaging? Why the shift from a language of pure abstraction to the figure and, in particular, that of man? Why does Socrates, just as dialectic is reaching its point of culmination, in the last passages of Book VI, choose to increase their distance from the good, to submerge in the shadows of the cave the interlocutors who were beyond the sun and enjoying the illumination of a higher realm in the abstract vision of the divided line? If it is not a pedagogical necessity, what compels him to this act of conversion? The displacement to the underground takes place as part of the philosophical discourse.[85] Shortly, such a retrogressive move will be bound up with the political demands of the polis,[86] but in the path of the argument itself, the return from the heights, or near heights of the divided line, from the almost contemplation of the good, seems a matter of course.

The question is all the more mystifying, given that turning of another order, a turning upward and therefore precisely in the opposite direction, is soon proposed as the path out of the dilemma and error of the cave. A repetition of sorts of the proposed ascent in Book VI[87] from the sun of the visible world up to the intelligible (but starting from a position that is literally *mise en abîme*). And if this turning promises both release and the eventual acquisition of the power of sight so lacking in the depths of the cave, a leading of such men "up to the light, just as some men are said to have gone from Hades up to the gods" (521c), nevertheless, there is much that is painful and unexpected in the process of the upward passage. What is at stake is both the polis and philosophy: "the *turning* of a soul around from a day that is like night to the true day; it is that ascent to what *is* which we shall truly affirm to be philosophy" (521c, first emphasis mine).

> "Then most certainly," I said, "such men would hold that the truth is nothing other than the shadows of artificial things."
>
> "Most necessarily," he said.
>
> "Now consider," I said, "what their release and healing from bonds and folly would be like if something of this sort were by nature to happen to them. Take a man who is released and suddenly *compelled* to stand up, to *turn* his neck around, to walk and look up toward the light; and who, moreover, in doing all this is in pain and, because he is dazzled, is unable to make out those things whose shadows he saw before. What do you suppose he'd say if someone were to tell him that before he saw silly nothings, while now, because he is somewhat nearer to what *is* and more *turned* toward beings, he sees more correctly; and, in particular, showing him each of the things that pass by, were to *compel* the man to answer his questions about what they are? Don't you suppose he'd be at a loss and believe that what was seen before is truer than what is now shown?" (515c–d, emphases mine)

The prisoner is compelled to stand up, to turn round, to walk, to look toward the light, to answer the questions posed to him. He suffers pain to the body and pain to the mind. Dragged along by force (515e), he takes each step on the path with nostalgia for the clarity of what he left behind. The entire path of the upward ascent (of the downward, too, as we shall see) is punctuated by a comparison to the "before." From the shadows and echoes of the cave, to the artifacts and statues of the carriers, and the light of the fire that illumined them, he is taken "the rough, steep, upward way" (515e) to see the shadows and phantoms of reflection in the realm above, the things lit by the light of the sun, until finally he can raise his eyes to the heavens and contemplate the sun itself.

But the job of the founders is "'not to permit them what is now permitted . . . [to allow the prisoners] to remain there.' 'What?' [Glaucon] said. 'Are we to do them an injustice, and make them live a worse life when a better is possible for them?'" (519d). Glaucon, it seems, has forgotten the thrust of the Socratic sense of justice, each one doing his own business but always in the service of the whole.

> "My friend, you have again forgotten," I said, "that it's not the concern of law that any one class in the city fare exceptionally well, but it contrives to bring this about in the city as a whole, harmonizing (*sunarmottôn*) the citizens by *persuasion and compulsion (peithoi te kai anankêi)*,[88] making them share with one another the benefit that each is able to bring to the commonwealth. And it produces such men in the city not in order to let them *turn* whichever way each wants, but in order that it may use them in binding the city together."
> (519e–520a, emphases mine)

Release from the bonds of the cave offers no simple liberation. Socrates' polis is a world of harmony, perhaps, but one mustn't forget the harsher sense detectable in *sunarmottôn*, that of governance by order and regulation, the "compulsion" or necessity that Socrates repeatedly insists on. "Compulsion" and "turning" pepper all these pages, pulling us up short whenever we imagine an oasis in "acts of divine contemplation" (517d), as a changeless union with what *is*, with "being" rather than "becoming" (526e), or, as Glaucon puts it, "a haven from the road . . . and an end of [the] journey" (532e). This becomes clear despite the fact that Socrates will tempt us to this surmise by saying that "the instrument with which each learns . . . must be turned around from that which is *coming into being* together with the whole soul until it is able to endure looking at that which *is* and the brightest part of that which *is*" (518c).[89]

How do we come to terms with this turning compulsion? It is a compulsion that in one form or another haunts the *Republic* to the very end. In the dialogue's closing passage, we come full circle. Socrates had begun by citing Odysseus as he describes his descent into Hades: "I went down" (327a).[90] He closes with the narrative of the visit to Hades by Er who explicitly alludes to Odysseus's tale (614b).[91] Er "become[s] a messenger to human beings of the things there" (614d) and he tells a tale with a topography not unlike the divided line or the cave of Socrates' allegory, the division between the upper world and the underground. As with dialectic, it is a question of a journey. More clearly than ever before, the issue is one of ethics.

> "And [the departed souls] came to a certain demonic place, where there were two openings in the earth next to one another, and, again, two in the heaven,

above and opposite the others. Between them sat judges who, when they had passed judgment, told the just to continue their journey to the right and upward, through the heaven. . . . The unjust they told to continue their journey to the left and down. . . . He saw there, at one of the openings of both heaven and earth, the souls going away when judgment had been passed on them. As to the other two openings, souls out of the earth, full of dirt and dust, came up from one of them; and down from the other came other souls, pure from heaven." (614c–e)[92]

If the almost endless ascent and descent in the dialogue's closing myth seems proposed as the inevitable and cosmic course of things, in the allegory of the cave Socrates will insist that the necessity of the return from the ascent to the good is political. In any state other than the one they have created in speech philosophers might be allowed to remain.

> "Well, then, Glaucon," I said, "consider that we won't be doing injustice to the philosophers who come to be among us, but rather that we will say just things to them while compelling them besides to care for and guard the others. We'll say that when such men come to be in the other cities it is fitting for them not to participate in the labors of those cities. For they grow up spontaneously against the will of the regime in each." . . . (520a–b)

It was under this necessity to "care for and guard the others," the necessity of returning to educate those who are left behind, under this pedagogical guise that one might choose to picture Socrates' turn from the divided line back down to the allegory of the cave, although Glaucon, at least, seemed not to be in need of the plunge back into imagination. It is possible, however, that the necessity is bound, not just to the political exigencies of a particular state or to the pedagogical needs of Glaucon, but rather to the demands of philosophical argument in general. It is possible that the argument has no other place to go. Despite the many pronouncements about the glories of "looking at that which *is*" (518c), nowhere in the *Republic* does Socrates claim that his own philosophical path has reached its goal, stepped out above the hypotheses (511a). We read of arguments "out of the range of our present thrust" (506e), places that Glaucon could not possibly follow because he "would no longer be seeing an image" (533a), tokens offered in place of the truth (506d–507a). The compulsion to turn, as in the pain-fraught ascent and descent of the allegory, is the compulsion to compare.

The Path of the Argument: The Turns of Analogy

Socrates' many undergrounds, it must be admitted, get us nowhere,
definitively. Metropolitans, subversive sub-ways, they are, at best, shuttles,
perpetually forcing us to turn around. The allegory of the cave makes this
most explicitly clear: it sends its philosopher-to-be to the upper world and
then forces him into darkness once again. And yet the underground is the
non-place from which the city, as Socrates puts it, is created in speech
(369c), a speech, we have seen, that threatens the logic of the city no less
than it fabricates it.

But there is another borderland to Plato's *Republic* far more difficult
to discern, although this too, it could be argued, is the non-place out
of which the polis is constituted. The topos of the underground in the
noble lie and the tale of Leontius, as also in the divided line of Book
VI and the cave of Book VII,[93] poses no obstacles to the imagination.
But the topography of the path, a metaphor to which Socrates insistently
returns, the path of the argument, cannot so simply be mapped. This is
not only because of the detours, announced and unannounced, and so
far flung that we repeatedly forget where we were headed to begin with.
Nor do we grope blindly simply because Socrates lets the argument go
wherever it might lead. We see clearly enough the points of call: justice in
the individual which leads to justice in the city and back again to justice
in the individual soul, the relations among the civic classes analogous to
the forms of the individual soul; along the way the education of youth,
the position of women, the attack on the poets, the denigration of other
forms of government, and so on.

Still, if the underground lies comfortably in the realm of the imagination, if the path of the argument is erratic but traceable, the path of the
path, that other non-place from which the polis is created, is of another
order. A question, then, not of what the dialogue produces, *not* of what its
speech declares must and must not come into being, but rather of *how* the
polis is created in speech. Socrates' manner of speaking may seem beside
the point, outside the city, real or imagined. It is what we can never view
properly, although it is always there under our feet. It is the hardest thing
to get a hold of: if our sight is "not rightly turned nor looking at what it
ought to look at" (518d). The form of the dialogue forever threatens to
"slip through somewhere and disappear into obscurity" (432b).

Socrates' philosophic discussion, his "dialectic" in the course of the dialogue, indeed aims for the region of intellection. Still this dialectic begins with the crossing of geographical borders to annex the land of the barbarian other. Along the way: according to its content, everyone is taken in, all classes of the regime and even the women; according to its form, all interlocutors are taken in. It harmonizes to unity any threat of the other or discord. It does so by separating out into forms (454a) the objects of its concern, a division that often comes forth as simile, or comparison. This is the critical activity of dialectic, the way in which philosophy discusses, the steppingstones and springboards that are never definitively left behind. Shadows and shades: these are what drive the dialectic, what so often allows it to move from one point to the next on its erratic path. Analogy makes dialectical thinking possible, productive thinking and thinking as production—as in the metaphorical intercourse between the "real lover of learning" and what *is*, where the organ of grasping is "akin" to that which it grasps, where it is the coupling of the philosopher with that which is similar that produces intelligence and truth.

Nevertheless, Socrates is bent on getting *beyond,* by bypassing such analogy that, perhaps not entirely incidentally, as in the *Symposium,* womanizes the philosopher as a source of reproduction (and not only as a result of the specificity of this image), and produces her/his subsequent labor pains. Socrates' goal is transcendence that guarantees both the power structure of the polis and the power of dialectic (532d). He achieves this by transforming analogy, the side-by-side (*paradeigma*) patterning of the merely similar, into the image. The conceptualization of the image enables a privileging of origin and a denigration of copy and thus allows the argument to hierarchize the otherwise neutral elements. This is, of course, the strategy of the infamous passage in the opening pages of Book X in which god, manual artisan, and painter are contrasted with respect to their proximity to what *is*, in which the imitation produced by the last of the three is proclaimed "third from . . . the truth" (597e).

That this distinction between analogy and image is difficult, perhaps impossible, to pull off becomes evident in Socrates' compulsive returns at all the most critical moments of the dialogue to a series of comparisons, often hybrids of analogy and image. One need only return to the divided line and the allegory of the cave where, in several versions, the relations between the intelligible and the visible are articulated as proportional analogies. It is around light, that which brings to light, that which gives sight to the eye and gives the object the power of being seen, that one of the central schemas of the dialogue turns. It is introduced to shed light on the matter, because we are not sharp of sight, ostensibly, to make Glaucon, we suppose, see more clearly. We have read it before but not in its schematic simplicity, in what Socrates calls a proportion (*analogon* [508b]), for here, Tiresias's warning notwithstanding, Socrates, like Odysseus before him, crosses paths with the sun:

the *idea* of the good : sun :: sun : fire

What makes the head spin here, what turns things around, in this summary of the allegory of the cave is that the sun is on the one hand the light of the visible realm in the first half of the proportion and on the other its contrast, an image of the *idea* of the good in the second. The double ratio blurs the divide between upper and lower realms, between that which enables knowing and that which enables seeing. It brings together precisely that which philosophy must separate. If one has a problem contemplating the sun in Plato, is this not the reason?

What also drives the discussion of justice (from Book II to Book IV) is an implicit proportional analogy with something fundamentally askew in the correspondences. The discussion leads to the creation of the city in speech and goes on to define the individual in a proportion that has man as the pivotal term: the city is to the three forms of man, as man is to the three forms of his soul.

Polis : three forms of Man :: Man : three forms of his Soul

Man is the common but absolutely incommensurable element here. Monolithic in the city, where he is *either* ruler *or* guardian *or* craftsman,[94] man as individual is nevertheless the locus of all three forces, similar to those in the forms of the city's classes, but dangerously different from one another, and sometimes at fractious odds. (The tale of Leontius was an eye-opener in this regard.) In this the governing Socratic simile that drives so much of the narrative, man, thus doubly and impossibly figured, is precisely the unfixable, indefinable, the uncontrollable. Man is the dismeasure of all things. The compulsion to turn things around in proportion (*analogon*) is the underground of the polis and also the state of philosophy.

But it is above all the relation of the terms of raw analogy that is intolerable for Socrates' model of either the polis or philosophy. What takes place in the course of philosophizing, as we have seen, is strangely akin to Socrates' proposals for the political operations of the state. The repressive assimilations of dialectic are quite analogous to Socrates' definition of justice and to the political structure of the polis. In the regime the hierarchy of classes takes place under the aegis of a moderation that represses difference in the name of harmony and unity, just as the dialectic of the *Republic*, producing agreement, represses difference in the name of Socratic mastery, leaving behind the manys for the one.

When the dialectic's path is forced to detour in analogies, then, the hierarchical structures of state and those of the individual soul are implicitly unsettled as well. And dialectic is at risk almost at the moment it first appears on the scene, when Socrates' initial mode of argument through elenchus gives way to the apparent mildness of a new form of discussion and new form of mastery. For shortly after eristic is ignominiously tossed out the front door in the name of dialectic,[95] analogy surreptitiously comes in the rear (368c–d). It is just at this juncture that Socrates proposes to seek out the justice that was so elusive in Book I by setting up the analogy between justice in the state and justice in the soul. Justice is invaded by the just as. This is a "just as" in which neither term, neither city nor individual, ultimately subsumes the other.[96] And because of this, analogy challenges the definition of justice to come, a definition whose principle is one of subservience. Justice guarantees the strict adherence to the one, to the ruler in the polis or to logos in the individual soul. It is, according to the tale of Leontius, the absolute obedience to what speech or reason declares. Dialectic may expel difference in an attempted univocity to silence disagreement, but difference comes back in the form of analogy, a differentiation of the dialectic voice with itself, taking place, making pace, throughout the dialogue. Thus the *production* of justice in Plato's *Republic* is at odds with its *concept, a production* through quite another act of language, taking place in speech. All this has been rolling around at our feet from the beginning: we saw it and did not see it. For it is a story that perpetually forces us, in Socrates' words, to turn our thought elsewhere. Dialectic, despite Socrates' call in the closing lines of the dialogue to "keep to the upper road" (621c), lets the argument go where it might: "wherever the argument, like a wind, tends, thither must we go" (394d).

There is danger, then, in analogy, as is evident in the opening gesture of the dialectic argument, and not only because it is kin to the images and shadows of the underground. Let us remember where we are. We find justice as or in a blank in our self-knowledge. It is what we are already holding but fail to see, what "we too didn't look at . . . [as we] turned our gaze somewhere far off" (432e). To find justice Socrates creates the city in speech and then searches for its analogon in the human soul. This is a mode of production whose risks Socrates, at least once, makes almost explicit, just when he tests his uncertainties with regard to the definition at which he has arrived. We are warned that something might well go awry when one argues by analogy, that is when one assumes that the same "classes of natures" (435b) that constitute the city might be found in the several natures of the soul of each man. The image that Socrates offers for testing the relationship between justice writ large and justice writ small is nothing short of incendiary. To be sure such pyrotechnics may not be warranted. Socrates and Glaucon will go on to agree that the city and man are in agreement, just as described in the preceding philosophic discussion. The threat of fire, which, not incidentally, is the light of the cave—the fire that produces the image, rather than the light of the sun or the *idea* of the good—may not be called for, or at least not openly called forth. Still, Socrates hesitates:

> "Now let's complete the consideration by means of which we thought that, if we should attempt to see justice first in some bigger thing that possessed it, we would more easily catch sight of what it's like in one man. And it was our opinion that this bigger thing is a city; so we founded one as best we could, knowing full well that justice would be in a good one at least. Let's apply what came to light (*ephanē*) there to a single man, and if the two are in agreement (*homologêtai*), everything is fine. But if something different (*allo*) should turn up in the single man (*en tôi heni*), we'll go back again to the city and test it; perhaps, considering them side by side (*allêla*) and rubbing them together like sticks (*tribontes, hôsper ek pureiôn*), we could make justice burst into flame (*eklampsai*), and once it's come to light (*phaneran genomenên*), confirm (*bebaiôsometha*) it for ourselves." (434d–435a)

Socrates wishes to confirm the truth to which dialectic leads him. Isn't this what dialectic is about, confirmation in the light of the good, a certain security given to those who follow its path?

Before we follow through here, however, let us nevertheless take a bit of a detour to explore another version of this, in one of the very few places in the *Republic* where dialectic is directly approached—and see what comes to light if we exhibit these two passages side by side.

"Then," I said, "only the dialectical way (*methodos*) of inquiry proceeds in this direction [of making agreement become knowledge], destroying the hypotheses, to the beginning itself in order to make it secure (*bebaiôsêtai*); and when the eye of the soul is really buried in a barbaric bog (*borborôi barbarikôi*), dialectic gently draws it forth and leads it up above, using the arts we described . . . in the turning around." (533c–d)

Can it be a coincidence that almost the same term appears in both passages to bespeak the security that dialectic guarantees? Can it be a coincidence, and is it not an irony that the very terms that promise the certainty and confirmation of the dialectic's drive to oneness, *bebaiôsometha*, *bebaiôsêtai*, stammer with their *be-bai*—the same *ba-ba*—that famously accounts in nonsense syllables for the barbarian, someone outside the Greek language culture, someone up to his ears and even his eyes in the "barbaric bog (*borborôi barbarikôi*)"?

Given this, what kind of confirmation of his argument can we expect when Socrates rubs the two terms of the analogy, justice in the city and justice in the one man, together? It is possible, we are reminded, that agreement might not immediately come to light. And if justice in the individual proves not the same, but other and different, we need to consider city and man side by side with one another, bring them together like pieces of wood rubbed one against the other to produce fire. This, we read, will make justice at last burst into flame: with this we will confirm justice, the goal of our search. But how assuring is the shining forth of justice as the two terms of the analogy burst into flame? It would be, after all, according to this image, not a factionless obedience to hierarchy, not the agreement of the terms of comparison, city and man, but their frictional non-identity that brings justice into being in a conflagration that threatens to consume all three, city, man, justice: such is the danger of analogy that we rarely choose to see. The repressive force of justice in the *Republic* that eliminates difference in the name of the one and promises harmony within and service to the polis, both arises from and is no less threatened by the fractious difference of the terms of analogy.

What the side-by-side of analogy, unlike the image, produces is not only a difference between terms, but an ineradicable difference in which neither term rules nor rules the other out. It produces neither the definitive differentiation of eristic nor the assimilation of all difference into agreement that takes place through dialectic. It violates the code of mastery that defines justice: "Isn't to produce justice to establish the parts of the soul in a relation of mastering, and being mastered by, one another that is according to nature?" (444d).

Analogy takes place as difference without hierarchy, a loophole in the structure of power. One can only try to imagine the political implications of a community so conceived. To be sure, nowhere in the *Republic* are the relations between individuals or between the polis and its barbarian other conceived in terms of analogy. One might well wonder whether such relations within the city could ever fall under the aegis of what we call a political system, or whether such a state so envisioned could be conceived as circumscribed by a border, like that dividing line between the polis and the barbarian with which the definition of the city in speech began.[97] Difficult, perhaps impossible, to imagine: similar but not identical, neither different nor the same; no citizen assimilable into the service of the other, a relation in which individuals are separate and unequal, but always comparable. There is no telling where all that might lead.

§ 4   Hamann Is a Nomadic Writer: "Aesthetica in nuce"

The sayings of the wise are like pegs of a tent.
> —Isaiah

Most blessed of women be Jael . . . of tent-dwelling women most blessed.
> —Song of Deborah, Judges V, 24

Hamann is a nomadic writer.[1] Just when you think you know where he is, just when you hear a voice beckoning you to "turn aside," and stay a while, it turns out he has pulled up stakes and pitched his tent elsewhere. Not without having displayed a certain hospitality to be sure. For when water might well suffice to quench your thirst, Hamann invariably gives you cream.

In 1761 Johann Georg Hamann writes his famous essay "Aesthetica in nuce," "Aesthetics in a nutshell" as the English speaking world inevitably translates it. It appears one year later in a collection of pieces entitled *Kreuzzüge des Philologen—Crusades of the Philologist*. How to judge this essay is now as then a critical problem. There are two things one can say with certainty about "Aesthetica in nuce." It is not a conventional aesthetics and it offers us nothing in a nutshell, if by that we are to understand a terse and unproblematic encapsulation of what it is Hamann has to say. This utter refusal to speak openly baffles the modern reader and yet he was no less obscure to his contemporaries. Goethe writes in *Dichtung und Wahrheit*: "there is again a sort of equivocal double light, which appears to us highly agreeable: only one must completely renounce what is ordinarily called understanding."[2]

A reviewer of Hamann's "Sokratische Denkwürdigkeiten" ("Socratic Memorabilia"), published just three years earlier, describes it as "a piece of writing that contains nothing but absurdity and nonsense. Anyone who does not wish to ruin his understanding should leave this unnatural offspring of a confused head unread" (N II, 87).[3] Nothing in Hamann denies this. It is Hamann, after all, who preserved this diatribe, choosing to publish it along with his response. Moreover he himself describes his own work in somewhat similar terms.[4]

If Goethe and Hamann's reviewer have nailed the experience of reading "Aesthetica in nuce," nevertheless, in a long tradition ever since, literary historians have rarely been at a loss to mark the essay's irrefutable place in the timeline of German letters.[5] "Aesthetics in a nutshell," they tell us is explained by what it clearly points to—what it points to in the past and what it points toward in the future. Hamann launches a passionate attack against the Enlightenment[6] and, as only the hindsight of posterity could see, is the father of Sturm und Drang and ultimately of Romanticism.[7] But reading "Aesthetica in nuce" in this manner is like contemplating a solar eclipse in a vessel full of water (N II, 199). Or as Hamann also put it, it is like looking at "the wrong side of a tapestry"[8]—it "shews the stuff, but not the workman's skill" (N, II, 199). What happens if we observe it more directly, even though just how Hamann went about it is not easy to unravel, even though directly observing how Hamann faced the Enlightenment is bound to bedazzle?

What are we to make of a writer compelled to write only on the occasion of, or in relation to, another text?[9] "Aesthetica in nuce" positions itself as a polemic against Johann David Michaelis in his commentary on Robert Lowth's *De sacra poesi Hebraeorum* (1758). In "Aesthetica in nuce" he sallies forth not only against Michaelis, but also against Lessing, Mendelssohn, Voltaire, and others. Very little is written in the essay, then, that does not pass by way of reading something or someone else. Even proper names are usually abandoned for circumlocutions that are sometimes less than evident:[10] Michaelis, against whom here as elsewhere Hamann is determined to do battle, appears as "the archangel on the relics of the **language of Canaan**" (N II, 197), as a "learned **commentator** [on] the oldest poetry" (N II, 198, 13–14), and as "a **master** in **Israel**" (N II, 201); Moses Mendelssohn appears as "a passing Levite of modern literature" (N II, 200), Lessing as "**Aesop** the **younger**" (N II, 201), Mahomet as "the Arabic prophet of lies" (N II, 213), and Augustine as "the good African shepherd" (N II, 213).

But what detours Hamann's reader is not only the disruption of proper names, personifying in another figure both those he questions and those he admires. As the closing lines of the essay remind us, much of the text is in the footnotes, often expansive ones that do not necessarily elucidate the text above. Moreover every other turn of phrase, it seems, even in the body of the text, is a call to or echo of either a biblical or a classical passage.[11] And when antiquity is not in question, Hamann's essay presupposes an equally impossible, detailed knowledge of the works of his contemporaries or near contemporaries.

Given Hamann's religious declamations, might we not cite the conclusions of previous commentators and think of his writing as typological?[12] As in the relation between the Old and New Testaments, one text gives a foretaste of the other, or refers back to the other as its prediction. Typology promises messianic access to revealed truth and a teleological movement toward a final judgment.[13] "Aesthetica in nuce" would then play a part in a redemptive history and also, perhaps, in history as redemption. For typology has a remarkable resonance with the ways in which we tend to narrate literary history—one era, even an individual author, as the precursor of another era in which its fulfillment takes place.

And would this not be of a piece with those most famous of passages from the essay? Be of a piece with them and place them in the context of a divine creation in which, as Hamann puts it in an early essay, "On the Interpretation of Holy Writ" ("Über die Auslegung der Heiligen Schrift"), God is a writer.[14]

> God, a writer! . . . (N I, 5)
> All works of God are signs and expressions of his attributes: and thus, it seems, all of physical nature is an expression, a simile, of the spiritual world. All finite creatures are only in a position to see the truth and the essence of things in similes/images. (N I, 112)

> Gott ein Schriftsteller! . . .
> . . . Alle Werke Gottes sind Zeichen und Ausdrücke seiner Eigenschaften; und so, scheint es, ist die ganze körperliche Natur ein Ausdruck, ein Gleichnis, der Geisterwelt. Alle endliche Geschöpfe sind nur im Stande, die Wahrheit und das Wesen der Dinge in Gleichnissen zu sehen.

Hamann's take on Genesis guarantees a reassuring place for the human reader. Just as a typological textual practice projects a harmonious and productive interrelation of images, so the divinely created world that Hamann describes in "Aesthetica in nuce" speaks of an unproblematic interpretive transition from the divine to the human.

> Poetry is the **mother-tongue** of the human race; as **gardening** is older than

farming: **painting**,—than writing: **song**—than declamation: parables—than arguments. . . .

The **senses** and the **passions** speak and understand nothing but **images**. In **images** the entire treasure of human **knowledge** is contained. . . . The first **explosion** of creation, and the first **impression** of its historian; the first **manifestation** and the first **enjoyment** of nature unite in the **word: 'Let there be light!'** . . . (N II, 197)

Speaking is **translation**—from a **tongue of angels** into a **human tongue**, that is, **thoughts** in **words**—**things** in **names**—**images** in **signs**. . . . (N II, 199)

> Poesie ist die **Muttersprache** des menschlichen Geschlechts; wie der **Gartenbau**, älter als der Acker: **Malerey**,—als Schrift: **Gesang**,—als Deklamation: Gleichnisse,—als Schlüsse. . . .
>
> **Sinne** und **Leidenschaften** reden und verstehen nichts als **Bilder. In Bildern** besteht der ganze Schatz menschlicher **Erkenntnis**. . . . Der erste **Ausbruch** der Schöpfung, und der erste **Eindruck** ihres Geschichtschreibers;—die erste **Erscheinung** und der erste **Genuß** der Natur vereinigen sich in dem **Worte: Es werde Licht!**
>
> Reden ist **übersezen**—aus einer **Engelsprache** in eine **Menschensprache**, das heißt, **Gedanken** in **Worte**,—**Sachen** in **Namen**, —**Bilder** in **Zeichen**. . . .

If poesy is the mother tongue of the human race, if parables or similes are older than conclusions, this is because the language of God's divine creation is in images. "Every phenomenon of nature was a word,—the sign, emblem, and pledge of a new, secret, inexpressible, but all the more intimate union, communication and community of divine energies and ideas" (N III, 32).[15] Every phenomenon of nature was a word, a speaking that undergoes translation from the heavenly to the human tongue. God spoke to man in images and ever since the entire treasure of human knowledge consists precisely in images. And yet strangely, perhaps incomprehensibly, Hamann also has this to say:

> In nature, we have only **jumbles of verse** and *disiecti membra poetae* left for our use. It is for the **scholar** to gather these; for the **philosophers** to interpret them; to imitate them—or even bolder!—to bring them to their destiny, is the part allotted to the **poet**. (N II, 198–99)

> Wir haben an der Natur nichts als **Turbatverse** und *disiecti membra poetae* zu unserm Gebrauch übrig. Diese zu sammeln ist des **Gelehrten**; sie aus-

zulegen, des **Philosophen**; sie nachzuahmen—oder noch kühner!—-sie in Geschick zu bringen des **Poeten** bescheiden Theil.

A nature made up of broken fragments of poetry but of broken pieces of poets as well. What might it mean that as scholars we must gather, as philosophers interpret, and as poets imitate these broken pieces—which is not to say to fashion them into a unified whole? What does it mean that Hamann calls on the poet not simply to gather or interpret but to imitate on the one hand the "jumbles of verse" and on the other the *"disiecti membra poetae,"* the dispersed, disjointed members of the poet?

This is not to say that Hamann's religion of a universe of images should not be taken seriously, even if it is no easy task to say just what he is after in his crusade against the Enlightenment. The *Kreuzzüge des Philologen* are indeed performed in the name of a radical reconception of the image. But how are we to understand "crusades" in a series of essays undeniably driven by Christianity? Is there a holy grail that Hamann seeks, some booty he sets out to bring back from afar? Or is he rather like the members of the Teutonic Order in Prussia whom he describes in a letter to Nicolai of March 4, 1763?[16] They constructed underground labyrinths and criss-crossed through them, fulfilling, in mock combat, their oaths to take part in the more easterly Crusades.[17] Is there not much that is subterranean and labyrinthine about Hamann's work if only we do not hesitate to go out and explore?[18]

And so we are making progress, you see, in reading "Aesthetica in nuce," if in a slightly zigzag fashion. We have read the title and the opening, ever citable, passages, and the title of the collection of essays in which it appears, and we are ready to dash on, though not without a detour, to the opening epigraph.

If Hamann's crusades are more an underground than a surface affair and ultimately get us nowhere, their apparently typological gestures too may also not fulfill the messianic promise of conventional Christianity. Less like typological interpretation, with its horizon of teleological redemption, "Aesthetica in nuce" rather resembles the cento of the decadent period of Latin literature, a mode of text that takes its name from a patchwork garment: it is "a composition formed by joining scraps from other authors."[19] A patchwork of citations, then, a long and repeatedly disrupted prosopopoeia in which the persona that Hamann assumes endlessly and abruptly changes. And is this not what the subtitle tells us?

For here at least one might take Hamann at his word: "Eine Rhapsodie in Kabbalistischer Prose." The term rhapsode comes from the Greek for stitching together and song. Cabbala (from the Hebrew for "tradition") is a traditional but esoteric mode of interpreting scripture.[20]

"Aesthetica in nuce," then, it is now more than evident, is hardly as self-contained as its title implies. Hamann frequently notes his sources but the reader is more often than not left to travel far and wide in different directions in order to stitch it all together. This explains the proliferation of remarkable and indispensable scholarly materials determined to lead us to the source of Hamann's allusions.[21] And yet crossing the hermetic borders of the essay only sometimes provides an answer. To take a less than neutral example: locating Hamann's scriptural sources might frequently make sense of otherwise obscure passages. In the words of the essay's closing lines, we might in this regard say of the scholars what Hamann writes of himself as rhapsodist: they have "read, observed, thought, sought for and found pleasant words, cited them faithfully, like a merchant ship which has obtained and brought its provisions from afar" (N II, 217). And yet if Scripture sometimes has the capacity to nourish our hunger for understanding, more often than not the biblical imagery rushes by in such orgiastic rapidity that there is no way to digest it.[22]

No doubt all this begins to explain the first epigraph, that biblical tatter heading the text, that shred that functions as a bizarrely latticed window opening out, or failing to, on what it is that follows. In this initial motto of "Aesthetica in nuce," just where we might expect to read "in a nutshell" what Hamann has to say,[23] Hamann makes certain we cannot miss the reference.

> spoil of dyed stuffs embroidered,
> two pieces of dyed work
> embroidered for my neck as
> spoil? (Judges V, 30)

The citation is printed in unpointed and therefore hardly accessible Hebrew,[24] but the source of the lines is nevertheless clearly marked. The fragment of verse (might we, citing Hamann [N II, 198], call it a "jumble of verse"?) comes from Judges, one of the "historical books" of the Old Testament, a book from which Hamann will cite, in pieces. Three lines into the main body of the text, again a phrase from the same chapter, identified in a footnote that reads: "Judges V, 10." And four pages later, again, a long paraphrase unmistakably from the same chapter. Every commentator feels called upon to point this out. Yet none I have read has noted a fourth and final allusion to the passage at the end of "Aesthetica in nuce." Why this repeated return to that part of Judges known as the Song of Deborah?

Hamann relates to it by way of Bishop Lowth's "Lectures on the Sacred Poetry of the Hebrews" to which Johann David Michaelis had added his commentary. Lowth celebrates the passage that Hamann cites in his motto as a most perfect example of prosopopeia, that kind of prosopopeia in which "fictitious speech is usurped to a real person."[25] In the prelude to Hamann's third allusion to Judges V he facetiously reminds us of Lowth's point. "Should this rhapsody indeed have the honour of being judged by a **master** in **Israel** [Michaelis], let us go to meet him in holy **Prosopopoeia**. . . . " (N II, 201). It is from this point of view that the motto has been interpreted. In whose voice, the question is inevitably raised, does Hamann speak in citing the Book of Judges? A question that makes sense only if we know the players and the tale.

The Song of Deborah (Judges V), composed by a contemporary of the battle it describes, tells of the struggle of the tribes of Israel against the forces of the Hazorite Sisera. Judges IV, written a century or two later, repeats the narrative. This later work tells of the prophetess Deborah who "at that time . . . was judging Israel" (Judges IV, 4). Because the "Israelites did what was evil" "the Lord [had] sold them into the hand of King Jabin of Canaan, who reigned in Hazor" (Judges IV, 4). Deborah summons Barak and exhorts him to lead his troops against Sisera, promising that God "will give [Sisera] into [Barak's] hand" (Judges IV, 7). But the shift of hand does not end here. For if God, who had given the Israelites into the hand of the Hazorites, now offers to deliver their leader, Sisera, into Barak's hand, Deborah takes back that promise almost as soon as she gives it: "the road on which you are going will not lead to your glory," she tells Barak, "for the Lord will sell Sisera into the hand of a woman" (Judges IV, 9).

Indeed, not only the conclusion but the entire story of Barak's battle undercuts the power of this would-be hero of Israel. For on the day on which the Lord had "delivered Sisera into [Barak's] hand," it is rather Yahweh who "[goes] out before [him]" (Judges IV, 14). "And the Lord threw Sisera and all his chariots and all his army into a panic before Barak" (Judges IV, 15). The Lord displaces Barak in battle, but it is a woman who displaces him in the smiting of Sisera. The Hazorite leader runs from the battle: and it is at the hands of Jael that Sisera falls.

> 24 Most blessed of women be Jael,
> the wife of Heber the Kenite
> of tent-dwelling women most blessed.
>
> 25 He asked water and she gave him
> milk,
> she brought him curds in a lordly
> bowl.
>
> 26 She put her hand to the tent peg
> and her right hand to the
> workmen's mallet;
> she struck Sisera a blow,
> she crushed his head,
> she shattered and pierced his
> temple.
>
> 27 He sank, he fell,
> he lay still at her feet . . .
> there he fell dead. (Judges V)

It is here one soon reads the lines of Hamann's motto, "spoil of dyed stuffs . . . " If Deborah's song celebrates first the exploits of certain tribes of Israel and then Jael above all women, now it abruptly turns to another, perhaps more unsettling scene. In the harem of Sisera his mother anxiously waits with the other women.

> 28 "Out of the window she peered,
> the mother of Sisera gazed
> through the lattice:
> 'Why is his chariot so long in
> coming?
> Why tarry the hoofbeats of his
> chariots?'
>
> 29 Her wisest ladies made answer,
> indeed, she answers the question
> herself:
>
> 30 'Are they not finding and dividing the
> spoil?—

A girl or two for every man:
Spoil of dyed stuffs for Sisera,
spoil of dyed stuff embroidered,
two pieces of dyed work
embroidered for my neck as spoil'" (Song of Deborah, Judges V)

The phrases Hamann cites as the opening and perhaps critical line of "Aesthetica in nuce" are the last in this passage. In what way might this motto give us, or can it give us, the summation of what is to come?

Much is at stake here. On the one hand Hamann's question of prosopopeia. The poet of Judges V writes in the voice of Deborah; Deborah speaks in the voice of Sisera's mother who poses a question to her ladies, which she then answers in their voice: "indeed, she answers the question herself" (Judges V, 29). It is also a question of spoils, of what one brings back from a battle won and what it means to assume a position of triumph. But following as these lines of the motto of "Aesthetica in nuce" (Judges V, 30) do on the narration of Sisera's violent death, it is no less a passage about delusions of victory.[26]

Still, why would Hamann, his commentators have been forced to ask, speak in the voice of Sisera's mother? Why would the committed Christian assume the role of the enemy of Israel? Lumpp, following Küster,[27] explains Hamann's prosopopeia by looking to the third allusion to Judges V. There the narrator exclaims that he waits for the appearance of the second half of Lowth's and Michaelis's work just as the mother of Sisera passionately awaited the return of her son. As Hamann's readers tell the story, this is because Michaelis, the object of Hamann's polemic, is thus pronounced dead before arrival. Dickson, however, understandably reluctant to equate Hamann with the mother of the enemy, replies he does not "put himself in the role of Sisera's mother, on the side of the enemies . . . ; he puts himself in the place of *Deborah*, impersonating her enemies; this Prosopopoeia is a double-personification."[28] But can we fix Hamann so definitively in the place of Deborah as the singer of the taunt song,[29] in the position of gloating triumph (a position on which Hamann's commentators, one way or another, all seem to insist)? The very lines Hamann chooses to cite, after all, are spoken by a woman who is ignorant of the death of her son, a murder brutally presented in the verses just preceding. Isn't this very passage, then, an admonition about delusions of victory, and a misplaced thirst for spoils? Isn't Hamann's theory of language, and, more compellingly the performance of his language, such that the will to control prosopopoeia on the part of his readers has to be read as ironically as the mother's expectations of plunder? (And perhaps no less ironical, however understated, is the booty that typology might be expected to bring.)

This is made all the clearer by the textual uncertainties of the biblical text. Above we have given a conventional English translation of verse 30 of the motto. It makes sense. But the Hebrew, as Hamann presents it and as biblical scholars have found it, leaves one at a loss. In the original Hebrew no one can be certain for whom the plunder is destined (only certain that it does not reach its destination). Thus some of the translations we encounter are: "'Two pieces of dyed work embroidered for my neck as spoil,'" but also "'for the neck of the spoiler?,'"[30] "'for the neck of the queen,'" "'for my shoulders,'" and, most puzzling of all, "'for the neck of the booty.'"[31] But in the literal English translation of Lowth's volume we read:

> To Sisera a spoil of divers colours,
> A spoil of needlework of divers colours,
> A spoil for the neck of divers colours,
> A spoil for the neck of divers colours of
> needlework on either side.[32]

With needlework on either side, one begins to suspect this text is much like that tapestry to which Hamann objects—refusing, doubly, as it does, to show "the **workman's** skill" (N II, 199), both to specify the recipient of the spoils and also the voice in which the motto speaks.

When Hamann returns to Judges for a third time then, as we have already seen, the position of the speaker seems unproblematically identified with Sisera's mother. The publication of the second half of Lowth's work with Michaelis's commentary has been announced and Hamann "lust[s] after it" like Sisera's mother yearning at the lattice for the return of her son.

> I burn for it—and wait in vain to the present day, as the mother of the Hazoritic captain looked out of the window for the chariot of her son, and howled through the lattice—Do not think ill of me, therefore, if I speak with you in **gestures** like the ghost in Hamlet. . . . (N II, 201)

> Ich brenne darnach—und warte umsonst bis auf den heutigen Tag, wie die

Mutter des Hazoritischen Feldhauptmanns nach dem Wagen ihres Sohns zum Fenster aussahe, und durchs Gitter heulte——Verdenken Sie es mir also nicht, wenn ich gleich dem Gespenst im Hamlet durch **Winke** mit Ihnen rede. . . .

However, the gesture Hamann makes here, which he more or less warns us is in need of interpretation, the way in which he speaks with us, is complicated by the preceding lines.

> Should this rhapsody indeed have the honour of being judged by a **master** in **Israel [i.e. Michaelis]**, let us go to meet him in holy **Prosopopoeia**, which is as welcome in the kingdom of the dead as in the kingdom of the living (—*si NUX modo ponor in illis* [if I can be numbered amongst them as a nut]). . . . (N II, 201)

> Sollte diese Rhapsodie gar die Ehre haben einem **Meister** in **Israel** zur Beurtheilung anheim zu fallen: so laßt uns ihm in heiliger **Prosopopee**, die im Reiche der Todten eben so willkommen als im Reiche der Lebendigen ist (—si NUX modo ponor in illis) entgegen gehen. . . .

The Song of Deborah always appears accompanied by the concept of judgment (here *Beurtheilung*) and not only because of its locus in the book of Judges. And if the issue of judgment is on the line here, so also, as in the motto, is the promise given in the title of "Aesthetica in nuce," the promise of summing up, encapsulating. For the voice that assumes the outlook of Sisera's mother is not precisely Hamann but rather the "NUX" or nut of the title *Aesthetica in nuce* ("—si NUX modo ponor in illis"). The nut speaks. Given the opinion of some of Hamann's contemporaries, this makes sense—in English if not in German. But what might it mean that it is neither Hamann who speaks, nor even as the title of the essay might suggest, his aesthetics, but rather the "nut"? With the nut of *in nuce*, after all, the philologist leads us to anticipate an easy and satisfying encounter with his aesthetic theory: summed up, neatly packaged, condensed.[33] And when this promise of succinct clarity speaks, when the nut speaks, the passage fails, at least as dramatically as the motto, to fulfill that expectation. The nut speaks to us in signs, in "gestures like the ghost in *Hamlet*" (N II, 201). It substitutes for its own voice the Song of Deborah or the voice of the yearning mother in that song which imagines spoils and power that will never materialize. The nut, then, may be the pledge of an encapsulated and repeatable communication, the promised booty of the aesthetic essay, but it rather holds up to view, or withdraws from view, gauzy pieces of embroidered textile intended for we know not whom.[34]

Let us follow this performance one last time in the essay's culminating statement that announces closure. Those lines sum up the entire essay; on the one hand they pass judgment on the vanity of "Aesthetica in nuce" and on the other they call forth the fulfillment of God's ultimate judgment. That final word appears as an "Apostille," variously translatable as an afterword,[35] a gloss, or as critical marginalia.[36] In the Apostille, Hamann offers us a first reading of his essay and a judgment of it as well, for reading and judgment, perhaps necessarily, go hand in hand. It is written, then, as a gesture to gather everything under one tent, so to speak, as a metacritique, once again in the voice of another: some critics hear the imagined voice of Michaelis, some that of Hamann himself. Here as throughout the "Aesthetica in nuce" we read the interpreter interpreting. "Interpreters of interpreters," a footnote reminds us, is the Socratic definition of the rhapsodists. That this is the practice of this "rhapsody in kabbalistic prose" cannot take us by surprise at the end of the text.

What might we expect from this interpreter of the interpreter? That with clarity he points us in the right direction? That he casts an all enclosing structure over the whole? That whereas we find ourselves in reading Hamann driven here and driven there, he will finally nail things down for us?

As the oldest reader of this Rhapsody in kabbalistic Prose I see myself obliged by the **the right** of **primogeniture** to leave behind for my younger brothers who will come after me, yet another **example** of **merciful judgment** (*Urtheils*), as follows:

Everything in this aesthetic nut tastes of **vanity!**—of **vanity!**—The **Rhapsodist**[*] has read, observed, thought, sought and found pleasant words, faithfully quoted, like a merchant's ship has obtained and brought his provisions from afar.

[*]—οι ραψῳδοι—ερμηνεων ερμενεις [the rhapsodists—interpreters of interpreters]. Socrates in Plato's *Ion*. (N II, 217, translation altered)

Als der älteste Leser dieser Rhapsodie in kabbalistischer Prose seh ich mich vermöge des **Rechts** der **Erstgeburt** verpflichtet, meinen jüngern Brüdern, die nach mir kommen werden, noch ein **Beyspiel** eines **barmherzigen Urtheils** zu hinterlassen, wie folget:

Es schmeckt alles in dieser ästhetischen Nuß nach **Eitelkeit!**—nach **Eitelkeit!**—**Der Rhapsodist**[*] hat gelesen, beobachtet, gedacht, angenehme Worte gesucht und gefunden, treulich angeführt, gleich einem Kaufmannsschiffe seine Nahrung weit her geholt, und von ferne gebracht.

[*]—οι ραψωδοι—ερμηνεων ερμενεις. Sokrates in Platons *Ion.*

To be sure this last simile (of the merchant's ship), like so many phrases in "Aesthetica in nuce," has a biblical source, even as the very topic of the passage concerns the way in which the text is woven from sources found elsewhere. But how can that source provide the meaning here, in a passage that speaks, and even speaks critically, of the rhapsodist's rhetorical practice?[37] And if that source is misleading, what is more critically at stake are two different ways in which the rhapsodist, having found his sources afar and cited them, uses them to fabricate his writing, as a cumulative addition of sentences on the one hand and as a performance of images on the other.

> [The rhapsodist] has ordered together **sentence** after **sentence**, as one counts the **arrows** on a **battlefield**; and marked out his **figures** as one measures out the **pegs** for a **tent** (*Nägel* zu einem **Gezelt**). Instead of **pegs** and **arrows** he has, with the *petits-maîtres* and **pedants** of his time, written * * * * * * * * and - - - - - - - - **obelisks** and **asterisks.**[38] (N II, 217)

> [Der Rhapsodist] hat **Satz** und **Satz** zusammengerechnet, wie man die **Pfeile** auf einem **Schlachtfelde** zählt; und seine **Figuren** abgezirkelt, wie man die **Nägel** zu einem **Gezelt** abmißt. Anstatt **Nägel** und **Pfeile** hat er mit den **Kleinmeistern** und **Schulfüchsen** seiner Zeit * * * * * * * * und - - - - - - - - **Obelisken** und **Asterisken** geschrieben.

These are the two different gestures, it seems, that constitute, and somehow explain "Aesthetica in nuce": adding together sentence on sentence, and marking out figures. They are, in turn, apparently to be transcended by a call to the last judgment of God. For the closing lines of the essay, which most commentators are content to leave in peace, are these:

> Let us now hear the **summation** (*Hauptsumme*)
> of his latest aesthetic, which is the **oldest**:
> **Fear God and give Him**
> **glory for the hour of His judgment** (*Gerichts*)
> has come, and worship Him who
> **made heaven and**
> **earth and the sea and the**
> **water fountains!** (N II, 217)[39]

> Laßt uns jetzt die **Hauptsumme** seiner
> neusten Aesthetik, welche die **älteste** ist,
> hören:
> **Fürchtet Gott und gebt Ihm die**
> **Ehre, denn die Zeit Seines Gerichts**
> **ist kommen, und betet an Den, der**
> **gemacht hat Himmel und**
> **Erden und Meer und die**
> **Wasserbrunnen!**

But how shall we judge these final lines that announce the last judgment in the phrases of the creation, when heaven and earth and the seas were divided from one another? How shall we understand this ultimate summation that announces the definitive end but does so in the language of the beginning, that announces ultimate resolution in the shadow, not only of division but also of a world whose creation, according to Hamann, you remember, was a vast production of images, the interpretation of which is bound to be disjointed?

So let us not jump to judgment, at least not *the* judgment. Given its double gesture, the Judgment (*Gericht*) the closing passage celebrates is perhaps the extension of rather than the counter-force to the judgment (*Urteil*) given at the beginning of the Apostille. The rhapsodist, Hamann or the first reader tells us, has brought his words from afar and produced his text in two different manners. On the one hand, he has added together sentence on sentence ("Satz und Satz zusammengerechnet" [N II, 217]), perhaps also proposition on proposition, as one counts arrows on a battlefield. An accounting, therefore, like the summation (*Hauptsumme*) of the closing lines, that adds up, taking place in the name of the "arrow," that sign that suggests simple direction and goal. If it is here a question of the arrow and a building of the logical linearity of propositions or sentences, also of the guidance to the source of words that come from afar, it is as well a question of the circle and the figure. The rhapsodist's second manner of composition takes place as he has "seine Figuren abgezirkelt" (N II, 217). He marks out his figures as one gauges the position of the pegs for a tent. This is hardly the same kind of measure entailed in adding together the number of arrows on a battlefield. One measures off (*abmißt*) the place of the pegs to a tent as one *abzirkelt*, as one marks with a compass, producing the form of a circle by piercing and fixing one point to determine the others at equal distance, producing a figure that is going neither here nor there. And we are still not there, at the culmination point of the meaning of these figures that might describe the workman's skill of Hamann. The oldest reader of the rhapsody now gives us, it seems, the literal meaning of his figures. He substitutes for pegs and arrows the asterisks and dashes, * * * * * * * * and - - - - - - - - , which in apposition he calls obelisks and asterisks.

In the body of an eighteenth-century text, as in the first edition of "Aesthetica in nuce," asterisks direct us to the footnotes, notes which are similarly marked at the bottom of the page by the same sign. Like the arrows of sentences built one on another, the asterisks of "Aesthetica in nuce" seem to set us in the right direction, pointing toward illumination and explanation, bringing us to references, biblical and otherwise, apparently provided by those nourishing notes.

If the asterisks mark the footnotes that promise an unproblematic shipping from afar of the explanations of textual opacities, how shall we read those figures marked out like the pegs of a tent? A footnote, the final footnote of "Aesthetica in nuce," explains further the significance of these signs. Hamann cites Jerome in the Preface to the Pentateuch: "Asteriscus illucescere facit; obeliscus iugulat et confodit" ["Asterisks illuminate; obelisks murder and stab"]. Hamann's note signals a warning. But his readers, the scholars whose task, we have read, is to gather (*sammeln*) "jumbles of verse" (N II, 198), nevertheless, have pointed us, it is no surprise, to a less threatening explanation, that falls within the welcoming safety of Holy Writ, in Ecclesiastes XII, 11:[40] "The words of the wise are like goads, and the words of scholars are like well-driven nails. . . . " The passage in the "Apostille," as the scholars read it, celebrates the wisdom of scholars. Thus they stand as sentinels guarding against a deadly danger. Small wonder they cannot take in, these readers, what is really at stake here, that they choose to sleep through the more compelling allusion, for the passage invites us back to Judges, this time Judges IV.

18 Jael came out to meet Sisera, and said to him, "Turn aside, my lord, turn aside to me; have no fear." So he turned aside to her into the tent, and she covered him with a rug.

19 Then he said to her, "Please give me a little water to drink; for I am thirsty." So she opened a skin of milk and gave him a drink and covered him. . . .

21 But Jael, wife of Heber, took *a tent peg* and took a hammer in her hand,

and went softly to him and drove the peg into his temple, until it went down into the ground—he was lying fast asleep from weariness and he died. (Judges IV, emphasis mine)

And yet this is not the complete explanation. Rather than getting its typo-logical nourishment solely from the distant text of Judges and bringing it back from afar, it is rather in Hamann's own domain that the "nail of the tent" ("ein Nagel des Gezelts," N I, 81) is most tellingly to be found.

Before we are drawn into that domain by the lure of the tent pegs we might return to the simile of arrows. If the asterisks are the arrows, how-ever much they illuminate they are nevertheless associated with a scene of carnage, the battlefield. They return us to that battle that has haunted the essay, that clear-cut struggle between good and evil in Judges IV and V. The first edition of "Aesthetica in nuce" makes this even clearer. There instead of arrows we encounter spears; and, as Deborah sings it, neither spear nor shield was seen among those in Israel, so poor were the people. In the Song of Deborah, therefore, spears can be the weapons only of the Hazorites. To count up the spears or arrows, then, is like the clear reckon-ing of that combat in which "all the army of Sisera fell by the sword [and] no one was left" (Judges IV, 16).

Still, it is not the "battlefield" alone, of course, in this closing passage of "Aesthetica in nuce" that beckons us back to Judges. Given what the narrator of the Apostille, the first reader of the rhapsody in kabbalistic prose, has to say of tent pegs, one cannot but hear a voice that calls to us: "'Turn aside . . . turn aside'" (Judges IV, 18). And if we turn aside, move sideways as it were rather than straight ahead, in contrast to the straight-forward battle, though with inextricable ties to it, there is another scene, not of accounting and illumination—but this time of the "murder and stab[bing]" of the final footnote. On the one hand the arrows one counts up are proof of definitive victory, of the slaying of every one of the enemy by that hero among the Israelites named Barak, proof as well of a clear-cut path to source and explanation, also the guarantee of spoils, both military and textual. Still, on the other hand, there is another scene. Not every one of the enemy has been slain by Barak. He has missed the one that really counts. Sisera has been called to the tent of Jael, has been induced to turn aside. Side by side with the arrows of direction are the figures marked out as with a compass, the tent pegs that do not quite encompass, enclose, sum up, present us with everything *in nuce*. Figures are measured and points are driven home in a manner one least expects.

Small wonder the scholars clap their hands to the sides of the head, not wishing to hear the allusion. For the story Hamann tells of figuration is hardly one of readerly triumph. And yet, from the very beginning, the reader has been our concern. What does it mean to understand Hamann or fail to, we have asked, if it is indeed Hamann who speaks? Is "Aesthetica in nuce" a typological text or are we to read it rather as a cabalistic rhapsody stitched together like a cento in which the source of the text is all but irrelevant to its significance? Is "Aesthetica in nuce" a crusade conducted to bring back meaning from afar or does it mark the point of a figural and nomadic language? How are all these questions of reading implicated in Hamann's tale of divine creation in which we inhabit a world of nothing but images, spoken by God, in the beginning, the translation of which is left to the human reader? Why is all this insistently and inevitably bound to the concepts of judgment and of decisive moral positioning? How does the Book of Judges frame "Aesthetica in nuce" from its opening motto to its closing Apostille?

If one listens carefully to these last lines, the rhapsode speaks, the interpreter of interpreters. Hamann reads. But he does not simply read Judges, nor for that matter does he simply perform reading as judgment. He reads himself reading the Song of Deborah.

In 1758, only three years before drafting "Aesthetica in nuce," while in the throes of his religious conversion, Hamann, as he tells it, goes through the Holy Bible for the second time.[41] And as he rereads he writes his *Biblische Betrachtungen*. There the Song of Deborah is the object of a long if less than straightforward meditation. Three times, let us remember, in the opening pages of "Aesthetica in nuce," Hamann has cited the biblical passage, twice with explicit footnotes that lead us to chapter and verse, once with details so lengthy and explicit, no reader can possibly miss the reference. In the Apostille just a brief phrase, "the nails of a tent (*die Nägel zu einem Gezelt*)," brings us unmistakably back to Judges, no longer to the prosopopeia of Sisera's mother, but rather to the triumph of Jael, and brings us back to Hamann rereading those same verses of Scripture.

Just as it is in the suffering of Jesus that we best recognize the abomination of sin, so we at the same time see in the prototypes of our victor images of the tyranny of the serpent which he overcame. What horrible enemies are those . . . who seem to be born to murder, who come as the emissaries of God. . . . What kind of a gruesome woman, who in the figure of a hospitable, peaceable, agreeable woman comes up to us, offers us her tent, covers us, instead of water gives us milk to drink and covers us again, to whom we are foolish enough to entrust our fear and to make her into a sentinel against danger, when all the time she has had no other intention with her friendliness, care and tending, than to see us in the sleep of security in order with an iron nail not only to bore through **our head**, but also to nail it **firmly** to her **ground and earth!** Thus God triumphed over Satan through his own tools, through the cunning which he had taught them, through the deceit which they had learned in his school, through the cruelties to which he had hardened them. Thanks be to God who has given us the victory, this magnificent victory, through our Lord Jesus.

A nail of the tent [*ein Nagel des Gezelts*; "Aesthetica in nuce": "nails of a tent],—a poison, a trick of Hell—with a hammer in the hand . . . yes a hammer for us—he slinks—he hits the spot which he knows to be the most dangerous—he fastens it to the ground, while we sleep, while we are tired from the flight which he had helped us to bring down upon ourselves, and whose victory he cannot prevent, however much he might try to thwart the fruits of it. (N I, 80–81, emphasis mine, 1758—published posthumously)

So wie wir in Jesu Leiden am besten die Abscheulichkeit der Sünde erkennen; so sehen wir zugleich in den Vorbildern unsers Siegers Bilder der Tyranney der Schlange, die er überwunden. Was für fürchterliche Feinde, die . . . zum Morden scheinen geboren zu seyn, die als Abgesandte Gottes kommen. . . . Was für ein grausames Weib, das unter der Gestalt einer gastfreyen, friedfertigen, gefälligen Frau uns entgegen gelaufen kommt, ihre Hütte anbietet, uns zudeckt, an statt Wasser uns Milch zu trinken [giebt] und uns wieder zudeckt, der wir thöricht genug sind unsere Furcht anzuvertrauen und sie zur Schildwache unserer Gefahr zu machen, unterdessen sie keine andere Absicht gehabt mit ihrer Freundlichkeit, Pflege und Wartung, als uns in dem Schlaf der Sicherheit zu sehen, um **unser Haupt** durch einen eisernen Nagel nicht nur zu durchboren, sondern auf ihrem **Grund und Boden** fest **zu schlagen!** So siegte Gott über den Satan durch seine eigenen Werkzeuge, durch die List, die er ihnen gelehrt hatte, durch die Falschheit, die sie in seiner Schule gelernt hatten, durch die Grausamkeiten, wozu er sie abgehärtet hatte! Gott sey Dank, der uns den Sieg, diesen herrlichen Sieg gegeben hat durch unsern Herrn Jesum Christum!

Ein Nagel des Gezelts ["Aesthetica in nuce": "die Nägel zu einem Gezelt"],— ein Gift, ein Kunstgriff der Höllen—-mit einem Hammer in der Hand . . . ja einen Hammer für uns—-er schleicht—-er trift den Ort, den er am gefährlichsten kennt—-er macht ihn fest auf dem Grunde, unterdessen wir schlafen, unterdessen wir müde sind von dem Fluch, den er uns geholfen hat auf uns zu laden, und dessen Sieg er nicht verhindern kann, so sehr er auch die Früchte desselben zu vereiteln sucht.

As in the Apostille, it is a question of figuration uneasily marked out. What is the relation, Hamann asks, between Jesus and his *Vorbilder*? In the proto-images of Jesus, in those who preceded him in the Old Testament, we see, counterintuitively, images of the tyranny of the serpent rather than Christ-like figures of suffering. Hamann, understandably, is overwhelmed by the gruesome violence of Jael as emissary of God. In this scramble of prose, moreover, Hamann, as relentlessly careful reader whatever the stakes, ever again identifies himself, not with Jael, "blessed among women," but with that wearied sleeping enemy of Israel, who, Christ-like, is nailed firmly and grotesquely to the earth.[42] What takes place in the turmoil of this his interpretation of Holy Scripture is that God's emissaries and Satan, the sentinels against evil and its perpetrators, even God himself and Satan, are entirely interchangeable and indistinguishable. Caught in the jumbles of the verses of Judges, Hamann no longer knows who the enemy is and who the defender of the Judeo-Christian tradition. The entire force of ungovernable prosopopoeia returns here: Hamann assumes the position and voice of Israel's enemy, Sisera, even as he celebrates the victory of the Scripture that brings him to turn topsy-turvy the object of his interpretation. Ethical decision is not a matter of fixing in place.

In this "Rhapsody in Kabbalistic Prose," "Aesthetica in nuce," in this text rhapsodically stitched together from cloths of diverse colors,[43] scraps from different authors (*OED*), tatters of the Song of Deborah come back to haunt us, like the ghost of Hamlet's father.[44] The grounding of Hamann's prose in the verses of the Old Testament brings about no typological closure, no messianic prediction and fulfillment, of question and answer, of text and explanation. No spoils come to us, no simple victory from its battles with the Enlighteners, not even a clear personification that lets us know who speaks to us in the essay. "Aesthetica in nuce" punctually and repeatedly renders definitive judgment in the name of Christianity, but it also practices another mode of critique that exposes the broken pieces to which the etymology of *Urteil* necessarily points.[45] Hamann himself, in the long passage we just read, is not unlike the *disiecti membra poetae* of whom we spoke earlier, torn between the positions that rigorous reading of even the holiest of texts is bound to impose. In the *Biblische*

Betrachtungen, confronted with the task of reading the *Gleichnisse* (similes, images) penned by God, Hamann sinks wearily into a pathos of defeat and victory. In "Aesthetica in nuce" he figures the task of interpretation quite otherwise and opens up a religion that liberates. Thus "Aesthetica in nuce" does not presuppose nor nostalgically long for either a definitive reading practice or a power-hungry certainty of judgment. The images of God's creation cannot be counted like the arrows in the aftermath of a triumphant battle with a certain outcome. Hamann attacks the site of certain illumination, not unlike the asterisks of his footnotes, no matter how holy their ostensible content. He does so in the name of a radical Christianity which as often as not seems to point to a final judgment, but as often as not also draws the reader into its unencompassable figures.

The ethics of "Aesthetica in nuce" are summed up in the incalculable after-math of the Apostille; which is not only to say that they are exemplarily laid out in the particular words of that last page. Hamann's ethics are a call to the perpetual performance of a "postil," a commentary as the dictionary tells us, upon a text of Scripture or upon any writing. The ethical act is one of commentary, of rhapsody, not only interpretation but a reading of oneself reading. This means reading with the rhapsodic risks we see Hamann to take in the *Biblische Betrachtungen*, fearsome risks to his preconceived concepts of good texts and bad, of right and wrong. Inevitably such an ethics leads to no simple mastery, to no assured sense of one's authority as writer or reader, to no spoils, as Hamann puts it, of "pleasant words, faithfully quoted," as provisions brought from afar. Before such reading looms no messianic horizon of redemption or of decisive judgment. But then again, already on the first page of "Aesthetica in nuce" we read: "it is in figures that the entire treasure of human knowledge is constituted" (N II, 197). This is one treasure whose summation cannot be calculated.

§ 5 What Does It Mean to Count? W. G. Sebald's *The Emigrants*

A beautiful protocol, an exact protocol. I will write a protocol of the sort that one doesn't experience everyday.

—From Werner Herzog's film *Kaspar Hauser*

Memory is fundamentally nothing but a citation.

Facing the title page of the Fischer Verlag edition of W. G. Sebald's *The Emigrants* (*Die Ausgewanderten*),[1] the following blurb appears, written, no doubt, with the best of intentions, but inevitably and understandably with an eye to selling books to the German public:

> With great sensitivity of feeling he describes the life stories and stories of suffering of four Jews driven from their European homeland. . . . W. G. Sebald writes in order to preserve memory. He thus did research and had conversations, gathered photos and documents as well as visiting the scenes.

> Mit großem Feingefühl schildert er die Lebens- und Leidensgeschichten von vier aus der europäischen Heimat vertriebenen Juden. . . . W. G. Sebald schreibt, um das Gedächtnis zu bewahren. Also hat er recherchiert und Gespräche geführt, hat Fotos und Dokumente gesammelt sowie Schauplätze bereist.[2]

Leave aside for the moment what it means to describe (*schildern*); discount the value of photos and documents to guarantee the worth of the accounts in question. How can it be they have gotten it all wrong—and in doing so have gotten it right?—"four Jews driven from their European homeland." Four Jews, four chapters, a full count.[3] Does it matter that Ambros Adelwarth, great uncle to the narrator, butler to a wealthy Jewish-American family, long years their son's lover, was himself no Jew? Does it make a difference that Paul Bereyter—dismissed by the National Socialists as schoolteacher because "he was only three-quarters an Aryan (*ein Dreiviertelarier*)" (50E, 74G), and called back to serve in the motorized artillery since "the draft notice . . . was also sent to three-quarter

Aryans" (55E, translation altered, 81G)—was only a quarter-Jew?[4] What
does it mean to be a quarter-Jew? What does it mean that instead of four
Jews there are only two-and-a-quarter in *The Emigrants*? And what does
it mean to count like a publisher? What is a Jew and how does one make
him count?

Ghost Quarter

From the story entitled "Dr Henry Selwyn":

Thus they turn back, the dead. (23E, translation altered; 36G)

How shall we quarter them, these dead, who seem to come back? Is this
not what *The Emigrants* is about, the question of quartering? In a volume
subtitled "Four Long Stories" ("Vier lange Erzählungen"), Dr. Henry Selwyn, Paul Bereyter, Ambros Adelwarth, and Max Aurach[5] find, perhaps,
a place to reside, or, at least to leave their residue and gain their due—a
remnant, the last that one might say about them. And yet the first that
one might say about them, the epigraph to the volume's first chapter, is
a call to destroy the remnant—while sparing, it seems, what Sebald calls
memory (*Erinnerung*):

Destroy the remnant
Not the memory. (1E, translation altered)

Zerstöret das Letzte
die Erinnerung nicht. (5G)

Then what shelter can be offered? And are these stories not like the Jewish
quarter (*Judenviertel*) that the narrator encounters in Manchester, emptied
before one's arrival of their inhabitants?

Little by little my Sunday walks would take me beyond the city centre to
districts in the immediate neighbourhood, such as the one-time Jewish quarter. . . . This quarter had been a centre for Manchester's large Jewish community until the inter-war years, but those who lived there had moved into
the suburbs and the district had meanwhile been demolished by order of the
municipality. (157E)

Allmählich kam ich auf meinen sonntäglichen Exkursionen über die Innen-
stadt hinaus in die unmittelbar angrenzenden Bezirke, beispielsweise in das

. . . vormalige Judenviertel. Bis in die Zwischenkriegszeit hinein ein Zentrum der großen jüdischen Gemeinde von Manchester, war dieses Quartier von seinen in die Vororte übersiedelnden Bewohnern aufgegeben und seither von der Stadtverwaltung dem Erdboden gleichgemacht worden. (231–232G)

What quarter can be given, what clemency shown, since there is no way to spare the lives of those already gone?[6]

From the story entitled "Max Aurach":

They come when night falls to search after life. (147E, translation altered)

Im Abenddämmer kommen sie und suchen nach dem Leben. (217G)

Does he fail, then, this narrator, does he fail those ghosts who inhabit the four divisions of his volume, by not bringing those seekers to life? At the moment of twilight ["im Abenddämmer"], he writes, in the afterlife, if I might shift the emphasis of the phrase "nach dem Leben," in the wake, as well, of the day's clarity, they seek. Does he fail, this narrator, who pens himself as W. G. Sebald, Winfried Georg Maximillian Sebald, whose friends called him Max—and so shall I? For I, too, want to befriend, however belatedly, the dead. Still, they may not return to life so much as turn us ever again to them.

From the story entitled "Paul Bereyter":

Again and again, from front to back and from back to front, I leafed through the album that afternoon, and since then I have returned to it time and again, because, looking at the pictures in it, it truly seemed to me, and still does, as if the dead were coming back *or* as if we were on the point of passing away into them. (45–46E, emphasis mine, translation altered)

Einmal ums andere, vorwärts und rückwärts durchblätterte ich dieses Album an jenem Nachmittag und habe es seither immer wieder von neuem durchblättert, weil es mir beim Betrachten der darin enthaltenen Bilder tatsächlich schien und nach wie vor scheint, als kehrten die Toten zurück *oder* als stünden wir im Begriff, einzugehen zu ihnen. (68–69G, emphasis mine)

Here, as Sebald's publishers promised, the "photos" gathered which will "reconstruct" "the past" and preserve memory. And if they are the same "Documents" we encounter in *The Emigrants*, ever again, after as before, forwards and backwards, we too are called on to leaf through the album

Sebald leaves *us* whose pages offer the same alternatives: either the dead return *or* we must be prepared for our own *Eingehen*—our passing away into their realm of image.

There are other leaves that have the same draw—those outside the window of the narrator's new house in the opening chapter.

> The trees stood scarcely fifteen metres from the house, and the play of the leaves seemed so close that at times when one looked out, one believed oneself to belong therein. (18E, translation altered)

> Die Bäume standen kaum fünfzehn Meter vom Haus entfernt, und das Blätterspiel war einem so nah, daß man manches Mal beim Hinausschauen glaubte, hineinzugehören. (30G)[7]

What does it mean in *The Emigrants*—on looking at the photographs, on leafing through the pages—that *either* the dead return *or* we are called into their photographic abode? In what way might these be alternatives, or equivalents? What is an image? What does it mean to look at an image? What is a photograph, those signature interspersions—*I* do not say documents, nor even illustrations—of Max's writing?

From the story entitled "Ambros Adelwarth":

> They were silent, as the dead usually are when they appear in our dreams, and seemed somewhat downcast and dejected. . . . If I approached them, they dissolved before my very eyes, leaving behind them nothing but the vacant space they had occupied. (122–23E)

> Wie meistens die Toten, wenn sie in unseren Träumen auftauchen, waren sie stumm und schienen ein wenig betrübt und niedergeschlagen. . . . Näherte ich mich ihnen, so lösten sie sich vor meinen Augen auf und hinterließen nichts als den leeren Platz. (180–81G)

So this is what happens when we draw close to them, when we pass too precipitously into their space.[8] This is not to say that we err if we believe ourselves "to belong therein" (18E, 30G) or if we stand "on the point of passing away into them" (46E, 69G). But we err if we think it easy to capture the souls of the dead, with photographs, with documents, with memories, with drawings, those souls which European mythology wisely casts as butterflies.

Perhaps this is what flits by in the mockery of the narrator's great-uncle.

Aunt Fini visits Adelwarth at the mental sanatorium he has chosen for his end:

> . . . when a middle-aged man appeared, holding a white net on a pole in front of him and occasionally taking curious jumps. Uncle Adelwarth stared straight ahead, but he registered my bewilderment all the same and said: It's the butterfly man, you know. He comes round here quite often. I thought I caught an undertone of mockery in the words, and so took them as a sign of improvement. . . . (104E, translation altered)

> . . . als dort ein Mann mittleren Alters auftauchte, der ein weißes Netz an einem Stecken vor sich hertrug und ab und zu seltsame Sprünge vollführte. Der Adelwarth-Onkel blickte starr voraus, registrierte aber nichtsdestoweniger meine Verwunderung und sagte: It's the butterfly man, you know. He comes round here quite often. Ich glaubte einen Ton der Belustigung aus diesen Worten herauszuhören, und hielt sie daher für ein Zeichen der . . . Besserung. (151G)

Adelwarth, of course, does not get better; but then, again, he was never mad.

Image of Max

So what is it that Sebald is after? And do we not find an image of him in Max Aurach, the artist, prominently placed as the volume's last entry,[9] in which narrator and author seem so drawn to one another? Just as the narrator, wandering through Manchester, finds a sign that guides him to Max the artist,[10] isn't Aurach the sign that might guide us to Max the writer? And what if we catch sight of him in the story of Aurach's most difficult work—a portrait of the Butterfly Man, that image that runs through *The Emigrants* from beginning to end? The Butterfly Man is an irrecuperable ghost from the past whose gesture, in turn, is to catch the souls of the departed and even to save the living from falling into the realm of the dead. He is the figure whose mode is unexpected recurrence, and who, nevertheless, obscures the particularity and possibility of memory. A chasm of amnesia separates the artist from the actual encounter with his subject. "For what reason and how far this lagoon of remembrancelessness had spread in him and how far it extended, had remained a riddle to him, despite his most strenuous thinking about it" (174E, translation altered; 259G). "Aus welchem Grund," for what reason, has the lagoon of oblivion taken him over—but, also, out of what ground? For the man with a butterfly net unsettles any sense we have of ground, in art, in reason.

If he tried to think back to the time in question, he could not see himself again till he was back in the studio, working at a painting which took him almost a full year, with minor interruptions—the faceless portrait "Man with a Butterfly Net." This he considered one of his most unsatisfactory works, because in his view it conveyed not even the remotest impression of the strangeness of the apparition it referred to. (174E)

Wenn er versuche, sich in die fragliche Zeit zurückzuversetzen, so sehe er sich erst in seinem Studio wieder bei der mit geringen Unterbrechungen über nahezu ein Jahr sich hinziehenden schweren Arbeit an dem gesichtslosen Porträt *Man with a Butterfly Net*, das er für eines seiner verfehltesten Werke halte, weil es, seines Erachtens, keinen auch annähernd nur zureichenden Begriff gebe von der Seltsamkeit der Erscheinung auf die es sich beziehe. (259–60G)

No way to go back to the time in question. A lesson perhaps for the dead who return searching for life, and for the living who, feeling they belong to an earlier world, are prepared to pass away into it. When Aurach tries to displace himself into the past of that encounter, chasing after the man who forever chases, he finds he has been already at work on the faceless portrait that will prove one of his most ill-conceived works. No meeting the past here, much less the object of his art, only the rupture of memory, the long experience of failing to have met him, to draw him, to capture him in an image, as in a net. Perhaps this is why it is the strangeness of the appearance, more precisely the apparition, and not the man himself, that Aurach attempts to but cannot produce.

Max travels to the Swiss Alps "to retrace another old memory (*Erlebnisspur*) that had long been buried and which [he] had never dared disturb" (172E, 256G). There he climbs to the summit of the Grammont, as he had done with his father in 1936 (173E, 258G), and finds himself drawn to the world below, the landscape of Lake Geneva.[11] It is, perhaps, not entirely unlike the lagoon of remembrancelessness that will soon gain ground within him. He would have fallen, it seems, become one of the dead, had not the man with the butterfly net caught him, rising up before him—"like someone who's popped out of the bloody ground" (174E, 259G).[12] This is, after all, what his net (which pops up so unexpectedly throughout the tales) captures—less the butterfly souls of the departed than the folly of feeling "compelled to fall into them" (174E, translation altered; 259G), the simple passing away into them ("[Eingehen] zu ihnen" [46E, 69G]). And is this not what the canvas (*Leinwand*) cannot subsequently contain—the play between catching and falling, production and destruction?

> Work on the picture of the butterfly man had taken more out of him than any previous painting, for when he started on it, after countless preliminary studies, he not only overlaid it time and again but also, whenever the canvas could no longer withstand the continual scratching-off and re-application of paint, he destroyed it and burnt it several times. (174E)

> Die Arbeit an dem Bild des Schmetterlingsfängers habe ihn ärger hergenommen als jede andere Arbeit zuvor, denn als er es nach Verfertigung zahlloser Vorstudien angegangen sei, habe er es nicht nur wieder und wieder übermalt, sondern er habe es, wenn die Leinwand der Beanspruchung durch das dauernde Herunterkrazten und Neuauftragen der Farbe nicht mehr standhielt, mehrmals völlig zerstört und verbrannt. (260G)

Perhaps all of Max's work is like that. Failed portraiture. The past, the person, replaced by the process of its reproduction. The "butterfly man" who is, after all, no one in particular and many in his multiplicity. A gesture toward "the picture of . . . " (174E, 260G), then again and again painted over,[13] scratched down, reapplied, finally, yet repeatedly destroyed. This is, of course, also the way Max Sebald works, or at least his narrator, and never more so than when he writes a portrait of Max Aurach.[14]

The scene of production, his "manner of working" (162E, 239G), is less the canvas than what falls away from it, drawn, it seems, by the same seductive force of gravity against which and in the name of which the Man with the Butterfly Net pops out of the bloody ground:

> Since he applied the paint thickly, and then repeatedly scratched it off the canvas as his work proceeded, the floor was covered with a largely hardened and encrusted deposit of droppings, mixed with coal dust, several centimetres thick at the centre and thinning out toward the outer edges, in places resembling the flow of lava. This, said [Aurach], was the true product of his continuing endeavours. . . . It had always been of the greatest importance to him . . . that nothing should change at his place of work . . . and that nothing further should be added but the debris generated by painting and the dust that continuously fell and which, as he was coming to realize, he loved more than anything else in the world. . . . (161E)

> Da er die Farben in großen Mengen aufträgt und sie im Fortgang der Arbeit immer wieder von der Leinwand herunterkratzt, ist der Bodenbelag bedeckt von einer im Zentrum mehrere Zoll dicken, nach außen allmählich flacher

werdenden, mit Kohlestaub untermischten, weitgehend bereits verhärteten und verkrusteten Masse, die stellenweise einem Lavaausfluß gleicht und von der Aurach behauptet, daß sie das wahre Ergebnis darstelle seiner fortwähren-den Bemühung. . . . Es sei für ihn stets von der größter Bedeutung gewe-sen . . . daßnichts an seinem Arbeitsplatz sich verändere . . . und daß nichts hinzukomme als der Unrat, der anfalle bei der Verfertigung der Bilder, und der Staub der sich unablässig herniedersenke und der ihm, wie er langsam begreifen lerne, so ziemlich das Liebste sei auf der Welt. (237–38G)

Aurach's failures are thus his success.

Art does not capture a lost object. It is not in search of times past, it is neither testimony, nor recovered memory—at least not only, not simply. It takes place when matter, the charcoal sticks Max uses up as he draws, the paint scratched off from the canvas, the coal dust that falls from the "continual wiping away of that which is drawn" (162E, translation altered; 239G) "when the matter, little by little, dissolves into nothing" (161E, translation altered; 238G) or almost nothing. His work "was in reality nothing but a steady production of dust, which never ceased except at night" (162E, translation altered; 239G).[15]

Butterfly Work

And yet, this is no doubt too precipitous. We cannot leave it there, on the floor, under the easel of what the narrator calls Aurach's study of destruction (180E, 269G). Let us rethink this production of dust. Aurach on seeing the narrator after a hiatus of many years has this to say: "there is neither a past nor a future. At least, not for me. The fragmentary images of memory (*bruchstückhaften Erinnerungsbilder*)[16] by which I am haunted have the character of obsessive ideas" (181E, translation altered; 270G).[17] For Aurach there is neither past nor future, rather memory's fragmentary and compulsive images: remnants that come home to spook, not only Au-rach, but the entire text of *The Emigrants*, crossing the borders of its four stories, disrupting the frames of the four portraits, making strange leaps and fissures (*seltsame Sprünge* [151G]), running through the text like the Butterfly Man, popping up here and there out of its bloody ground.

"Dust production," then, but as *Bestäubung*,[18] as cross-pollination, what, say, a butterfly might accomplish as it flits erratically from flower to flower; here a cross-pollination of memory's fragmentary images from one chapter to another; such are the ghosts of *The Emigrants*. Perhaps this explains why Max's portraits, belonging to no individual, can have no face, no definitive identity:[19] their greatest achievement is their refusal to portray, won by long labors of obliteration. The butterfly chaser, the mountain scene overlooking the land beneath, the landscape of Lake Geneva: unbound to the particularity of singular identity, like the dead they are ever returning to us.

We find these same revenants flit through the first of the stories.[20] The narrator and Clara join Dr. Henry Selwyn and his friend Edward Ellis for dinner. The scene is set, like others as well, with blind mirrors, flickering lights, and uncertain images. "High on the walls mirrors with blind patches were hung, multiplying the flickering of the fire and letting unsteady images appear in them" (12E, translation altered; 21G).

The foreigners who grew up in the mountains are asked their impression "of England, and particularly of the flat expanse of the county of Norfolk" (12E; 21–22G). No need to delineate, really, since the unsteady images, a flickering of who is who and where is where, have already transformed the flatland of Norfolk into the Alps. "The light of the west still lay on the horizon, though, with mountains of cloud whose snowy formations reminded me of the loftiest alpine massifs, as the night descended" (13E, 22G). "Dusk fell" (12E). It is, as always in *The Emigrants*, the hour of ghosting.

Like Aurach after him, in the pages that follow, it is of the Alps that Selwyn will speak, and this, too, is a tale of falling. Berne, 1913, and Selwyn is "more and more addicted (*verfallen*) to mountain climbing" (13E, translation altered; 23G)—addicted as well to the friendship of his alpine guide: "Nothing fell so hard upon me (*[ist mir] so schwergefallen*) . . . as the departure of Johannes Naegeli" (14E, translation altered; 24G). This is a loss soon to be doubled when, a few months later, Naegeli, in an accident, falls "into a crevasse in the Aare glacier" (15E, 24G). Selwyn is left in "a deep depression" during which it was as if he "was buried under snow and ice" (15E, 25G). Here Sebald places a photo of the glacial scene: it is duplicated, more or less, at the close of the chapter, though in a second incarnation (Fig. 5.1).[21]

A man has popped up in the originally deserted snowscape: his back to us, he poses faceless. He offers us the shoe he extends behind him (Fig. 5.2).

Between these twin images,[22] like the covers of a slim volume, the story of Dr. Selwyn's life, the home in Lithuania that he must leave behind, his

FIGURE 5.1.   Mountain panorama (W. G. Sebald, *Die Ausgewanderten*. © Eichborn AG, Frankfurt am Main, 1992).

childhood in London, a failed marriage, the *Heimweh* that subsequently overwhelms him, his suicide. Before that life and after, as preface and afterword, the mountain scenes that flicker in all their multiplicity. Not least the passage that closes the chapter in which the second photo appears as a critical document.

It is July 1986. The narrator takes the train from Zurich to Lausanne.

> As the train slowed to cross the Aare bridge, approaching Berne, I gazed way beyond the city to the mountains of the Oberland. . . . Three quarters of an hour later, not wanting to miss the landscape around Lake Geneva, which never fails to astound me as it opens out, I was just laying aside a Lausanne paper I'd bought in Zurich when my eye was caught by a report that said the remains of the Bernese alpine guide Johannes Naegeli, missing since summer

FIGURE 5.2.   Newspaper clipping (W. G. Sebald, *Die Ausgewanderten.* © Eichborn AG, Frankfurt am Main, 1992).

1914, had been released by the Oberaar glacier, seventy-two years later. Thus they turn back, the dead. (23E, translation altered)

Als der Zug . . . über die Aarebrücke nach Bern hineinrollte, ging mein Blick über die Stadt hinweg auf die Kette der Berge des Oberlands. Wie ich mich erinnere oder wie ich mir vielleicht jetzt nur einbilde, kam mir damals zum erstenmal seit langem wieder Dr. Selwyn in den Sinn. Eine Dreiviertelstunde später, ich war gerade im Begriff, eine in Zürich gekaufte Lausanner Zeitung, die ich durchblättert hatte, beiseitezulegen, um die jedesmal von neuem staunenswerte Eröffnung der Genfer Seelandschaft nicht zu versäumen, fielen meine Augen auf einen Bericht, aus dem hervorging, daß die Überreste der Leiche des seit dem Sommer 1914 als vermißt geltenden Berner Bergführers Johannes Naegeli nach 72 Jahren vom Oberaargletscher wieder zutage gebracht worden waren.—So also kehren sie wieder, die Toten. (36G)

How *do* they come back, these dead?—unhoped for, unsuspected, less in body than in letters, less in the landscape of their disappearance that the

narrator is bent on *not* missing, than in the scriptscape of the newsprint
that actually catches his eye, the tale of a "guide disparu,"[23] the documentation of a repeated image that now calls on us to consider the remains of
Naegeli as a pun on the dead man's name. "Sometimes . . . they come out
of the ice and lie on the border of the moraine, a small heap of polished
bones, and a pair of hobnailed boots (*ein Paar* genagelter *Schuhe*)" (23E,
translation altered; 36–37G, emphasis mine).

Slide Shows

A few pages before this alpine tale, the narrator and Clara, that vague
promise of light and clarity, attend a slide show presented by Selwyn and
his friend Edward Ellis. They revisit the mountains of Crete on a wood-
framed screen[24] that finds its appropriate place, before the mirror.

> Once or twice, Edwin[25] was to be seen with his field glasses and a container
> for botanical specimens, or Dr Selwyn in knee-length shorts, with a shoulder
> bag and butterfly net. One of the shots resembled, even in detail, a photo-
> graph of Nabokov in the mountains above Gstaad that I had clipped from a
> Swiss magazine a few days before. (15–16E)

> Ein paarmal sah man auch Edward mit Feldstecher und Botanisiertrommel
> oder Dr. Selwyn in knielangen Shorts, mit Umhängetasche und Schmetter-
> lingsnetz. Eine der Aufnahmen glich bis in Einzelheiten einem in den Bergen
> oberhalb von Gstaad gemachten Foto von Nabokov, das ich ein paar Tage
> zuvor aus einer Schweizer Zeitschrift ausgeschnitten hatte. (26G)[26]

As the narrator says of another butterfly man, we have "not even the remotest concept of the strangeness of the apparition" (174E, translation altered; 260G)—all the more so when one returns to the pages that precede
it. Between the photograph dust covers that enclose Selwyn's life-story,
alongside that tale that begins in the Alps and ends in the pages of a Swiss
newspaper, other mountains come flickering to us in a manner so natural,
or is it so artful, we forget their origin. With Nabokov on the scene, the
mountains of Crete slide to those of the Alps, and again, soon, to those
of the Caucasus. The Greek, the Western European, and the Asian are as
interchangeable as the names Selwyn gives his old horses: Hippolytus,
Humphrey, Herschel, the last a version of Hersch and Henry in a study
of the letter H.[27]

Aurach's Grammont, Naegeli's Oberaar, Nabokov's Gstaad are reflected mirage-like,[28] in the view from the heights around the Lasithi plateau in Crete that Selwyn wishes to share. It is a view that cannot but strike the onlooker at Selwyn's dinner party, and, all the more so, the reader.

> To the south, lofty Mount Spathi, two thousand metres high, towered above the plateau, like a mirage beyond the flood of light. . . . We sat looking at this picture for a long time in silence too, so long that the glass in the slide shattered and a dark crack fissured across the screen. That view[ing] of the Lasithi plateau, held so long till it shattered, impressed itself deeply on me at the time, yet I forgot it for a considerable time thereafter. (17E, translation altered)

> Der im Süden die Ebene überragende, über zweitausend Meter hohe Berg Spathi wirkte wie eine Luftspiegelung hinter der Flut des Lichts. . . . Auch vor diesem Bild saßen wir lange und schweigend, so lang sogar, daß zuletzt das Glas in dem Rähmchen zersprang und ein dunkler Riß über die Leinwand lief. Der so lange, bis zum Zerspringen festgehaltene Anblick der Hochebene von Lasithi hat sich mir damals tief eingeprägt, und dennoch hatte ich ihn geraume Zeit hindurch vergessen gehabt. (28–29G)

The image that trembles lightly on the screen now bursts (*zerspringt*) its frame: it breaks not only the glass of the slide but sends that crack—perhaps not unlike the fissure into which Naegeli has fallen—to the wood-framed screen on which the image is projected, the deep impression of which shatters, in turn, the view of the narrator. He is left like Aurach before that other white canvas in a state of remembrancelessness ("Erinnerungslosigkeit" [259G]). But whereas Aurach sets about to re-produce the lost figure (of the Butterfly Man), the narrator's glance (*Anblick*) here is brought to life once again—not by a return of the windmills of Lasithi but by a dream force outside him, another landscape that dreams him involuntarily back to Lasithi. It comes to him, if not under the light green veil (15E, 26G) of Crete, then overcast by another sort of film.

> It was not until a few years afterwards that [the view] returned to me, in a London cinema, as I followed a conversation between Kaspar Hauser and his teacher, Daumer. . . . Kaspar was distinguishing for the first time between dream and reality, beginning his account with the words: Ja, it dreamed me. I dreamed about the Caucasus. (17E, translation altered and somewhat forced)

> Wiederbelebt ist [der Anblick] worden erst ein paar Jahre darauf, als ich in einem Londoner Kino das Traumgespräch sah, das Kaspar Hauser mit seinem

Lehrer Daumer . . . führt und wo Kaspar, zur Freude seines Mentors, zum erstenmal unterscheidet zwischen Traum und Wirklichkeit, indem er seine Erzählung einleitet mit den Worten: Ja, es hat mich geträumt. Mich hat vom Kaukasus geträumt. (29G)

Not "es träumte mir"[29]—for Kaspar, it seems, is both dreamer and the dreamed.

The camera then moved from right to left, in a sweeping arc, offering a panoramic view of a plateau ringed by mountains, a plateau with a distinctly Indian look to it, with pagoda-like towers and temples . . . in a pulsing dazzle of light, that kept reminding me of the sails of those wind pumps of Lasithi, which in reality I have still not seen to this day. (17–18E)

Die Kamera bewegt sich dann von rechts nach links in einem weiten Bogen und zeigt uns das Panorama einer von Bergzügen umgebenen, sehr indisch aussehenden Hochebene, auf der . . . Follies, die in dem pulsierend das Bild überblendenden Licht stets von neuem erinnern an die Segel der Windpumpen von Lasithi, die ich in Wirklichkeit noch gar nicht gesehen habe. (29G)

Into *The Emigrants* Sebald inscribes Kaspar Hauser, a narrative, we are repeatedly told, which leaves unsolved the enigma of origin.[30] He substitutes instead the gestures of *Bestäubung* (cross-pollination), returning the narrator only by way of a film to Lasithi, which in reality he has never seen. This takes place by bursting and fragmenting the frame of narration among various narrators, realities, views, viewers, and images.

It seems we've been at the flicks, the motion pictures. The flickering on the movie screen that disturbs the images of Kaspar's Caucasus dream is that of the unsteady images (*unstete Bilder* [21G]) that Sebald's narrator, too, insists on.[31] It returns once more, as Kaspar lies dying. His final act is that of narration: a story as Kaspar tells it, of which he knows the beginning, but not the end. A caravan passes through a desert that is surrounded, of course, you will have guessed it, by mountains, even if the mountains are declared, for this is the point of his fragment: to be "merely your imagination (*nur Eure Einbildung*)" (*Kaspar Hauser*). The mountains are a question of imagination.

The caravan approaches the spectator: human figures, camel legs, seem to graze the focal point of the lens and step out this, our, side of the screen, bursting the bounds, violating the rules, of the cinematic contract.

The same violation—to the point of madness—takes place in Cosmo Solomon's retelling of a scene from the film *Dr. Mabuse, the Gambler*. It is the spectacle staged by a hypnotist who produces "a sort of collective hallucination in his audience" (97E, 141G): a caravan passes from the mirage of an oasis on stage out into the audience, drawing Solomon with it as it leaves the hall. Kaspar is right: his story has no end and has no limit. It steps into Sebald's narrative, here in the story of Henry Selwyn, there in that of Ambros Adelwarth, and again in that of Max Aurach.

It oversteps the border of the final chapter as well. In the story of Max Aurach, narrator and painter sit in the flickering light of the Wadi Halfa café.

> Lit by flickering, glaringly bright neon light . . . when I think back to our meetings in Trafford Park it is invariably in that unremitting light that I see [Aurach], always sitting in the same place in front of a fresco painted by an unknown hand that showed a caravan moving forward from the remotest depths of the picture, across a wavy ridge of dunes, straight toward the beholder. The painter lacked the necessary skill, and the perspective he had chosen was a difficult one, as a result of which both the human figures and the beasts of burden were slightly distorted so that . . . the scene looked like a mirage, quivering in the heat and light. And especially on days when [Aurach] had been working in charcoal, and the fine powdery dust had given his skin a metallic sheen, he seemed to have just emerged from the desert scene, *or to belong in it*. (164E, emphasis mine, translation altered)[32]

> Durchstrahlt von einem flimmernden . . . Neonlicht, . . . sehe ich Aurach, wenn ich zurückdenke an unsere Begegnungen in Trafford Park, ein jedes Mal sitzen, stets auf dem selben Platz, vor einem von unbekannter Hand gemalten Fresko, das eine Karawane zeigte, die aus der fernsten Tiefe des Bildes heraus und über ein Wellengebirge von Dünen hinweg direkt auf den Betrachter zu sich bewegte. Infolge der Ungeschicktheit des Malers und der schwierigen Perspektive, die er gewählt hatte, wirkten die menschlichen Figuren sowohl als die Lasttiere in ihren Umrissen leicht verzerrt, so daß es . . . tatsächlich war, als erblicke man eine in der Helligkeit und Hitze zitternde Fata Morgana. Und insbesondere an Tagen, an denen Aurach mit Kohle gearbeitet und der pudrig feine Staub seine Haut mit einem metallischen Glanz imprägniert hatte, schien es mir, als sei er soeben aus dem Wüstenbild herausgetreten *oder als gehöre er in es hinein*. (243G, emphasis mine)

And have we not come full circle—to our question of how to quarter the dead? Difficult to say if Aurach has come out of the desert image (*Wüsten-*

bild)[33] or whether, though denizen of this side, he nevertheless belongs within. Hovering between, or perhaps straddling both at once, in this flickering light, it's hard to tell. He is neither saved by the markings that create the picture, nor sent back to the unskilled fresco of unknown hand. But this his portrait tells us: Aurach becomes his own work of art: his fate, perhaps, that of the photographer whom he finds in a similar fix, in the pages of yet another newspaper.

> But anyway, he went on . . . the darkening of his skin reminded him of an article he had recently read in the paper about silver poisoning, the symptoms of which were not uncommon among professional photographers. According to the article, the British Medical Association's archives contained the description of an extreme case of silver poisoning; in the 1930s there was a photographic lab assistant in Manchester whose body had absorbed so much silver in the course of a lengthy professional life that he had become a kind of photographic plate, which was apparent in the fact . . . that the man's face and hands turned blue in strong light, or, as one might say, developed. (164–65E)

> Im übrigen, so fuhr er . . . fort, erinnere ihn die Verdunkelung seiner Haut an eine Zeitungsnotiz, die ihm unlängst untergekommen sei, über die bei Berufsfotografen nicht unüblichen Symptome der Silbervergiftung. Im Archiv der Britischen Medizinishcen Gesellschaft werde beispielsweise, so habe in der Notiz gestanden, die Beschreibung eines extremen Falls einer solchen Vergiftung aufbewahrt, derzufolge es in den dreißiger Jahren in Manchester einen Fotolaboranten gegeben haben soll, dessen Körper im Verlauf seiner langjährigen Berufspraxis derart viel Silber assimiliert hatte, daß er zu einer Art fotografischer Platte geworden war, was sich . . . daran zeigte, daß das Gesicht und die Hände . . . bei starkem Lichteinfall blau anliefen, sich also sozusagen entwickelten. (244G)]

A martyr of sorts to his art of photography. That long practice of taking in silver. What does it mean to take in silver? And where does Sebald stand in all this? What does he develop? What his narrator tells is surely no "beautiful protocol, no exact protocol," but he develops "a protocol of the sort that one doesn't experience every day" (*Kaspar Hauser*). Such writing leaves its subject and subjects, the author too, an enigma, even if, by the light of publication, in the many documents and photographs, their memories may *seem* preserved.

The uncertainty of the light in which that leaves them all hardly escapes the narrator. It is the closing pages of *The Emigrants*. He returns from visiting the ash-gray Aurach who, so close to death, has a voice like the rustling of dried leaves in the wind (231E, 345–46G)] that recalls, in another incarnation, the leaves outside the narrator's window. In a room he has taken in the Manchester hotel where Aurach has also resided—an act of solidarity, perhaps? certainly not identity—in that room the Polish industrial center of Łódź once known as the Polish Manchester comes to him (352G). Manchester—Łódź—or as the Nazis renamed it Litzmannstadt, a name that hints of the entangled web into which we have already entered.[34]

In the narrator's imagination, then:

> On those flats [of an infinitely deep stage], which in truth did not exist, I saw, one by one, pictures from an exhibition that I had seen in Frankfurt the year before.[35]
>
> They were colour photographs, tinted with a greenish-blue or reddish-brown, of the Litzmannstadt ghetto that was established in 1940 in the Polish industrial centre of Łódź, once known as *polski Manczester.* (235–36E)

> Auf diesen in Wahrheit gar nicht vorhandenen Seitenprospekten aber erschienen eines ums andere die Bilder einer Ausstellung, die ich im Vorjahr in Frankfurt gesehen hatte. Es waren grünblau beziehungsweise rotbraunstichige Farbaufnahmen aus dem Ghetto Litzmannstadt, das 1940 eingerichtet worden war in der polnischen Industriemetropole Łódź, die einmal *polski Manczester* geheißen hat. (352G)

Something of a second slide show, you see, whose relation to the first should be preserved. A color-slide show ("Farbdia-Serie")[36] out of memory and imagination.

> The photographs, which had been discovered in 1987 in a small suitcase, carefully sorted and inscribed, in an antique dealer's shop in Vienna, had been taken as personal souvenirs by a book-keeper and financial expert named Genewein . . . who was himself in one of the pictures, counting money. . . . (236E)

> Die Aufnahmen, die 1987 sorgfältig geordnet und beschriftet in einem hölzernen Köfferchen bei einem Wiener Antiquar zum Vorschein gekommen sind, waren zu Erinnerungszwecken gemacht worden von einem in Litzmannstadt tätigen Buchhalter und Finanzfachmann namens Genewein . . . den man selber auf einem der Bilder sehen konnte beim Geldzählen. . . . (352–53G)

FIGURE 5.3. Litzmannstadt chief accountant (Jüdisches Museum Frankfurt am Main).

The ghetto's chief accountant, bookkeeper, financial expert, counter of money (*Buchhalter*, *Finanzfachmann*, *Geldzähler*), and as history judged him later (if not the courts), embezzler and thief of the worst order.[37] Genewein obsessively documented the ghetto in almost four hundred color slides—for the purpose of memory (*Erinnerungszwecken*) and to celebrate the Nazi sense of "organization." "The photographer had also documented the exemplary organization within the ghetto: the postal system, the police, the courtroom, . . . the laying out of the dead, and the burial ground" (236E, translation altered; 354G). He celebrated no less, and perhaps above all, what he regarded as his own cutting-edge photographic experimentation.

The last of these photographs, rather a matter of his imagination, fixes the narrator's gaze. It is a question of how to frame all these documents, a question, you see it now, no doubt, of another screen and another frame, this time, and out of time, the frame of a loom.

> Behind the perpendicular frame of a loom sit three young women, perhaps aged twenty. . . . Who the young women are I do not know. The light falls

FIGURE 5.4.   Litzmannstadt weavers (Jüdisches Museum Frankfurt am Main).

on them from the window in the background, so I cannot make out their eyes clearly, but I sense that all three of them are looking across at me, since I am standing on the very spot where Genewein the accountant stood with his camera. (237E)[38]

Hinter einem lotrechten Webrahmen sitzen drei junge, vielleicht zwanzigjäh-rige Frauen. . . . Wer die jungen Frauen sind, das weiß ich nicht. Wegen des Gegenlichts, das einfällt durch das Fenster im Hintergrund, kann ich ihre Augen genau nicht erkennen, aber ich spüre, daß sie alle drei herschauen zu mir, denn ich stehe ja an der Stelle, an der Genewein der Rechnungsführer, mit seinem Fotoapparat gestanden hat. (355G)

Sebald places his narrator, himself, of course, too, on the spot—on the spot where the accountant, the *Rechnungsführer*, had stood, that keeper of books and financial expert, who was so good at taking in silver and no doubt knew all too well how to count by quarters.[39]

At stake, the names of the weaving young women, how they are woven together: with one another, with their German analogues,[40] and what the shift from the individual to the abstract mythological frame might signify. Also what it might mean, as the publisher has it, to preserve memory, to collect photos and documents.

The young woman in the middle is blonde and has the air of a bride about her. The weaver to her left has inclined her head a little to one side, whilst the woman on the right is looking at me with so steady and relentless a gaze that I cannot meet it for long. I wonder what the three women's names were—Roza, Lusia[41] and Lea, or Nona, Decuma and Morta, the daughters of night, with spindle, thread and scissors. (237E, translation altered)

Die mittlere der drei jungen Frauen hat hellblondes Haar und gleicht irgend-wie einer Braut. Die Weberin zu ihrer Linken hält den Kopf ein wenig seit-wärts geneigt, während die auf der rechten Seite so unverwandt und unerbit-tlich mich ansieht, daß ich es nicht lange auszuhalten vermag. Ich überlege, wie die drei wohl geheißen haben—Roza, Lusia, und Lea oder Nona, De-cuma und Morta, die Töchter der Nacht, mit Spindel und Faden und Schere. (355G)

At the close of 350 pages, the narrator stands in the place of Genewein. He is no longer, necessarily, like the besilvered Manchester photographer, a martyr to his art. He does not take a picture so much as await his fate.

We cannot count on him. *The Emigrants* does not and cannot save Henry Selwyn, nor Max Aurach, nor the quarter of Paul Bereyter that is Jewish, nor the one-and-three-quarters gentiles whose fates are just as tragic.[42] The dead cannot come back nor can one go into them, what-ever the temptation. Still, in strong light ["bei starkem Lichteinfall"], something *develops*, even though we may have lost the negative—even though we may know neither the original story nor its end for sure.[43] The interwovenness of all four, better still their *Bestäubung*, their cross-pollination, the way in which anything can rupture into anything else, challenges a politics based on identity,[44] and bursts the gazes (of author, narrator, reader) that have been held fast (*zerspringt die festgehaltenen An-blicke*): a liberation of sorts, that shatters the frame and keeps alive the resistance—the resistance to thinking in terms of bio-logical definition, believing it might yet mean something to count as a Jew. I break off by once again citing Kaspar Hauser, this time his dying words: "I thank you for having listened to me."

§ 6   Playing Jane Campion's *Piano*: Politically

I'm asking the sea to welcome me.

—Tungia Baker

A catholic priest, a protestant minister, and a rabbi were walking along the beach together when a great angel with diaphanous wings approached them.[1] He announced an apocalypse near at hand, telling them of a great flood that was to come the very next day. The priest hurried back to his church, with a deeply troubled visage. "The end of the world is at hand," he intoned: "we must all make our last confessions, receive absolution, and prepare for the hereafter." The protestant minister returned to his flock. "In just one day," he called out, "all the land will be covered with water. We must find it in our hearts and minds to accept the will of God." The rabbi, she too, made her way back to her congregation. With a great sense of urgency she turned to her audience and announced: "We have just twenty-four hours to learn to live underwater."

In the end we must learn to live underwater. If Jane Campion's film *The Piano* has a moral, this is surely it. Or rather we must come to terms as best we can with the realm this film envisions, and which we too more or less inhabit, as underneath the sea, a new sealand, so to speak. Still, no viewer can fail to sense that this film shrouds itself in the unholy suspicion that *The Piano* may not have any moral after all. It will be difficult to make this clear.

The politics of this film, set in mid-nineteenth-century New Zealand, unmistakably confront the contemporary issues of feminism, colonialism, and environmentalism: they speak eloquently as a protest against brutal and artificial hierarchies. In answer to this, almost everything in the land- and bodyscape of *The Piano* seems to make a call in the name of Nature. To the tyrannies of colonial rule and its violence to the ecology, the figures of the Maori natives and the unfettered growth of the bush are offered as the morally satisfying counterpoise. To the Victorian strictures imposed on women, imaged in the prison of their formal clothing, the film replies with a feminism that boldly defines itself in terms of desire and its naked satisfactions.

I will confess that the initial attraction of this film lay for me first and foremost in what seemed its feminism, in its concern for a woman who knows her own mind and asserts her own voice. And yet it is a film that insists on forcing us from the covert of a certain blind analphabetism, and on making us read aloud in a voice that is perhaps not our own; it is a film that insists on making us see. Like a dog coaxed from under the verandah during a heavy rainstorm, we are bound to get wet.

If *The Piano* clearly focuses on familiar issues of our day, if its seductions are such that a certain concept of Nature seems the solution to political inequities, if the viewer is "magnetically drawn to the spectacle" (35), and is bound to see it this way, such a point of view is not ultimately locatable in the film. There is throughout, but especially at the enigmatic horizons of its opening and closing scenes, another mode of (I hesitate to say theorizing) the political. Still this imaging and imagining of the political, alongside what takes place with regard to particular social issues, has everything to do with the performance. It suggests the possibility, if not quite the realization, of another mode of liberation, a liberation unwound from the wound of specific hegemonies. It comes to this film as second nature, silently, and often without self-consciousness, which is to say it comes to this film almost without our noticing it.

To be sure all of this is endlessly disturbing. It perhaps accounts for the unsettling qualities of the work. We find evidence of this in reactions from critics and viewers alike.[2] Is this a disturbed film? To paraphrase Mary Cantwell writing in the *New York Times*, the first thing one wants to know of Jane Campion, who both wrote and directed the film, is "if she's sane."[3] Or, as Stewart, Ada's husband, reflects about his new wife, even when one accepts her strange mode of communication, one still wonders whether it's not more than that, one wonders "if she's not brain-affected" (39). But perhaps Harvey Keitel has phrased it more precisely: "[Jane Campion] is at play, like a warm breeze."[4]

That play means telling a good story. It is a suspiciously symmetrical tale, framed at beginning and end by sea journeys. The first is preceded by a voice-over from civilized, nineteenth-century Scotland, the last followed by a voice-over from the beginnings of the city of Nelson. Voice-overs because Ada McGrath has chosen not to speak since the age of six. "The strange thing is," she tells us, "I don't think myself silent, that is, because of my piano" (9). She, her young daughter, Flora, and, of course, her piano, arrive on the desolate shores of New Zealand. She has been married by her father before her departure to a man she has never met, a middle-aged *pakeha*,[5] Alisdair Stewart.

If Ada is unable to speak, Stewart, it is obvious, is unable to hear. He ignores, at least, her requests to have the piano (which he tellingly mistakes for a bedstead) carried from the beach where, to her increasing anger, it remains exposed to the rain and tides. Ada and Flora induce the reluctant George Baines, European by birth but Maori in spirit, to take them to the beach where they landed. There, in a scene of extraordinary beauty, as Ada plays the soaring "uninhibited, emotional" (35) music which will haunt the rest of the film, she is transformed into a joyous creature of remarkable abandon. For if she has chosen the piano to replace her speaking voice, the instrument, it is clear, is more natural than the original, not only a more genuine expression of the inner Ada (that goes without saying), but identified, moreover, both with the sunlit beauty of the outdoors and later with the indoor sensuality of sexual passion. It is here as Baines watches her play, as he listens to her true voice, so to speak, that he is smitten.

Baines is a man who knows what he desires. He easily convinces Stewart to swap the piano and Ada's lessons for his eighty acres of land. Stewart takes him for something of a fool, for Stewart expends his daily energies acquiring the land of the Maori people, "very reasonably" (32) as he puts it. We see him offering the natives blankets and guns with disingenuous smiles of goodwill. And when they refuse to part with the land, we hear him complaining to Baines, his interpreter and his right-hand man:

BAINES *and* STEWART *walk through the bush,* STEWART *laden down with his blankets, red-faced and irritable.*

STEWART: What do they want the land for? They don't do anything with it. They don't cultivate it, they don't burn it back, nothing. How do they even know that it's theirs . . . ? (70)

Stewart, however, knows the land is his. The scene around his house is wounded with charred, dead, amputees of trees, "muddy . . . acres of . . . slash and burn" (140). When he is not buying land or burning it back he splits fence posts, marks them with his initials and small blood-red ribbons, and drives them into the ground to mark the border of his possessions. It makes perfect sense, therefore, that later in the film, to contain the passions of his wife whom he has discovered with Baines, he nails planks he has hewn to window and door to secure the boundary of his marital chattel.

He is outraged, moreover, on seeing those trees transformed into emblems of sexual gratification when Flora instigates a game with the Maori children.

> *The children rub up and down against the tree trunks, kissing and hugging them. The game has an edge of promiscuity to it as they exchange trunks. . . . Unseen by the children,* STEWART *marches toward* FLORA. *He pulls her off the tree.*

STEWART: Never behave like that, never, nowhere. You're greatly shamed and you have shamed these trunks. (72)

The same scene that shames the *pakeha* amuses the native women. For the Maoris, we are made to understand, delight in a range of free sexual pleasures, including cross-dressing, occasionally even crossing the screen in the open undress that the Europeans have so to labor to achieve.

And how can it be unrelated, then, that they stand as guardians of the earth? But where are we heading here, if not to that great commonplace that native peoples and women are closer to nature and unfettered sexuality? Hollywood has a history of the first at least from *Little Big Man* to *Dances With Wolves*. Both feminist and antifeminist writing have a history of the second. Yet the Maoris do not precisely play the role of nature to Stewart's colonial culture. Harvey Keitel may suggest that the Maoris "tend to have a more profound relationship to the earth and the spirits than the *pakeha* do" (143), but that relationship is never unmarked by culture. Maori land is not the locus of the pristine untouched, the banal counter to Stewart's slash to possess. It is insistently respected, rather, as the site of human mortality, either as the burial ground of the ancestors in general (69) or as the place of a particular death (27). It bears silent and perhaps threatening witness to human finitude, a witness to which the closing lines of the film will return us.[6]

Let us just say for now that it is certainly not as the noble savage that we encounter this other culture. "All of them are clothed in a mixture of native and European costume" (17). The costume of civilization is never quite complete and the Maoris are from beginning to end imperfect repli-

cas of a European world that has almost destroyed them. Campion originally planned to present them covered with sores,[7] the obvious victims of
the white man's diseases and the white man as disease. She opts instead for
a different commentary on the colonial invader which tosses to the winds
any pathos of native purity.[8] The Maoris enter to a carnival music, strung
out across the screen like happy-go-lucky counterparts to the darkened
figures in *The Seventh Seal* or as the exotic answer to the closing scene
of *8 1/2.* The effect is far less pathetic than parodic. The utter absurdity
of Stewart's formal clothes is underscored by the figures of two similarly
behatted Maoris, one of whom tilts his head in exact unison with each
movement of the officious, questioning white man.[9]

Nor does the figure of Ada act out the litany of clichés attached to a
certain feminism. She never engages in any menial household chores. If
she is something of an exemplary mother to begin with—a captivating
storyteller and always affectionate—this is only until her overwhelming
passion for Baines brings her to shut her daughter out, to cut her daughter off.

The political message of *The Piano* is never simple, never straightforward. Neither native nor woman is there simply as victim in relation to
the hegemonic figure of the white man—not even when Stewart attempts
rape, not even when, in a horrifying rage of jealousy, he drags Ada to his
chopping block and hacks off her forefinger like yet another limb of a
felled tree.

Perhaps it's just as well that I've let the ax fall. It was bound to happen
sooner or later. In some ways, we could start again for we must get on,
you see. Things will not really be different from now on, no different
from what they were before. In *The Piano* Ada is not defeated by the
disembodiment of her bloody finger at the fall of the ax. On the contrary.
Her will becomes stronger than ever.

The will of this film, like Ada's, or at least that which drives it, is mute.
In the words of Hira, it is "beyond the veil" (117), and that is what makes
it so difficult to apprehend. Yet therein lies its most overwhelming political thrust. We might say of *The Piano* what Nessie says of herself just
when the film is about to take a critical turn: "[it's] in costume"—in ways
we have not begun to see. In ways we may never quite fully take in.

Let us take, to begin with, its most obvious disguise: the play within
the play at its very center. The community assembles one evening for a
double performance. The children, dressed variously as clouds and angels,

are there to present a vision of heaven. The adult contribution is a tale of evil, a counterbalancing glimpse of the underworld.[10] The story is that of Bluebeard, taken from Charles Perrault's "La Barbe bleue," a narrative that in its printed version is followed by no fewer than two instructive morals. This is a community, no less than our own, that knows the difference between heaven and hell, between the moral and the immoral.

The play we see has been much anticipated, for we witness in advance its careful preparations and hear the explanations of how the props work, how the stage is set, and how the illusion is to be created.

> AUNT MORAG (*Looking carefully at* STEWART. . . . *Without pause, but referring to the sheet*). You see, these are the slits that the heads will go through, show him Nessie . . . they'll be dead, the Reverend is going to use animal blood, no doubt it will be very dramatic. (39)

First prop, then: a "*double white sheet*" (38). In this story of luring an object of desire into bed, how can sheets be insignificant? The scene depicts the closet of horrors, the chamber in which Bluebeard's wife discovers her predecessors and victims of her husband's crimes. The white expanse is stretched across half the stage, the heads of the "dead" wives placed through the slits, blood dripping from their severed necks: Nessie passes in front illuminating each with a plate of candles in her hand. The sheet forms the opaque line of demarcation between the theatrical presentation of morbid heads in front and the very live bodies that it hides.

The play whose effect is "very dramatic" indeed now reverses the logic of inside and out. The illusion of the first scene: actual heads, however disguised, appear before the sheet, each illuminated in turn by a light held in front of it. Nessie puts her candles down and, leaving the chamber, shifts to the left side of the stage. Here the rest of the tale is played out, not in front of but behind a second sheet stretched out a few feet closer to the audience. What we witness is a shadow play, action beyond the veil or sheet (a presentation of which Socrates, no doubt, would have disapproved). For this, too, we have been prepared.

> *Inside the* REVEREND *is closely watched by* STEWART, AUNT MORAG *and* NESSIE. . . . *A lamplight flickers warm tones across their faces while the rest of the room is dark, giving it a conspiratorial air.*
>
> REVEREND: Nessie, . . . come put your hand out. . . .

NESSIE: Oh, no, use Mr. Stewart.

REVEREND: Nessie, please.

. . . .

NESSIE *hesitatingly puts her arm out toward him and the* REVEREND *chops away in the air two feet in front of her.*

. . . .

REVEREND: Put out your hand. Look, look, you are being attacked!

The REVEREND points to the opposite rose-papered wall, where his shadow and paper axe now look very real as they loom large above the crouching Nessie, chopping into her. NESSIE *squeals, as does Mary.*

REVEREND: And with the blood it will be a very good effect. (58)

In the second scene, light passes from behind through a no longer opaque cloth on which the silhouette of Bluebeard enters from the left, that of his wife from the otherwise staged scene on the right. The cardboard ax with which he prepares to attack her *"now [looks] very real,"* the critical distance between ax and victim collapsed.

What lies in the balance here—it leaps to the eye—is the staged difference between two kinds of representation, a difference on which we have only begun to reflect. If there is a lesson in the production of *Bluebeard* it has something to do with the double narrative it presents, on the one hand with the real before the eye (the heads of the murdered wives before the sheet), on the other with the action through the translucent screen, as film. But at the same time, it is made crystal-clear, in this film so fraught with viewers and voyeurs, that it is not only a question of what one sees but also of how one sees it. As the performance takes place there are no less than three audiences, each with a different perspective. The cinema audience is certain that the tale of Bluebeard is purely staged. The *pakehas,* in turn, know more or less, more rather than less, that it is all illusion. But as the Maori warriors take in the scene, they are taken in. They charge the stage to right the wrong that threatens to take place and menace the villain with very real retribution. The movie audience roars with laughter, but the *pakehas* are rather in an uproar. For if the natives tend (as on the beach) to unsettle the seriousness of the white man through acts of theatrical parody, they also unsettle the white man's sense of the purely theatrical through acts potentially quite serious. Perpetual irony and uncertainty in the distinction between playful distance and the grave.

But what is also at stake therein, one cannot avoid seeing it too, is the possibility of moral action. Does such moral action require a sense of certainty with respect to reality? Perhaps. That the mode of the moral is one of retribution, that it is in the Maori warrior that the wife killer could meet his match, violence for violence, hegemonic power overturned by might making right, to this we will have to return.[11] In contrast, does the possibility of defying the immoral, then, require a sense of certainty with respect to reality? Not necessarily, perhaps. Nor is defying the immoral necessarily the same as doing the right thing. Let us just say for now, not precisely by way of explanation, that what one cannot avoid seeing, at least here, if not clearly elsewhere in *The Piano*, is that this is less a play within a play than a film within a film. The shadow play of Bluebeard and his wife enacts the principles of cinema in its most primitive form.

How does one account, then, for that same primal scene of feminine violation reenacted? Ada removes a key from the piano on which she engraves a message of love to George. This she wraps and ties in a napkin and instructs her daughter, Flora, to carry to her lover. It is this gesture that precipitates Stewart's rage. Ada finds Flora outside laundering her doll's clothes. The child sits surrounded by hanging linens and the camera lingers long enough on Ada's silhouette against a sun-illumined sheet to remind us where we are because of where we've been. As Campion's stage direction puts it: "*Her black shadow behind the sheet recalls the macabre play*" (94). As Ada is dragged to her punishment she grasps at another sheet to stay the inevitable. Bluebeard and his wife are now played by Stewart and Ada at the chopping block:[12] it is no laughing matter. No one in the audience is unaffected. Still, the filmic maneuvers that produced this scene are obviously no less manipulated to create illusions than the theatrics of the schoolhouse presentation, even if the "blood [here as there] no doubt [is] very dramatic" (39), even if Stewart and the "*axe now look very real*" (58). Yet in the many times this film was shown, no one in the audience has charged the screen to save the heroine. "Why is that?" (84).

Wherein lies then the politicality of *The Piano*? Certainly not in a call to immediate action. Nor can we append to it as Perrault does to his tale a maxim or two that might specify its doctrinal truth (although, to be sure, a somewhat parodic version of Perrault's morals will have a critical role to play). If *The Piano* performs an exceptional and fierce feminism[13] this will have much to do with the apparently anticlimactic events that follow the scene of Stewart's brutality and also with the commentary that the haunting repetition of its visual images enact throughout.

For *The Piano,* like Ada, is something of a mute. It moves silently, as it signs. The material of these visual images is, above all, the fabric that sets the stage for the film's play—and not only in the sheets, both whole and torn, that make the performance possible.[14] If the scene of Perrault's play presents the film within the film, in a sense we are never far away from it. Never far away, that is, from one of its modes of presentation—on the one hand the opaque, on the other the translucent. The distinction makes all the difference in the world and yet none whatsoever.

And the garment that captures the imagination above all in this tale of desire is, of course, the skirt: it has, in a sense, a life of its own. It marks from the beginning the place of reproduction, both on the cinematic screen and in the female body. On the desolate beach where they have just landed a seaman asks Ada if she has things for shelter. That shelter turns out to be the great meshed hoop skirt (which reappears so often) covered with a petticoat which is rendered translucent by a light within. As we first see it, Flora stages a shadow-play against the cloth, with her hands, of course: "Look, I'm a very big moth.[15] Will it catch fire?" (film).

This is indeed where everything catches fire. The great underskirt of cinematic projection, source of storytelling[16] and of the story, place of risk. It delivers Ada the next morning to the disappointed eye of her new husband as she backs out like the offering of a breech birth. It receives her just before she kisses Baines for the first time and as she sinks down after Stewart's attack. Covered with clothing it marks the distance and formality of Victorian repression. Yet it is the same skirt under which her lover's head disappears as Ada stands in obvious delight. This image, like the others in *The Piano,* guarantees no symbolic continuity or stability. It haunts the film, rather, with the possibility of contradiction, inversion, difference. Filmic figure of shelter, of cold distance, of utter intimacy, the skirt becomes a shroud as Ada plunges beneath the water at the end of the film. No longer surrounding the locus of sexual pleasure, we witness the reversed order of layers—outer skirt innermost, hoop outermost. As she descends to the bottom tied to her piano, they cover the upper body, no longer from waist to ankle, but now from waist to crown.

The cloth that covers the head, of course, is no sign of tragic conclusion but rather the condition of *The Piano* to begin with. This is less because of those bonnets that engender a complex study in black and white than because of the cloth that shuts out light and belongs to the photographer.

The very first scene after mother and daughter arrive at their new home is that of the wedding picture. "AUNT MORAG: If you cannot have a ceremony together, you have at least a photograph" (film). The photograph replaces the ceremony which had already taken place weeks earlier on the same day the film's story begins, with Ada in Scotland, Stewart in New Zealand. "ADA: Today [my father] married me to a man I've not yet met" (9). The photograph, then, is not that of the event itself, nor is it a reproduction of the natural scene. The scenic view, rather, in the conventional Victorian manner, consists of a backdrop behind the human figures, in this case an ironical substitution of trees for the scene of actual trees behind it. Moreover in this costume drama in which the director of photography, Stuart Dryburgh insists, "[Campion's] approach has been totally irreverent" (141), Ada wears "*not a normal wedding dress but a backless one used again and again as a photographic prop*" (29). That prop which, we are constantly reminded, is fragile and bound to tear (and so it does), is donned for the acting out of a wedding that has never really taken place and a marriage that never really will.

The camera stands facing the screen on which the rural scene is imaged. As Ada comes on stage to assume her place Stewart goes behind the camera, pulls its cloth over his head and, as the cinema viewers observe from just the other side of the lens, peers first with one blue eye and then with the other. How shall we understand that we are made to come eye to eye with the object of the photo who has displaced himself to the site of the photographer? For the cloth as we have already seen marks both the place of the object to be viewed and desired and also that of the viewing.[17]

How shall we come to terms with this in a film that openly takes the history of photography as the model for its own imaging? "For the cinematography, we've used a nineteenth-century colour stills process—the autochrome—as an inspiration" (141), Dryburgh says. If he doesn't have the dates of the autochrome quite right,[18] *The Piano* is nevertheless situated at a critical moment in the history of photography. Taking place in the 1850s, it is but a few years since Daguerre had, in 1839, sold his process to the French government with the arrangement that the technical details would thereupon be made available to the public. The passion for photography was immediate and overwhelming.

The rhetoric, even before its realization, had always been in the name of nature.

> The physical aid of camera obscura and camera lucida had drawn men so near to an exact copying of nature and the satisfaction of the current craving for reality that they could not abide the intrusion of the pencil of man to close the gap.[19]

Thus Daguerre spoke of giving "Nature the ability to reproduce herself." The brother of Nicéphore Niepce, one of the earliest pioneers, writes of Daguerre: "These representations are so real, even in their smallest detail, that one believes that he naturally sees rural and primeval nature." Niepce himself defined the "sole object" of his project of *point de vue* as that of "copy[ing] nature with the greatest fidelity."[20] In the wedding picture, however, as we have seen, it is hardly a question of fidelity.[21]

In the decade in which the film is set, new processes made possible a frenzy of fixing the human image in portraits. Stewart on both sides of the camera is part of that craze to engage the real, to capture nature. Even earlier in the film, in our very first glimpse of him, we see Stewart as an ardent image catcher. As he and Baines and their troop of Maoris traipse through the wooded brush on the way to the beach, Stewart stops for a moment to set his hair in order. It is here that we find out the answer to a question only subliminally posed throughout. What is it that the *pakeha* and father of the family actually has in his pocket? (The question, you remember, has a cinematic resonance in the voice of Mae West.) If in the previous scene the film placed itself under Ada's skirt, the pocket of Stewart, it makes sense, is the logical and symmetrical space to fathom.

> DRYBURGH: The camera's viewpoint on all this is that of a witness directing the viewer's attention in a very intimate way. Sometimes we go places where the camera can't really go. We've been . . . inside Stewart's pocket, right down at the level of hands and fingers . . . It wouldn't be a Jane Campion film without some wittiness in the framing. (141)

What Stewart has in his pocket, besides the hand which fondles it, is a photograph which he touchingly and surreptitiously takes out to admire, just before he must confront the real thing. We see him gazing at the stiffly posed Ada, but then, with a change in the angle of the light (that shift in the position of illumination which later proves critical in the performance of *Bluebeard*) the photograph becomes a mirror in which he scrutinizes himself. As Stewart's self- and husbandly possessions flicker uncertainly, the mirroring glass also repeatedly catches the less elusive objects of his ownership, the trees of the bush behind him.[22]

In the photograph lies the will to possess, however melancholy and disappointed, to possess woman, nature, and self.[23] It has its counterpart in a far wittier and freer medium. For while outside the "pencil of nature"[24] is taking the staged "wedding" portrait against the backdrop of simulated trees, while Ada, clothed in her costume of fragile lace, is getting soaked through by the rains of New Zealand, Flora sits inside telling Aunt Morag of another wedding and another storm:

AUNT MORAG (*Frowning*): And where did they get married?

AUNT MORAG *checks to see if someone is coming.*

FLORA (*Her Scottish accent becoming thick and expressive.*): In an enormous forest, with real fairies as bridesmaids each holding a little elf's hand.

AUNT MORAG *sits back, regarding* FLORA *with obvious disapproval and disappointment. She smooths back her hair.*

FLORA: No, I tell a lie, it was in a small country church, in the mountains . . .

AUNT MORAG *is becoming involved again. She leans forward.*

AUNT MORAG: Which mountains are those, dear?

FLORA: The Pyrenees.

AUNT MORAG: Ohhh, I've never been there. (*She leans forward.*)

FLORA: Mother used to sing songs in German and her voice would echo across the valley . . . That was before the accident . . .

AUNT MORAG: Oh, what happened?

AUNT MORAG *looks over her shoulder as* FLORA *continues to talk; so persuasive is* FLORA's *storytelling that the scene comes vividly to life, albeit in* FLORA's *dark pupil.*

FLORA: One day when my mother and father were singing together in the forest, a great storm blew up out of nowhere. But so passionate was their singing that they did not notice, nor did they stop as the rain began to fall, and when their voices rose for the final bars of the duet a great bolt of lightning came out of the sky and struck my father so that he lit up like a torch . . . And at the same moment my father was struck dead my mother was struck dumb! She—never—spoke—another—word.

AUNT MORAG: Ohhh . . . dear! Not another word. Well, from the shock, yes it would be. (31–32)

This wedding is not copied by the pencil of nature but rather created by the brush of a (rather diminutive) woman. Literally, one is tempted to say. For as Flora tells her story, just as lightning bursts simultaneously in her narrative and outside the house, on the screen (painted directly on the film, it seems) we see childlike pictures of a man. In rapid succession, like a jumping-jack whose string is pulled suddenly, we see him in two positions, first standing stiffly, arms to the side, then, as the thunder rolls, arms up, flames behind him. Like a primitive cinematic sequence, we see frames of a motion picture that abruptly refuse to portray the real world.[25] Singular and startling break in the narrative continuity[26] of a story that for all its strangeness is nowhere else otherwise quite so unreal or surreal. A radical gesture of fiery image-ination (like its tamer counterpart, the illumined skirt on the beach), Flora's recast lie places the origin of her mother's muteness as the culmination of a perfect artistic achievement, as the moment of exquisite passion, as the filmic disruption of her own narrative, and simultaneous with the death of the father as composer.[27] Why is that?

What takes place here is not simply photographic reproduction of the real and natural on the one hand (however ironized) and filmic imagination on the other, no more than in the double scene of *Bluebeard*. It all depends on what light you see it in and above all on the point of view.

Isn't this, after all, what the initial frames of *The Piano* are about? Long, uneven shafts of reddish-pink light fan out across the screen, unfocused, like a failed and undeveloped color negative of translucent vessels of blood. The view we have is that of Ada (that almost Adam of a name). Yet it is nearly no view at all—an almost blindness, with distance so minimal between eye and object that what we see is an unrecognizable blur. Still it is, no doubt, the representation of what Ada's mind sees, visual analogy of the voice that refuses to become her speaking voice. "The voice you hear is not my speaking voice, but my mind's voice" (9). These are the opening words of the film, and from what one can see also the opening as film. What does it mean to hear a voice that is not a speaking voice, to hear a voice that speaks in place of speaking and therefore *in the place of* silence?

The voice we hear is a voice of the mind, but it affords us no simple access to Ada, its source, accompanied as it is by a visual image we cannot possibly understand. The image we first see is from the other side, from Ada's perspective, her fingers, liquid fingers, substitutes for the speaking voice; these are the fingers with which Ada in her muteness will sign, write, and, above all, play the piano. And these fingers render us just as illiterate here, just as unable to read them, as they will later—in all those scenes where fingers talk with no subtitles to explain them. Ada peers out from hands held and spread against her face, yet what we witness is no child's game of hide and seek, but rather a prefiguration both strange and ominous. They form the veil between the mind and the gaze of the other, like the sheet in the performance of *Bluebeard,* like the reddish-pink diaphanous curtain that separates Baines' bed from the site of the piano; they display the blood of the horrific and apparently decisive event—unspeakably, unreadably before us.

We see Ada's fingers pierced through with sunlight, from her perspective, as we hear the voice of her mind, but then, immediately thereafter, we see them from the clear perspective of the onlookers that we are, as they become matter-of-fact objects to the lens of the camera. The screen is never again troubled by the unbearable and blinding proximity of its filmed object, film as object. Nor between this opening and the closing moments of the film do we hear her mind's voice.

Still, Jane Campion's *The Piano* seems to be about a woman who knows her own mind. Anyone who has truly seen it (although, to be honest, I'm not sure that I have) can tell you that. But what might it mean to know one's own mind? *The Piano* opens to view the mind's voice, yet what opens to view is the point of articulation of the entire film as an unfixable movement between subjective and objective, translucent and opaque, presence of the hand only as prefiguration of its wounding, instrument for speaking in the place of silence, site of language as unreadability.[28] If the wedding photograph followed by Flora's filmic imagination and then the double theater of the Bluebeard play place fixed representation and its emancipation side by side, the opening shots make Ada's fingers both of these almost at once and also the veil between. Moreover, all that bound up with the ostensible difference between an interior monologue and the equivalent of objective, third-person narrative as which the film continues. Given this, it is altogether possible that "knowing one's own mind" in both senses of that phrase, and with all the political and philosophical resonances it might have, is no certainty at all.

What Ada tells us of in her mind's voice is precisely that the absence of her speaking voice is a question of will.

> I have not spoken since I was six years old. No one knows why, not even me. My father says it is a dark talent and the day I take it into my head to stop breathing will be my last. (9)

A question of will, but a will that is strangely disconnected from conventional concepts of volition. If Ada has not spoken since the age of six, not even she knows why. A will, then, that is like a passion outside the realm of tame self-interest and self-knowledge.

That will is ultimately what overwhelms Stewart. For when he goes to see Baines, after violating Ada in the only way of which he is capable, after failing to violate her in the ways in which he desires, he has this to say:

> STEWART: (*Slowly*): I heard it here. (*He presses his forehead with the palm of his hand.*) I heard her voice here in my head. I watched her lips, they didn't make the words, yet the harder I listened the clearer I heard her.

> . . . .

> STEWART: She said, "I am afraid of my will, of what it might do, it is so strange and strong." She said, "I have to go, let me go, let Baines take me away, let him try and save me." (114–15)

What is the strength of woman's will—this will that "lay[s] out thoughts like they were a sheet" (51)? Wherein lies its strangeness? For in some sense Ada is the freak version of the possibility of woman's will, even though that means rethinking the concept of woman and that of will.

Almost at the end of the movie, almost at the end of her life, Ada's will reasserts itself. It seems that the dark talent of which her father spoke, which might be the refusal to speak or simply the will that enables her to stop speaking, that dark talent of a will indeed allows her to take it into her head to stop breathing. But having plunged with her piano into the sea, she struggles to free herself from her shoe and then finally breaks the surface of the water.[29]

Ada—speaking in her mind's voice:

ADA (V.O.):

What a death!

What a chance!

What a surprise!

My will has chosen life!?

Still it has had me spooked, and many others besides! (121)

Ada's will, it seems has been a force to overcome the power of death. And yet in the list of descriptions of what has taken place we hear "What a death!" In what way this choice for life is also death, we will have to see. Whatever her will ultimately does, it does so as chance and as surprise. It is not that Ada has chosen life, but that her will has chosen it. She is not the locus of decision of mind. And therefore that choice will spook her no less than others.

But who is it that had chosen death to begin with? Has there been a choice for death to begin with? Why is Ada first taken into the depths with her piano? Does Ada's foot find its place among the coils of rope attached to the piano by choice or by chance? The script reads:

> *As the piano splashes into the sea, the loose ropes speed their way after it. ADA watches them snake past her feet then, out of fatal curiosity, odd and undisciplined, she steps into a loop.* (120–21)

The text tells us that the step into the loop is out of fatal curiosity, odd and undisciplined. This is no dramatic gesture in the name of following her true voice, but is rather the quirk of a will to that which escapes the rigor of logic, a choice in the name of odd, if fatal curiosity, one, moreover, that can and does reverse itself with the same lack of discipline. The will of Ada—if we can in any accurate sense call it Ada's will after all we have seen—is no more a force for life than it is for death.

Besides, that will is thoroughly entangled in the unsettling morality that threads its way through the story line as well as with the strange an-aesthetic treatise that is silently developed alongside it. An a-morality that is difficult to put one's finger on and which is not altogether indistinguishable from the radical politicality of *The Piano*. We might rebegin to read that force (which in fact we have always been reading, if never in a disciplined and direct manner) in contrast to the morals that Perrault appends to his tale.[30]

Perrault's Bluebeard is run through by his wife's brothers. A bit like the Maori, they arrive just in time, as he prepares to punish his wife for her curiosity, the curiosity that led her to the knowledge of the forbidden chamber. Since Bluebeard has no other heirs, his widow can use her great wealth to arrange her sister's marriage, and to pay a "dowry for her own marriage with a very worthy man, who banished Bluebeard from her mind."[31] The bad man exchanged for the worthy by a circumspect use of wealth.

Moral

Curiosity, in spite of its great charms,
Often brings with it serious regrets.
Every day a thousand examples appear.
In spite of a maiden's wishes, it's a fruitless pleasure,
For once satisfied, curiosity offers nothing,
And ever does it cost dearly.[32]

If curiosity in Perrault is that which can be satisfied, if its expenditure can be measured in cost or loss, curiosity as Campion describes it is quite another matter. Also a question of risk to be sure, its stakes, however, are immeasurable, and it offers no promise of closed satisfaction (the kind of satisfaction, say, of learning the contents of the locked chamber or the satisfaction that the economy of buying one's husband affords). Ada's curiosity is rather chance and surprise; and the concatenation of endings or failures to end that crowd the last minutes of the film are evidence of that.

Another Moral

If one takes a sensible point of view
And studies this grim story,
He will recognize that this tale
Is one of days long past.
No longer is the husband so terrifying,
Demanding the impossible,
Being both dissatisfied and jealous;
In the presence of his wife he now is gracious enough,
And no matter what color his beard may be
One does not have to guess who is master![33]

Perrault's second moral has something to say, as does Campion's film, of the relation between man and woman. It displaces the horrific events of the tale to "one of days long past." From this "sensible point of view" (quite at odds with the undisciplined curiosity and the filmic disbalance with which *The Piano* is shot through) one must see, writes Perrault, that husbands are no longer terrifying and dissatisfied. Women, he insists, have assumed a position of mastery.

Yet nothing in Campion's film of some three centuries later claims that such a repositioning has been either possible or desirable. For if a certain liberation of woman takes place in *The Piano*, it is not circumscribed by the resistance, however obligatory, to the imposition of authority identified as male. Such resistance, after all, is inevitably determined by the authority against which it struggles and it falls under the aegis of a conventional concept of will that is no less a desire for power.

Side by side with that absolutely necessary, and yet necessarily limited, political gesture (that at least partially defines the relation of Ada to Stewart) is, of course, the involvement of Ada with Baines. George offers Ada a "deal" (52): she can earn her piano back with a lesson for every key of the piano: but during each lesson there are "things" he would like to do. Passion as perversion, perhaps. Baines bargains for gradual possession of Ada's body and love; she bargains for gradual repossession of her piano and, it would seem, of her proper voice. Right from the beginning and throughout neither Baines nor Ada is independently able to set the terms of the exchange. Baines wishes "one visit for every key," but Ada will only agree to a visit "for every black one" (52). "That's a lot less than half" (52), as Baines ruefully notes. As the lessons progress Baines convinces Ada to do what she would rather not, but he must agree each time to an increase in the number of keys he will thereby forfeit: two for touching her arms, five for lying with clothes on, ten for lying without—until Ada arrives to find the Maoris carrying the piano away.[34] Baines has given the piano back to her with no further demands. It is then and only then, as she sits in Stewart's house in possession of her piano, as she plays its keys apathetically (for there is no Baines to observe or caress her), only then that she conceives her desire for him. Baines has given her the piano and given up his hold on her; she gives herself to him now just as freely. (The script declares them "*profoundly equal*" [32].) No longer an exchange with designated limits, it exceeds any economy that Stewart (or even Perrault) could envision.[35]

Still, one might—one must—observe, it is Stewart's envisioning of the scene (although not his alone), his arrival in time to take it all in (first through a chink in the side of the house, later from under the floorboards) that makes impossible any lasting exaltation of their passion. At once viewer and voyeur, in a narration that never lets us forget their potential coincidence, we watch Stewart watching the lovemaking of George and Ada, *under the skirt*, so to speak, in all the ways we have been given to understand that space from the beginning of the film. This is not only because they become the performance that engrosses Stewart, but because, at least in the rapture and interruption of the moment, their relation casts aside the will to possess we have rather seen bound to the aesthetics of photography. The force that pervades this scene is like the fatal curiosity that places Ada's foot in the loop of rope—odd, undisciplined. It is entangled in a will, a-moral, not immoral, that makes no definitive move toward closure but rather toward death with life, and both of these with chance.

How then to explain that the film has three endings, which is not to say conclusions? Isn't the first of these, in which Ada gives up her lover's bed to share the bed at the bottom of the sea with her piano, the aesthetically correct one? To be sure she would be leaving chance, surprise, and life aside, in the name of death. But for the first time Ada's will would know its own mind. This is what we might once have called a poetic ending (although Campion has poetry of another order in store for her viewers). As Ada's true voice goes so would Ada go; moreover, it is all too understandable a seduction to associate the piano in its full emotional appeal, not only with the voice of woman, but also with the art this film wishes to be. Attached in an umbilical relationship, the piano as her voice and self, a true relationship of mother to daughter would be preserved, underwater. Isn't the tragic ending the artistically apt one, then, as opposed to the Hollywood ending of commonplace contentment with which the film seems to close in Nelson? Isn't the artistically satisfying that which does not locate its closure in the conventions of human passion? In this film which seems to be about the desperate hunger for sexual satisfaction, isn't it a refusal of that hunger that makes art possible?[36] Perhaps. Couldn't we read in her death a lesson about the ultimate defeat of woman by male brutality, a reading satisfying from the point of view of a certain politics? Perhaps. Wouldn't this be Ada's total liberation from men (assuming that were the film's definition of liberating the feminine)? Perhaps.

Yet, one might say, Campion chooses none of these—if the question of Campion's intentionality were really to be taken seriously. Why, then, does Ada's will change? Why does *will* in this film enfold aberration in its own impossible definition? Why are chance, surprise, and life incorporated within death and vice versa?

Much to the consternation of the critic John Simon, who bemoans the flightiness of woman's mind, Campion gives us a second ending. Simon writes:

> At a New York Film Festival press conference, Jane Campion said she had originally intended to have . . . *The Piano* end with the drowning of the heroine. Instead, she has her going off to live happily ever after with her lover. I wonder about a writer-director who ends up making the opposite of what she set out to do.[37]

You would think that a critic old-fashioned enough to call the director "*Miss* Campion" (as Simon does elsewhere in the article) would also believe it is a woman's prerogative to change her mind. Just how menacing that change of mind is, we will have to see.

In the notes to the script we read:

> CAMPION: One of the major changes to the script was to give the ending a more poetical, more psychological finish.
>
> CHAPMAN: It really needed the right ending or it could have been too soft. But basically Jane—with our help—came up with the idea of the erotic focus shifting for Ada, from the lover Baines to her husband Stewart. I think this is the thing that makes the film modern actually, and not sentimental.
>
> CAMPION: Ada actually uses her husband Stewart as a sexual object—this is the outrageous morality of the film—which seems very innocent but in fact has the power to be very surprising. . . . It becomes a relationship of power, the power of those that care and those that don't care. I'm very interested in the brutal innocence of that. (138–39)

The apparently prosthetic change, it seems, is not simply from drowning to "living happily ever after." Chapman's sense of the ending, at least, is the upending of romantic conventions as Ada shifts the erotic focus from George to Stewart. Campion calls this "very surprising," the "outrageous morality of the film." If neither this temporary turn of events nor the scene in Nelson is a "more poetical, more psychological finish," both are certainly calculated to outrage the John Simons who are watching.

Still it takes a certain deafness to regard the return to civilization as "living happily ever after." In Nelson, Ada gives piano lessons.

ADA: I teach piano now in Nelson. George has fashioned me a metal fingertip; I'm quite the town freak, which satisfies. (122)

If this seems to provide closure, it is also a breach of all that came before. Ada was right when she said that her piano was spoiled. Spoiled by the ax buried in it by Stewart, spoiled by the key that has been removed,[38] spoiled because the playing of that piano can never be the same once passion of another order has been, even momentarily, satisfied. Yet another kind of satisfaction has been found now. A satisfaction on another piano, played with a different hand. This hand has a metal fingertip which means, not that Baines has made her whole again, but (how can we avoid hearing it) the click of the metal against the keys as a constant reminder of its artifice, a tap, moreover, strangely noncoincident with the new piano's sound. But it is precisely the metal fingertip, says Ada, that brings satisfaction. "I'm quite the town freak, which satisfies." Satisfaction is not from a body reconstituted, nor from the perfect, full round sounds of the piano but from the playing interrupted by the click, the undisciplined and the odd.

It makes perfect sense, then, that Ada should be learning to speak. The beautiful tones of the piano gone, there is room now for the voice that she will describe and that we will hear.

ADA (V.O.): I am learning to speak. My sound is still so bad I feel ashamed. I practise only when I am alone and it is dark.

ADA's *hands move across the piano keys; her metal finger shines in the dull light.*

. . . .

ADA *paces up and down. . . . Over her head she has a dark cloth; her voice makes low guttural sounds. . . .* (122)

What Ada speaks with is hardly the operatic voice that Flora wished to attribute to her in her tale to Aunt Morag. She speaks the low guttural sounds of no content. Over her head once again the photographer's hood, the dark cloth seeming to impose a blindness in place of the muteness she has put aside. No full recovery of senses here, no recuperation of voice, of finger, nor of her (and our) gaze, which from the opening frame was already questionable. The insistence is on a certain deprivation or at least deformity, a certain freakishness with which Campion's films have all been obsessed.

Bourgeois bliss, nevertheless, which in the film takes place in the garden, though hardly a Maori Garden of Eden,[39] is confirmed by the kiss that George gives Ada there (lifting the cloth like a bridal veil); yet this familial joy is less completion than irony, and in its own way it is as unsettling as what came before. For lest we mistake this scene, lest that kiss allow us to float in the belief that (their) sexual passion can achieve a sustained and unfreakish satisfaction, lest the bed of George and Ada implied by that final embrace seem the fairytale ending usually produced only this side of the Pacific, a third voice-over and third scene announce themselves.

ADA (V.O.):

At night I think of my piano in its ocean grave, and sometimes of myself floating above it. Down there everything is so still and silent that it lulls me to sleep. It is a weird lullaby and so it is; it is mine. (122)

What is Ada's is no longer the piano[40] but thoughts of it and of her self, underneath the sea. Her music is now punctuated by the freak click, her life by the imagining of her own death.

The first ending, it would seem, has not been entirely displaced. Narrative as progression and resolution (here as before) becomes something of an illusion.[41] (Walter Benjamin had much to say of the political implications of that.)[42] If we seem to move from bed to bed, from that of the sea to that of Baines, the scene of drowning returns, nevertheless, forever there to haunt in this, the imaginary ending of the film. An unremitting underwater lullaby of mother to daughter who has not been released to the surface to be born (again). A perpetually changing announcement of the grave as well. Less as the "happily ever after" that life in Nelson might seem, less as a continuous hereafter as which the initial drowning could be conceived (constructs, moreover, that our notions of political revolution too often resemble) than as an ever insistent and repeated apocalypse rupturing (and setting) the limits of life. Death in life, over and over. As for the Maori whose land was marked as the site of death, here another, very different, nature is the locus of the grave. Flood. It comes with a rhythm as interruptive and unavoidable as night is to day ("At night I think of my piano"), the filmic invasion of natural ground. The closing scene is therefore not the cultivated Garden of Nelson but Ada's body floating in a murky underwater realm, her skirts ballooned up, this time over her entire body from ankle to head.

Ada's voice recites the first lines of a sonnet by Thomas Hood, who, Scottish like Ada, would have lived (and died) just before the era in which the film takes place.[43]

THERE IS A SILENCE WHERE HATH BEEN NO SOUND
THERE IS A SILENCE WHERE NO SOUND MAY BE
IN THE COLD GRAVE, UNDER THE DEEP DEEP SEA. (123)

It goes without saying that it makes all the difference to end the film with this recitation and this image. It is not the closing of Ada sacrificed with her piano, recuperation through negation. It is not the resolution of conjugal happiness, bad husband exchanged for good lover. It is Ada's mind's voice that once again speaks as in the film's first scene and once again speaks of silence, this time, however, in the words of another. It is a return to the mind's eye and voice (though whose is unclear) with which the film began and the underwater realm one already senses in the translucent fingers of the opening frames.

In a sense the cinematography of *The Piano* hardly leaves that realm. Taking us on the first journey viewed from under the boat, floating us from hilltop to hilltop soon after our arrival in a shot that makes the bush seem (as it does throughout) the bottom of the ocean.[44] Then taking us on that other journey as we plunge with Ada and her piano, and finally to Nelson where Ada's thoughts return us to the image of the ocean grave.

The cinematography of under the sea is now accompanied by the verse of Thomas Hood, the lines of a dead poet. They are not only the final words voiced both by Ada and the film, they take their place as well as the final visual image, typographically.[45] Suddenly fixed on the screen as a strange invasion of the letter of the script, the three lines appear, but only after the long list of credits. Just before the copyright (that documented protection against reproduction and imitation), just before the copyright and along with it, in the very last frame of the film: the opening verses of the sonnet "Silence." And then—"Thomas Hood (1799–1845)": appended to the poet's name the dates that circumscribe his life. How to read this invasion and this juxtaposition? What do they say, if anything, about the film, the poem, the questions of authorship, imitation, and mortality so manifestly framed there? How do these in turn implicate a politicality to be read in conjunction with *The Piano*? Ironically, they take their place in relation to the film that precedes them as the self-assured morals of Perrault do in relation to his tale. Ironically, because the particular lines we hear of Hood suggest neither the economy of learning nor the promise of power implicit in the closing lines of *Bluebeard*. For if the sonnet has a lesson to teach, it is less because of what Ada cites than because of what she silences by excision: the rest of the poem. Hood's lines continue:

> Or in wide desert where no life is found,
> Which hath been mute, and still must sleep profound;
> No voice is hush'd—no life treads silently,
> But clouds and cloudy shadows wander free,
> That never spoke, over the idle ground:
> But in green ruins, in the desolate walls
> Of antique palaces, where Man hath been,
> Though the dun fox, or wild hyena, calls,
> And owls, that flit continually between,
> Shriek to the echo, and the low winds moan,
> There the true Silence is, self-conscious and alone.[46]

Ada's final words, the opening lines of Hood's sonnet, can only be understood in contrast to "the true Silence" of its closing lines that bring a guarantee of truth and the authority of self-consciousness. Ada's recitation disrupts the more banal tendencies of the film's first two endings, while the sonnet's sestet would read as their affirmation, running counter as it does to everything the film most radically performs. The poem of Hood functions in the film as at once the final word and also the disruption of teleology. For these verses come, we are told, as a lullaby that repeatedly reasserts the possibility of the first underwater ending, thus disrupting the marital bliss at Nelson, which then has only seemed to eclipse and go beyond the initial scene of drowning.

The Piano, in its muteness, is neither "true" nor precisely self-conscious, if self-consciousness be thought, as it is in the sonnet, as bound to a concept of self-possession and knowledge rather than to fatal curiosity. Alongside those clear scenarios of hegemony, resistances to hegemony, and therefore its inevitable return and reimposition (even in the name of the moral), what the film plays out are—in Hood's phrasing—"cloudy shadows wander[ing] free." There are many forms those shadows take, none of them fixed. There are many names for them although Campion, like Ada, never speaks clearly enough for us to fully grasp them. As when Baines' index finger finds the hole in Ada's stocking, even if we catch sight of and put our finger on them for a while, the scene is still bound to be abruptly cut. Will, curiosity, passion, film . . . having been spooked by these and many others besides, it no doubt makes no sense to rehearse them.

What *The Piano* wills, though not in any simple sense, is like the emergency brake of revolution of which Walter Benjamin speaks.

> Marx says—revolutions are the locomotives of world history. But perhaps it is entirely different. Perhaps revolutions are the grasp of the human race traveling in this train for the emergency brake.[47]

See here, if you will, revolution in the names of feminism, anticolonialism, environmentalism, but they do not take place as that which we could rightfully call identity politics. This revolution holds out no promise of the happily ever after, the hereafter, banal redemption. If you are waiting for these to come definitively, don't hold your breath. And yet, if we are willing, by chance, to take it into our heads to stop breathing, now and again, surprisingly, when we least expect it, what undisciplined curiosity might lead us to see here, however intermittently and unclearly, is an astonishingly political performance. It implicates, inextricably, theories of aesthetics, narration, representation, self, authority, power, language, imagination—as the political inevitably does: though a certain politics will inevitably attempt to deny it.

There is no moral to this story, then, at least no language that can contain the generalized truth of its statement. The politicality it poses (though not its politics) is performed as a punctual a-morality. Always embedded in a particular moment, in the specificity of a particular image, differently, it liberates from a politics of hegemony and identity with unforeseeable force.[48] At the critical turn of ethical crisis it disrupts the inevitable (re)assertion of structure, power, hierarchy. Not irresponsible a-morality, but respons-ability at its most vigilant, if also most unpredictable. Rendering the translucent opaque, the opaque translucent, in its opening and in its closing moment, here, there, and everywhere throughout—yet nowhere, really: *The Piano* "is a weird [film] and so it is. . . . "

Notes

Prologue

1. In the case of Plato, especially in the *Republic*, representation would, no doubt, have to be thought in radical terms, and certainly not as re-presentation. Dialectic promises knowledge not mediated by the senses, although philosophical language stakes out the path to intellection.

2. The ethical force of *Antigone*, for example, is not simply Antigone's devotion to divine law over and against Creon's insistence on the law of state.

3. The project of J. Hillis Miller's *The Ethics of Reading* (New York: Columbia University Press, 1987) would be exemplary in this regard.

Chapter 1. Dusting Antigone

1. Except where indicated otherwise, translations of Sophocles are from *Antigone*, ed. and trans. Andrew Brown (Warminster: Aris & Phillips, 1987) and are marked by line numbers. In those places where I did not rely on Brown's translation, I am exceptionally grateful to Molly Ierulli who so generously read and commented on my use of the Greek text with the rigor of a true classicist.

2. Irigaray calls *Antigone* "The work of Sophocles, which marks the historical bridge between matriarchy and patriarchy" (*Speculum*, 270F, 217E). Luce Irigaray, *Speculum de l'autre femme* (Paris: Minuit, 1974) and *Speculum of the Other Woman*, trans. by Gillian C. Gill (Ithaca: Cornell University Press, 1985), hereafter referred to as *Speculum*. Throughout this chapter, page references to French editions are followed by an F, to English editions by an E.

"This tragic episode in life—and in war—between the genders represents the passage into patriarchy" (*Sexes*, 14F, 2E). Luce Irigaray, *Sexes et parentés* (Paris:

Minuit, 1987) and *Sexes and Genealogies*, trans. Gillian C. Gill (New York: Columbia University Press, 1993, hereafter referred to as *Sexes*).

3. G. W. F. Hegel, *Phenomenology of Spirit*, trans. A. V. Miller (Oxford: Oxford University Press, 1977), ¶ 475, 288. References in the text are marked by *Phenomenology* followed by paragraph and page numbers.

My reading of Hegel throughout this essay is singularly devoid of irony, taking the philosopher at his word, more seriously than I can say. Werner Hamacher has offered thoroughly convincing arguments toward a less one-sided reading of Hegel's position on woman, one in which woman functions as absolute individualization, as a (necessary) punctual disruption of the polis. If what I propose here, nevertheless, stays its ground (that is the ground and positions that Irigaray erects both for herself and Hegel) this is to set the philosophers as the backdrop for the shadow play on the conception of motherhood I wish to produce. The irony of this will to production (by way of negation) must be borne for the sake of staging a vigilant reading of *Antigone*.

4. Luce Irigaray, *Éthique de la différence sexuelle* (Paris: Minuit, 1984) and *An Ethics of Sexual Difference*, trans. Carolyn Burke and Gillian C. Gill (Ithaca: Cornell University Press, 1993), hereafter referred to as *Ethics*.

5. "Antigone is working in the service of the god of men. . . . It is no longer a case of her fulfilling her role as a member of the *female gender*. Antigone already serves the state. . . . She now performs only the dark side of that task, the side needed to establish the male order as it moves toward absolute affirmation" (*Sexes*, 125F, 110–11E).

6. Luce Irigaray, *Le Temps de la différence: Pour une révolution pacifique* (Paris: Librairie Générale Française, 1989) and *Thinking the Difference: For a Peaceful Revolution*, trans. Karin Montin (New York: Routledge, 1994), hereafter referred to as *Difference*.

7. This trajectory is outlined by Luisa Muraro in "Female Genealogies," in *Engaging with Irigaray*, ed. Carolyn Burke, Naomi Schor, and Margaret Whitford (New York: Columbia University Press, 1994), 327–30.

8. More literally, the French reads, "according to her and according to me" (*Difference*, 87F).

9. "She has no a priori contempt for those who govern" (*Difference*, 83F, 69E).

10. "Antigone respects the natural and social order by genuinely (not metaphorically) respecting the earth and the sun, respecting maternal ancestry as a daughter, respecting oral law rather than a written law. . . . She reminds us that the earthly order is not a pure social power, that it must be founded upon the economy of the cosmic order, upon respect for the procreation of living beings, on attention to maternal ancestry, to its gods, its rights, its organization" (*Difference*, 84F, 69–70E).

11. Robert Graves, *The Greek Myths*, vol. 2 (London: Penguin, 1960), 380.

12. Thus the title to section A.a. of the chapter entitled "Spirit" is "The ethical world. Human and Divine Law: Man and Woman" ("Die sittliche Welt, das menschliche und göttliche Gesetz, der Mann und das Weib").

13. Jacques Derrida speaks of "the family, the natural moment of the ethical" (162F, 143E). Jacques Derrida, *Glas* (Paris: Galilée, 1974), and *Glas*, trans. John P. Leavey, Jr. and Richard Rand (Lincoln: University of Nebraska Press, 1986). He clarifies this positioning of the natural earlier in the volume, a positioning that, if anything, makes more striking Antigone's radical and complex relationship to Nature.

> Nature is not a determinate essence, a unique moment. It overlays [*recouvre*] all the forms of the spirit's exteriority to self. Nature appears then—while progressively disappearing therein—in each stage of the spirit's becoming. (*Glas*, 45F, 37E)

That the family is "natural" is hardly the same, then, as being Nature.

14. "This relationship is at the same time the limit at which the self-contained life of the Family breaks up and goes beyond itself. The brother is the member of the Family in whom its Spirit becomes an individuality which turns toward another sphere, and passes over into the consciousness of universality. The brother leaves this immediate, elemental, and therefore, strictly speaking, negative ethical life of the Family, in order to acquire and produce the ethical life that is conscious of itself and actual" (*Phenomenology*, ¶ 458, 275).

"He passes from the divine law, within whose sphere he lived, over to human law. But the sister becomes, or the wife remains, the head of the household and the guardian of the divine law" (*Phenomenology*, ¶ 459, 275).

15. *Hegel's Lectures on the History of Philosophy*, ed. and trans. E. S. Haldane, vol. 1 (London: Routledge and Kegan Paul, 1955), 441.

16. See Tina Chanter's exemplary reading of Irigaray's reading of Hegel on *Antigone* in *Ethics of Eros* (New York: Routledge, 1995), 80–126: "The irony of women's position, in this account, is that they make possible the integrity of the *polis*, yet remain defined in opposition to it, as outsiders who threaten its equilibrium. Hegel thus both transcends women's definition as natural beings, and confines women to their naturalness" (88).

17. G. W. F. Hegel, *The Philosophy of Fine Art*, trans. F. P. B. Osmaston, vol. 2 (London: G. Bell & Sons, 1920), 215; hereafter referred to as Hegel, *Fine Art*.

Perhaps, but when Hegel speaks of Sophocles here and there, it is less to the details of particular moments he turns than to Sophocles as characterizing the generalizations the philosopher makes. In the "Lectures on the Philosophy of Religion" he speaks of *Antigone* as "the absolute example of tragedy" (Georg Wilhelm Friedrich Hegel, "Vorlesungen über die Philosophie der Religion," in *Werke*, vol. 17 [Frankfurt: Suhrkamp, 1969], 133.)

One might feel compelled to consider as well the thematization of generality and universality in the examples that follow, particularly in light of the force of the universal in Hegel's *Phenomenology* and its relation to the distinction of gender. (There are many other instances of this in *The Philosophy of Fine Art* as well.)

> The sphere of this content, although capable of great variety of detail, is not in its essential features very extensive. The principal source of opposition, which Sophocles in particular . . . has accepted and worked out in the finest way, is that of the *body politic*, the opposition, that is, between ethical life in its social universality and the family as the natural ground of moral relations. These are the purest forces of tragic representation. (Hegel, *Fine Art*, 4:318)

> The personalities in the lofty tragedy of the ancients such as . . . Antigone, and Creon have, it is true, among other things a personal object; but the substantive thing, the pathos, which as the content of their action is the compelling force behind them, is of absolute authority, and for this very reason, is also itself essentially of universal interest. (Ibid., 2:344–45).

18. This was Antigone's point to begin with in the opening lines of the play.

> Eteocles, they say, he has laid beneath the earth with due observance of propriety and custom [?], to be honoured by the dead below. But as for the wretched corpse of Polynices, they say that Creon has proclaimed to the townsfolk that no one may lay him in a tomb or mourn for him; they must leave him unwept, unburied, a delightful treasure-house for the birds which will gaze upon him as their welcome prey. (23ff.)

19. "I shall take her where men's feet do not tread and bury her alive in the rock, providing just enough food for expiation, to avoid pollution of the whole city" (773ff.).

20. In *Speculum*, 282–98F, 227–40E.

21. Luce Irigaray, *The Irigaray Reader*, ed. Margaret Whitford (Oxford: Basil Blackwell, 1991), 53.

22. Not only *anthrôpos*, but also, in line 334, *touto* as a stressed neutrality.

23. Charles Segal (*Tragedy and Civilization: An Interpretation of Sophocles* [Cambridge: Harvard University Press, 1981], 163) notes that the word used here for the plow's movement in conquest of the earth resurfaces when Antigone menaces Creon with the disloyalty of his people: "'They see the truth,' she continues, 'but make their tongues cower to you' [509]. The verb translated 'cower,' *hypillein*, is used of animals putting their tails between their legs in fear. It is also the word used of the plow's movement in the conquest of the earth in the first stasimon" (340). If we are to take seriously this connection between *illein* and *hypillein*, Antigone's speech ironizes the apparent power of man (the subject of the choral ode) by linking it to the cowering in male hierarchies, here a hierarchy that represses speech.

24. J. C. Kamerbeek (*The Plays of Sophocles* [Leiden: E. J. Brill, 1978], 93) points out that elsewhere in the play "exactly the same words are used to refer to [the act of removing the dust, 428] and to Antigone's deed" of sprinkling the dust (384). It is as though the difference between the two cannot be marked, as though the dust is forever neither here nor there.

25. Irigaray speaks of Creon's "privilege of being the sole safeguard of speech, truth, intelligence, reason" (*Speculum* 273F, 219E).

26. Jebb and Campbell suggest it is a term that also refers to the lips: it is as though what takes place precludes not only the guards' capacity to see but also to speak. Sophocles, *The Plays and Fragments*, pt. 3, trans. Richard Jebb (Cambridge: Cambridge University Press, 1928), 85, and Sophocles, *The Plays and Fragments*, ed. Lewis Campbell (Hildesheim: Georg Olms, 1969), 494.

27. George Steiner suggests rightly that "earth and air are violently confounded" here, one of several moments in the *Antigone*, therefore, where the above and the below are not so easily distinguished. George Steiner, *Antigones* (Oxford: Clarendon Press, 1984), 224.

28. S. Benardete ("A Reading of Sophocles' *Antigone*," *Interpretation: A Journal of Political Philosophy* 4.3, 5.1, 5.2 [1975]) insists on distinguishing "the two dusts," that of the storm and that of Antigone. He speaks of the two as opposite forms of "unseemliness," rightly sensing that thinking them together implies a certain menace that confuses "the marks of human artifice" and "chance" (5.1:4). The passage is particularly interesting because in the course of his highly intelligent and subtle interpretation Benardete seems to shift positions: first regarding as a "most uncanny event" that "moist and putrescent flesh should be as bare of dust after such a storm as before it" (ibid.), then implicitly accepting the inevitability of the covering of dust from the storm, but distinguishing it from Antigone's which carries "her own signature" (ibid.).

George Steiner, realizing that the demarcation is not so easily made, sets himself squarely in the comfortable position the chorus had assumed (278f.), reading the possible confusion of the two as dramatizing "the problematic contiguities between the acts of Antigone and of the gods" (Steiner, *Antigones*, 225). It could be, however, that something far more unsettling is at stake.

29. One sees and hears the resonance between Tiresias's report of failed interpretation and the guard's image of Antigone as bird (*ornithos*, 424) in the term for augury (*ornithoskopos*), made up of the terms for bird and sentinel (*ornithos* + *skopos*): *skopos* is the same term, moreover, that Creon uses when asking the chorus to be his watchmen (215).

30. The parallel between the remains of the dead and the burnt sacrifice is apparent in the ritual Creon did not perform: "If the Homeric usage was followed, when the flesh had been burned the bones would be washed with wine

or oil, wrapped in fat, and placed in an urn" (Jebb, explication of line 1203, in Sophocles, *The Plays and Fragments*, pt. 3, 213).

31. And also the shrill cries of the eagle who "could glut his jaws with [Theban] blood" to which the chorus compares the warring man of Argo (110ff.).

32. Graves, *The Greek Myths*, 2:750.

33. Homer, *The Odyssey of Homer*, trans. Richmond Lattimore (New York: Harper and Row, 1965), 245. Brown makes the connection of this image both to Homer's *Odyssey* and to Aeschylus's *Agamemnon*.

34. Seth Benardete's careful reading points to Aeschylus's *Agamemnon* as the probable source of the simile (V,1,5). In Aeschylus's simile he shows (as we have pointed out in the case of Homer) that the parallelism of the figure is blatantly inexact.

35. In the context of Irigaray's sense of place, it is difficult to situate. She too frequently meditates the place of a mother, but often in the sense that woman can establish no maternal filiation and so can only replace and displace the mother.

> The love of self among women, in the feminine, is very hard to establish. Traditionally, it is left in the undifferentiation of the mother-daughter relationship. . . . A dimension that must be denied in word and act if the good health of family and city is to be ensured, Hegel wrote. Does this mean that love of the mother among women can and may be practiced only through *substitution*? By a taking the place of? (*Ethics*, 100F, 101–2E)

36. Ten years later, in *Ethics*, Irigaray will write, however: "Antigone's actions must not be dismissed as respect for her father's family, fear of the gods of the underworld, or obedience to order in a state that forbids her any ethical action of her own" (*Ethics*, 106F, 108E).

Still Irigaray attributes, it seems, Antigone's fate to a failure in the relationship between mother and daughter, as though Antigone's identification with the mother in the moment of death could promise nothing revolutionary—and this, despite the fact that elsewhere in *Speculum*, in "The Blind Spot of an Old Dream of Symmetry," Irigaray writes of Antigone: "In patriarchy, the revival of relations between mother and daughter always creates conflict" (147F, 118E).

37. An act whose inefficacy, in any case, is already marked by the resemblance of Creon's ritual burning of body parts to Tiresias's equally failed rituals of augury.

38. Thus earlier in this same passage Irigaray leaves Antigone's intention where her body is—up in the air: somewhere between having given in and still staging her revolt.

39. The first was as the mother bird, in the words of the sentinel.

40. Henry George Liddell and Robert Scott, *A Greek-English Lexicon* (Oxford: Clarendon Press, 1968).

41. See Segal, *Tragedy and Civilization*, 181.

42. This is my translation from Irigaray's French. The English translation has a shortened version of the passage and, of course, a different translation. The passage comes from Hegel's *Philosophy of Nature*.

What Jacques Derrida writes of the seed in Hegel (*Glas* 35–36F, 27–28E) as well as his reading of this particular passage (*Glas*, 128ff.F, 111ff.E) are exceptionally relevant here. Antigone's conception of Haemon, like her motherhood in the figure of the sentinel's report, does not follow the logic of Hegel's seed.

43. Aeschylus, *The Eumenides*, in *Greek Tragedies*, vol. 3, ed. David Grene and Richmond Lattimore (Chicago: University of Chicago Press, 1960).

44. See Segal, *Tragedy and Civilization*, 183:

> In this same speech Creon confronts an opposing principle of an especially feminine kind, Antigone's "reverence for those of the same womb" *homosplanchnoussebein* (511). On this basis Antigone defends herself against the male-oriented, civic ethic of the polis. She makes kinship a function of the female procreative power: she defines kinship in terms of the womb (*splanchna*).

45. A concept of space surprisingly fixed—in contrast to what she had written earlier in "Volume-Fluidity" (*Speculum*), 282F, 227E.

46. See also the several references to the myth of Persephone, references in which, as Segal points out (*Tragedy and Civilization*, 180), there is no allusion to the return of the daughter, where it is a question of a Demeter therefore who has lost her child to the house of the dead.

47. Ibid., 187.

48. Derrida writes:

> Is it thus simply a matter of struggling against a material decomposition, against a simple dissociation that causes the organic to return to the inorganic? Is the force against which the funeral rite works, under the name death, is it a mechanical and anonymous, a physical, nonconscious exteriority? The analysis would be banal. The feminine operation of burial does not oppose itself to the exteriority of a nonconscious matter; it suppresses an unconscious desire ["the cannibal violence of the survivors' unconscious desires" (165F, 146E)]. The family wants to prevent the dead one from being "destroyed" and the burial place violated *by this desire*. (*Glas*, 163–64F, 144E)

In the figure of the bird Antigone at once fulfills and represses this desire.

49. Luce Irigaray, *This Sex Which Is Not One* (Ithaca: Cornell University Press, 1985), 78.

50. Hegel, "Vorlesungen über die Philosophie der Religion," 133.

51. Philippe Lacoue-Labarthe, "La Césure du spéculatif," in *L'Imitation des modernes* (Paris: Galilée, 1986), 39–69, and "The Caesura of the Speculative," in *Glyph* 4, ed. Samuel Weber and Henry Sussman (1978): 57–84.

52. Ibid., 39–40F, 49F; 57–58E, 66E.

53. Ibid., 52F, 68E.

54. No doubt, from a certain, well-rehearsed, point of view, this will seem a betrayal. For what takes place in this essay is not through the will of or in the voice of the heroine. We have not "[abstracted] Antigone from the seductive, reductive discourses [to] listen to what she has to say" (*Difference*, 84F, 70E) as Irigaray called for. It might seem that, once again, we have let man speak for woman and have placed her outside the symbolic order. But neither have we taken the words of the sentinel and that of Tiresias according to their will and intention. No one's language here controls the fitful starts, neither that of Antigone nor that of the two seers, and not even that of Sophocles.

55. Lacoue-Labarthe, "The Caesura of the Speculative," 53–54F, 70E.

Chapter 2. Virtue Inside Out

1. The citations from Plato's *Symposium* are from the Loeb Classical Library edition, vol. 3 (Cambridge: Harvard University Press, 1996). On occasion, small changes to the translation have been made.

2. A great many readers of the dialogue have noted this. See, for example, on this and many other points I touch on, the careful and extended reading of Robert Lloyd Mitchell, *The Hymn to Eros* (Lantham: University Press of America, 1993), 177.

3. Something approaching the opposite of this assertion is in the *Republic* 395a–b. (Stephanus references are used throughout.)

4. In this particular instance of Socrates' resistance to rhetoric, he also substitutes himself for Odysseus, a character renowned for manipulative rhetorical skills, for lying, for deviousness of phrase.

5. The term holds an important if denigrated place in Plato. It occupies the lowest level of the divided line in Plato's *Republic*. See Jean-Pierre Vernant, *Mortals and Immortals* (Princeton: Princeton University Press, 1991), 179–80.

6. When he speaks again, it is in his closing speech on the strange intersections of the comedian and tragedian.

7. See, for example, Plutarch, "Alcibiades II," in *Plutarch's Lives* (Cambridge: Harvard University Press, 1968), 7–9. Plato also rails against the flute in the *Republic* 399c–e and 411a.

8. See the *Republic*:

"But, rather, because he sees and contemplates things that are set in a regular arrangement and are always in the same condition—things that neither do injustice to one another nor suffer it at one another's hands, but remain all in order according to reason—he imitates them and, as much as possible, makes himself like them. . . .

"Then it's the philosopher, keeping company with the divine and the orderly who becomes orderly and divine. . . . (500c–d, Plato, *The Republic of Plato*, trans. Allan Bloom [New York: Basic Books, 1991])

9. See the *Republic*:

"About philosophic natures, let's agree that they are always in love with that learning which discloses to them something of the being that *is* always and does not wander about, driven by generation and decay." (485a–b)

10. See Luce Irigaray's exceptional essay to which my early thoughts on the dialogue owe much: "Sorcerer Love: A Reading of Plato, *Symposium* 'Diotima's Speech,'" in *An Ethics of Sexual Difference* (Ithaca: Cornell University Press, 1993), 20–33 ("L'amour sorcier [Lecture de Platon. Le Banquet, 'Discours de Diotime']," in *Éthique de la différence sexuelle* [Paris: Éditions de Minuit, 1984]). Irigaray reads Diotima's speech and praises its original insistence on the "*between*" (21) and the "*intermediary*" (20), love as the mediator that is always in movement, in a state of becoming. She contrasts this to the conclusion of Socrates' report of Diotima's speech. A miscarriage of method, Irigaray writes, which might be regarded as "the foundation act of meta-physics" (27), a "teleological quest for what is deemed a higher reality" (29).

11. Stanley Rosen suggests that the skin is the satiric cover of Socrates (Stanley Rosen, *Plato's Symposium* [New Haven: Yale University Press, 1987]), 298. This may well be Alcibiades' apparent intention. But removing the skin, as we shall suggest, does not necessarily shed the irony.

12. *Atopian* is the term that Alcibiades uses to speak of Socrates' eccentricities. It suggests the impossibility of holding place.

13. There is much to be said here, therefore, of the relationship between this passage and the speech of Aristophanes.

14. Robert Graves, *The Greek Myths*, vol. 1 (London: Penguin, 1960), 77.

15. Socrates then may be like certain images, those of the Silenuses and satyrs, but he is also the force of a comparison that refuses to be fixed in place. The threat to the state in the pages that follow may be less the hacking of the statue than the impossibility of the concept of statue to begin with.

16. This is a theme that wanders in and out of the dialogue; see, for example, the cloak of Alcibiades with which he covers Socrates (219b), and Socrates covered in turn with his own cloak (219b and 220b).

17. This is the reading of Rosen, *Plato's Symposium*, 320.

18. The source of the dialogue's narrative is "Aristodemus of Cydathenaeum, a little man, who went always barefoot" (173b). He encounters Socrates on the way to Agathon's wearing what the Liddell and Scott *Greek-English Lexicon* defines as a kind of slippers worn by fops (*blautas*, 174a). But then again Alcibiades describes Socrates going barefoot even in the bitter winter of a war, and Socrates tells the myth of Eros who is "ever poor . . . hard and parched, shoeless and homeless" (203d).

19. And this is after all what Diotima's ascent to heaven proposes, which is what Socrates' speech does.

20. Rosen makes a connection between the slicing of the circle men and the opening of the Silenus figures (*Plato's Symposium*, 297).

21. Let me insist that this description in no way characterizes Stanley Rosen's rather extraordinary accomplishment in general. His volume of the *Symposium* is a model of classical scholarship and interpretation. As a theatrical gesture, and with a good sense of its absurdity, I read only the implications of a single footnote. This is a note that attributes to Leo Strauss the surmise that Plato dates the ostensible drinking party as a means of creating a history with political intent.

22. See, again, Luce Irigaray, in "Sorcerer Love" (31).

23. See, among many others in this regard, Bury's discussion of the possible dates of the symposium (Plato, *The Symposium of Plato*, ed. R. G. Bury [Cambridge: W. Heffer & Sons, 1932], lxvi). Mitchell, *The Hymn to Eros*, although early in the book (5) suggesting the conventional date of 416, is later on (176) one of the few to take seriously into consideration the possibility that the symposium took place in 415, with all the ramifications of that date.

24. As Mitchell notes, this would be just before the ill-fated Sicilian expedition. Thirty-thousand combatants, over 130 triremes, and 5,000 hoplites are sent to expand the borders of the Athenian empire at Alcibiades' urging. From this expedition, Alcibiades will be ordered brought back to Athens to stand trial for his life, an arrest from which he breaks away to betray Athens by serving Sparta, to betray Sparta by serving Persia, and then to betray Persia by serving Athens.

25. "The entire occasion is heightened by its proximity to the castration of the Hermae and the profanation of the Eleusinian mysteries." The footnote continues:

> "Leo Strauss has suggested, in lectures he left unpublished, that the banquet is meant to take place on the very night of the religious crimes; thus the *Symposium* clears Socrates and his companions from implication in acts against the polis by showing 'what really happened.'" (*Plato's Symposium*, 285)

26. Still history leaves the question of Alcibiades' guilt or innocence more or less ambiguous and it was rather, specifically, with profanation of the Eleusinian Mysteries that he was charged.

27. But it is also the issue of all the discourses whose topic as proposed by Eriximachus is to do honor to the god of Love (177a–b).

28. Thucydides, *History of the Peloponnesian War* (London: Everyman, 1993), 309.

29. *A Dictionary of Greek and Roman Antiquities*, ed. William Smith (London: John Murray, 1875), 603.

30. Plato, *Hipparchus*, 228–29.

31. *Dictionary of Classical Antiquities*, ed. Oskar Seyffert and Henry Nettleship (London: William Glaisher, 1895), 285–86.

32. *A Dictionary of Greek and Roman Antiquities*, 603. Can it be entirely irrelevant that the commonly held, if unverified, belief concerning the occupation of Socrates' father is that he was a sculptor?

33. The etymology of the term is from Hermes and from the verb meaning to carve, cut out with a knife, engrave, note down, as though the menacing cutting of the mutilations were already within.

34. *Dictionary of Classical Antiquities*, 286.

35. Or, perhaps, given the total abstraction of the pillar, a challenge to representation. Robin Osborne, in a superb article that informs much of this discussion, speaks at one point of the archaic Herm as a "denial that it is anything other than a piece of sculpture" (52). Robin Osborne, "The Erection and Mutilation of the Hermai," *Proceedings of the Cambridge Philological Society*, no. 211 (1985): 47–73.

36. Thucydides, *History of the Peloponnesian War*, 309.

37. Other sources suggest it was both.

38. The attack on figuration would be coincident with the violent attack on the state: it is in the *Republic*, of course, and not only in the most obvious ways, that one must trace figuration in its uneasy relation to the polis.

39. Alcibiades' attack on figuration is not simply a slicing of the Herms, but an undoing of the possibility of Herms, as monument, simple figuration, adoration of the gods. It brings into play the entire issue of body and its other at work in Socrates' speech (211a–c).

40. Plutarch, "Alcibiades II," 49.

41. For example, if one takes the Greek literally, Alcibiades regards his beauty as a gift from Hermes and good luck (217a).

Chapter 3. Subversions of the Political

1. The quotations in the epigraphs, and all subsequent references to the English translation of the *Republic*, are from Plato, *The Republic of Plato*, trans. Allan Bloom (New York: Basic Books, 1991), unless otherwise specified. Stephanus references are used for Plato's text, page numbers for Bloom's notes and interpretive essay.

2. Johns Sallis, "The Upward Way: *Republic*," in *Being and Logos* (Bloomington and Indianapolis: 1996), 318. In this splendid and lengthy essay Johns Sallis preceded me by many years on the road to Hades. His learned and original interpretation of the dialogue posits the trajectory of the *Republic* as an ascent culminating in Book VII, followed by a descent. Along the way one finds careful and illuminating readings of the text. I owe much to his many insights.

3. See J. Hillis Miller, "Plato's Double Diegesis," in *Reading Narrative* (Norman: University of Oklahoma Press, 1998).

4. Eric Voegelin and others after him have noted that this as a citation from Homer, Book XXIII of *The Odyssey* (Eric Voegelin, *Order and History: Plato and Aristotle* [Baton Rouge: Louisiana State University Press, 1957], 52ff.). Voegelin draws the parallel between Hades and the Piraeus, marking the connection as well to the allegory of the cave and the myth of Er. His insights are the point of departure both for Salis and for certain central issues in this essay. See Sallis, "The Upward Way," 316.

5. "We were pressing homewards" (327b).

6. Homer, *The Odyssey*, trans. Robert Fagles (New York: Penguin, 1996).

7. On the term *Politeia* see Bloom, *The Republic of Plato*, 439–40, and Sallis, "The Upward Way," 313.

8. One needs to think of this in relation to the movement upwards that, in the light of the divided line passage (Book VI) and the allegory of the cave (Book VII), might be the gesture that brings one to the idea of the polis.

9. See the allegory of the cave (515c, 518d, 519b), for example.

10. See 439e–440b, to which we will come.

11. It is where the dialogue takes place and also the place from which it is most likely retold the next day (see Sallis, "The Upward Way," 314).

12. See ibid., 316.

13. Alexander Sesonske, "Plato's Apology: *Republic I*," in *Plato's Republic: Interpretation and Criticism* (Belmont: Wadsworth, 1966), 42.

14. "Wherever the argument, like a wind, tends, thither must we go" (394d).

15. Bloom, *The Republic of Plato*, 311. Plato seems to make the same distinction elsewhere. "What about the man who labors a great deal at gymnastic and feasts himself really well but never touches music and philosophy?" (411c). "Then, I suppose, such a man becomes a misologist and unmusical. He no longer makes use of any persuasion by means of speech but goes about everything with force and savageness" (411e).

16. Homer, *Iliad*, XXII, 60, XXIV, 487 and *Odyssey*, XV, 246. See Bloom, *The Republic of Plato*, 441 n. 12.

17. See the speech of Socrates in the *Symposium*, *Phaedo*, 65e–66a, and *Republic*, 439e–440b.

18. This is essentially what the myth of Er will also suggest.

19. *The Encyclopedia of Philosophy*, ed. Paul Edwards, vol. 5–6 (New York: Macmillan, 1967), 319, for example, speaks of such a plan.

20. Sesonske writes: "His method, in *Republic I* as throughout the early dialogues, is to seek truth via refutation" ("Plato's Apology: *Republic I*," 45). In contrast, Sesonske speaks of Plato abandoning the Socratic method of eristic in Book II with a turn to dialectic (ibid., 42 and 45–46). Charles H. Kahn, on the

other hand, in *Plato and the Socratic Dialogue* (Cambridge: Cambridge University Press, 1996, xiv), disputes the traditional division of Plato's works into three periods.

21. "I say that to talk every day about virtue and the other things about which you hear me talking and examining myself and others is the greatest good to man, and that the unexamined life is not worth living . . . ." (*The Apology* [38a], in Plato, *Euthyphro, Apology, Crito, Phaedo, Phaedrus*, The Loeb Classical Library [Cambridge: Harvard University Press, 1914], 133).

22. See especially the opening passages of Book III (386–91).

23. There is a subtle parallel to be drawn between the gesture of giving up eristic, the struggle for a position of advantage, and the assurance of the conventional supremacy of males in Greek culture. Whereas the practice of eristic leaves the opponent defeated, it leaves the opponent's difference intact. Paradoxically, therefore, it is with the turn to dialectic, just when Socrates seems to make a radical move toward the equalization of women, that he repeatedly declares the ultimate supremacy of the male. The female, as we will see, is the "same," but always weaker and thus, as Irigaray might phrase it, assimilated to the same.

24. Henry George Liddell and Robert Scott, *A Greek-English Lexicon* (Oxford: Clarendon Press, 1988) entry *elenkhos*. (Hereafter referred to in the text as LS.)

25. He wins each round through negation, proving the other's assertion falls into contradiction, exteriorizing his opponent. And yet, as the mode of argument changes in Book II the discussion takes place much as one would acquire points, property even, not unlike the invasion and seizing of the land of the other, the barbarian, which will be the point of departure for the founding of the new polis in Book II. The various and changing definitions of faction and war must be rethought in relation to dialectic and eristic (Book V, 470–71).

26. See the entry on Plato in *The Encyclopedia of Philosophy* which offers a clear description of eristic (316–17) as well as its role in the evolution of Plato's dialogues (319). Still, the passage conflates eristic and dialectic, whereas in the *Republic* this is clearly not possible.

27. All this while seeming to remain a friend (333e). Eristic forces Polemarchus, for example, into admitting that justice is operative when things are useless (333c–e) or that the just man is a thief (334a), into paths he didn't chose to tread (341a).

28. This mode of argument parallels the way the philosopher relates to disciples and women alike, as we will see.

29. One can choose most any page at random in Books III–X to produce a similar litany of responses.

30. Bloom explains: "There was a popular belief in antiquity that if a wolf sees a man first, the man is struck speechless" (*The Republic of Plato*, 444).

31. "Socrates can get away with his usual trick; he'll not answer himself, and

when someone else has answered he gets hold of the argument and refutes it"
(337e).

32. Socrates' power is in his voice. And his battle with Thrasymachus, from
the beginning of their exchange, is a struggle for the imposition of voice.

> I was astounded when I heard him, and, looking at him, I was frightened. I think that
> if I had not seen him before he saw me, I would have been speechless. As it was, just
> when he began to be exasperated by the argument, I had looked at him first, so that I
> was able to answer him. . . . (336d)

33. Charles H. Kahn offers an excellent gloss on dialectic in Plato's dialogues
(*Plato and the Socratic Dialogue*, 292–309). This meticulously thorough text is
particularly instructive in tracing and understanding Plato's concept of dialectic
through other dialogues.

34. This is a story that is and is not from Herodotus's *Histories*. It tells a story
so similar, it is impossible not to read them side by side; it tells a story so signifi-
cantly different, one cannot but note the disparities. Scholars are sometimes at
a loss to know what to do about that fact, since the story that Herodotus tells in
his *Histories* does not quite gibe with the story we have here in Plato, does not
quite gibe on the one hand because Glaucon talks of the ancestor of Gyges, but
there are other distinctions as well.

The nineteenth-century Plato scholar Adam insists, in *The Republic of Plato*,
that Glaucon must have been talking about an ancestor of Gyges and not about
the Lydian of whom Herodotus speaks (see Sallis, "The Upward Way," 350).
Other scholars back him up. But Bloom tells us to look to Herodotus and other
contemporary scholars seem to have no trouble supposing that Plato is working
from the account that Herodotus gives us.

35. Herodotus, *The Histories*, I, 9 and I, 8 (London: Penguin, 1972), 6.

36. The shepherd has played a role in the exchange with Thrasymachus whom
that cynic sees as a figure for a leader who betrays those in his care (343 and
345), who "looks to his master's good and his own" (343b) rather than caring for
things for their own sake.

37. See Sallis, "The Upward Way," 351.

38. Thrasymachus had compared searching for justice to looking for gold.

39. This despite Schleiermacher's claim to the contrary: Friedrich Daniel
Ernst Schleiermacher, "Der Staat," in *Über die Philosophie Platons* (Hamburg:
Felix Meiner Verlag, 1996), 338–39.

40. Likeness was used earlier in the eristic mode of the dialogue in order to
separate out—to defeat Thrasymachus.

41. A sense of the side by side rather than the hierarchical is evident in the
final lines of the extended comparison, at the end of Book VII, where Socrates
speaks of "this city and the man like it" (541b).

42. "Only in the *Republic* do we learn that 'dialectic' has been chosen as the
official designation for the highest kind of philosophical knowledge, the knowl-

edge that is identical with, or indispensable for, the art required of the states-man: the *politikê technê.* . . . " (Kahn, *Plato and the Socratic Dialogue*, 293).

43. It is hard to miss that in overstepping the bounds of the first city one encounters all those future threats to philosophy: the imitators, those concerned with "figures" (the poets), and "actors," those who have to do with the feminine and feminine adornment (373b).

44. See the concept of the scapegoat (*pharmakos*) in Jacques Derrida's "La Pharmacie de Platon," in *La Dissemination* (Paris: Éditions du Seuil, 1972), 146ff. Other versions of this gesture are described at several points of *De la Gramma-tologie* as well.

45. "Won't they consider differences with Greeks—their kin—to be faction and not even use the name war? . . .

"Therefore, as Greeks, they won't ravage Greece or burn houses nor will they agree that in any city all are their enemies . . . but that there are always a few enemies who are to blame for the differences. . . .

"I for one," he said, "agree that our citizens must behave this way toward their op-ponents; and toward the barbarians they must behave as the Greeks do now toward one another." (471a–b)

"I assert that the Greek stock is with respect to itself its own and akin, with respect to the barbaric, foreign and alien." (470c)

46. There is a complex relationship among these four, a relationship that is not always consistent. Those Socrates speaks of here as "guardians" are yet to be further articulated into auxiliaries, on the one hand, and rulers to be chosen from the best of this class. "The young, whom we were calling guardians (*phu-lakas*) up till now, we shall call auxiliaries (*epikourous*) and helpers (*boêthous*) of the rulers' (*arkhontôn*) convictions" (414b). Still when Socrates arrives at his ultimate definition of justice, he calls the guardian class what he earlier referred to as rulers:

"Meddling among the classes, of which there are three, and exchange with one another is the greatest harm for the city and would most correctly be called extreme evil-do-ing. . . .

"Then that's injustice. . . . The opposite of this—the money-making (*khrêmatis-tikou*), auxiliary (*epikourikou*), and guardian (*phulakikou*) classes doing what's appro-priate, each of them minding its own business in a city—would be justice and would make the city just." (434b–c)

47. This is, paradoxically, precisely the argument that Socrates dispatched in 332–35.

48. There is a small slip here in the implicit definition of the philosopher that we encounter later in the *Republic*. It is not that the philosopher, like the dog, is alien to that of which he is ignorant, alien to those whom he does not know. Rather, the philosopher, as lover of knowledge, will be alien to ignorance

altogether. However philosopher-like the guardian-dog may be here, that they are not one is evident in the split that soon ensues between philosopher-rulers chosen from among the best guardians and an auxiliary soldier class that they rise above.

49. This becomes obvious in the allegory of the cave where the question of the philosopher as ruler is at work in the allegory and the necessity of his return to liberate and rule the city is made explicit.

50. In the famous passage that follows, in a similar twist, Socrates illustrates the dangers of Homer's assumption of the voice of his characters. Under the pretext of explanation to Adeimantus who doesn't quite follow, in order to show the superiority of narrative over imitation, and thus running the danger of "turn[ing] our thought elsewhere" (393a), Socrates, nevertheless, imitates the voice of Homer. (See Miller, "Plato's Double Diegesis.")

51. Derrida's many comments on the binary logic of Plato's work would be relevant here. See for example "La Pharmacie de Platon," 96.

52. This is evident in the repeated rhetoric of purging. After the discussion of the appropriate musical instruments for the guardians, for example: "'And, by the dog,' I said, 'unawares we've again purged the city that a while ago we said was luxurious'" (399e). The act of expunging through citation would be just one example of many.

53. Socrates speaks of this as something "that requires a great deal of persuasion" (414c). Persuasion, it must be remembered, is what he proposes as the possible antidote to the strength of body and strength in numbers of Polemarchus and his companions in the opening lines of the dialogue (327c).

54. This is precisely what dialectic is also about, a separating out and a harmonizing into one. There are, of course, less cynical ways of reading the relation between the one and the many in the polis. See Sallis, "The Upward Way," 362, for example.

55. This tale of the benign mother under whom all unite as brothers stands in contrast to the theogony of Hesiod where sons serially murder and castrate the father, source of generation.

56. The dialogue is punctuated with reminders of this power structure, for example in the already cited passage in which Socrates renames the guardian class as the auxiliary: "'The young, whom we were calling guardians (*phulakas*) up to now, we shall call auxiliaries (*epikourous*) and helpers (*boêthous*) of the rulers' (*arkhontôn*) convictions'" (414b).

57. One would have to think the closing passage of Book III in this regard. Socrates makes taboo for the guardians any contact with gold or silver, proposing to tell them, rather, "that gold and silver of the divine sort from the gods they have in their soul always and have no further need of the human sort" (416e).

The privileging of the metaphorical over the literal would establish complex parallels and distinctions with the privileging of the intelligible over the visible on the one hand (the divided line in Book VI) and of "one particular form" (596a) or idea over its "particular 'manys'" in the work of the manual artisan (596a).

58. Unsettling, moreover, that as this takes place, just as Socrates is about to insist on a strict hierarchy among the three classes of rulers, auxiliaries or soldiers, and craftsmen, the myth surreptitiously upends that hierarchy. For all men are said to be "molded" as though created by the lowest of these classes, the artisans ("in truth, at that time they were under the earth within, being fashioned and reared themselves, and their arms and other tools being crafted" [414d]).

59. Even before we embark on the tale of Leontius, we are at a loss. If the analogy between polis and individual is strictly to hold, the courage and rage of the warrior class would then no longer be directed toward the barbarians on the other side of the border, but, in parallel to the tale of Leontius, toward the craftsmen within the city. This is one of other, more indirect, among a legion of warnings signaling the violence of the state.

60. Thus Bloom, for example, will speak of the *Republic* as "the true *Apology* of Socrates," Socrates on trial for his life (Bloom, *The Republic of Plato*, 307).

61. Injustice, according to one of its earliest descriptions, has much to do with the scene of Leontius. "And, if, then, injustice should come into being within one man . . . will it lose its power or remain undiminished?" . . . "Then does [injustice] come to light as possessing a power such that, whenever it comes into being . . . it first of all makes that thing [the man] unable to accomplish anything together with itself due to faction and difference" (351e–352a).

62. Socrates insists on this repeatedly in the coming discussion.

"Now what would be the remaining form (*loipon eidos*) thanks to which the city would further partake in virtue? Plainly, this is justice." (432b)

"In my opinion," I said, "after having considered moderation, courage, and prudence, this is what's left over (*to hupoloipon*) in the city; it provided the power by which all these others came into being; and, once having come into being, it provides them with preservation as long as it's in the city. And yet we were saying that justice would be what's left over (*to hupoleiphthen*) from the three if we found them." (433b–c)

63. See Bloom, *The Republic of Plato*, 457, who speaks of this moment as "a new beginning of the book."

64. See ibid., 457 n. 4 and 458 n. 12.

65. It is in beginning to take this outrageous position that Socrates will violate his own stylistic law that "the poet himself [should speak and not] attempt to turn our thought elsewhere, as though someone other than he were speaking" (393a). Strangely, in arguing for the quasi-equality of woman, Socrates insists

on arguing both sides of the question. "'Do you want us,' I said, 'to carry on the dispute and represent those on the other side ourselves so that the opposing argument won't be besieged without defense?'" (453a). To this Glaucon eventually replies: "'But I . . . beg you, to interpret the argument on our behalf too, whatever it may be.'" (453c).

66. See also 457a, 454c, 455c–d, 456b, 387e, 395d, 398e, 469d.

67. See Luce Irigaray, *Sexes et parentés* (Paris: Minuit, 1987), 125, and *Sexes and Genealogies*, trans. Gillian C. Gill (New York: Columbia University Press, 1993), 111, who writes of Antigone, and by extension all women, as the "representative of the other of the same."

68. Plato, *Laches; Protagoras; Meno; Euthydemus*, trans. W. R. Lamb, The Loeb Classical Library (Cambridge: Harvard University Press, 1999).

69. See Kahn, *Plato and the Socratic Dialogue*, 305.

70. See Bloom, *The Republic of Plato*, 459 n. 16, who points out that words relating to the first meaning abound in the *Theaetetus*.

71. To be sure "faction" (*stasis*) functioned quite differently earlier in the dialogue where it signified the seemingly irreconcilable difference of injustice.

72. Derived from *paradeiknumi*—to display side by side (LS).

73. If Socrates goes on to suggest that the man who merely opines is "not healthy" (476e), one might wonder about the significance of the fact that the argument above is couched entirely in the mode of opinion.

74. Bloom has this to say: "This is the word used for the activity of discerning the *forms* or classes to which things belong. It is the fundamental task of dialectic to define things according to natural divisions existing in the world; diairesis is the way of discovering such definitions" (Bloom, *The Republic of Plato*, 453 n. 50).

75. In this last phrase I am using Bloom's alternate translation (given in his footnote) rather than the one that appears in the body of the text.

76. The reference is actually to "calculation" here, but Socrates uses the same terminology for dialectic.

77. See Plato's *Phaedo*:

"Don't you think that the person who is likely to succeed in this attempt most perfectly is the one who approaches each object, as far as possible, with the unaided intellect, without taking account of any sense of sight in his thinking, or dragging any other sense into his reckoning—the man who pursues the truth by applying his pure and unadulterated thought to the pure and unadulterated object, cutting himself off as much as possible from his eyes and ears and virtually all the rest of his body, as an impediment which by its presence prevents the soul from attaining to truth and clear thinking." (65e–66a)

The Collected Dialogues of Plato, ed. Edith Hamilton and Huntington Cairns, Bollingen Series, LXXI (Princeton: Princeton University Press, 1989).

78. See also 537d.

79. The following passage from the *Sophist* gives something of a sense of this, although the hierarchization we encounter in the *Republic* is here not as acute.

> Stranger: Dividing according to kinds, not taking the same form for a different one or a different one for the same—is not that the business of the science of dialectic?
>
> Theaetetus: Yes.
>
> Stranger: And the man who can do that discerns clearly *one* form everywhere extended throughout many, where each one lies apart, and *many* forms, different from one another, embraced from without by one form, and again *one* form connected in a unity through many wholes, and *many* forms, entirely marked off apart. (253d–e)

Hamilton and Cairns, *The Collected Dialogues of Plato*.

80. For other schemas of the divided line see Bloom, *The Republic of Plato*, 464 and Nickolas Pappas, *Plato and the Republic* (London: Routledge), 140.

81. See Sallis, "The Upward Way," 439–41.

82. See the remarkable reading of Jacques Derrida in "La Pharmacie de Platon" (92 ff.), to which this reading owes a great deal.

83. See Sallis, "The Upward Way," 405. Perhaps even a hotbed of the reproduction of reproduction. One need only think of the philosopher who couples with what really is, and generates intelligence and truth, like a woman in labor (490b).

This is a generation of intelligence and truth by the lover of learning, an intelligence that is akin to, or con-genital with, produced simultaneously with, the object of truth, what *is*.

84. See, for example, 344d and 349–50.

85. See Sallis, "The Upward Way," 445 ff.

86. Whoever reaches the highest realm of knowledge will not be permitted to remain, but rather will be compelled to return to the cave.

87. Not unlike that of Diotima's speech in the *Symposium*.

88. Compulsion and persuasion, which seemed to distinguish the force of Polemarchus from the persuasion offered by Socrates in the opening lines of the dialogue, are now both commended by the voice of philosophy.

89. Just how to think the relation among turning, the seductive stasis of *what is*, and compulsion is also Heidegger's preoccupation: Martin Heidegger, "Platons Lehre von der Wahrheit," in *Wegmarken* (Frankfurt am Main: Vittorio Klostermann, 1967), 203–38 ("Plato's Doctrine of Truth," in *Pathmarks* [Cambridge: Cambridge University Press, 1998], 155–82).

The essay opens with a shift from science to doctrine. It turns from a conventional conceptualization of knowledge as a language of expression and proposition that produces results and the graspable to doctrine (*Lehre*), concerned rather with the unsaid in the thinker's saying: enabling no grasp, no results, no use. As Heidegger goes on to speak of Plato's allegory, we are led to believe that the unsaid in Plato, too, is a shift in the essence of truth. It is a shift in the essence of any truth that the allegory or *Gleichnis*, as Heidegger calls it, might have to offer. To begin with it is a shift in the way in which the *Gleichnis* must and must not be read or interpreted. The unsaid of the allegory is not a matter of finding the allegorical equivalent of Socrates' description of the cave and what lies outside it to our human state. The unsaid, and education (*paideia*) as well, Heidegger will insist, have to do with movements, "incidents" and "transitions" (*Vorgänge* and *Übergänge*), with a passage between states, with defamiliarization, with a changing of our habituation, with inversion and turning around.

But Heidegger will shift from this reading of Plato's cave to another in which truth (*alêtheia*), no longer a question of the unsteadiness of transitions of which he has spoken of up till now, becomes, rather, a question of perception, knowing, and reason. He speaks of the accessibility of the phenomenal, of consciousness in the light of steady appearance, of presence and the idea. He writes above all of the Idea of the Good in its relation to the morally Good. A language of mastery enters, in which the idea lords it over the unhidden. Adequation determines the relation between the seen and the seeing. Moreover unhiddenness or truth becomes a characteristic of humans toward being, a correct way of their seeing. The title of Heidegger's essay notwithstanding, Plato, it seems, is after the graspable; practicing science (*Wissenschaft*), striving for truth as correctness. Philosophy, metaphysics, theology, and humanism—all these are at stake, mired as they are in a certainty of the correct, of the fixed. In a sense Plato, in this inverted reading, has returned us to the cave. Having lost our freedom definitively, we see only straight ahead.

And along the way Heidegger will have turned things upside down or at least plunged the discourse into that contamination of forms of the soul that Socrates so warned against. Socrates' realm of the supersensuous is invaded by the third form of the soul; for what truth as the "correctness of apprehending and asserting" (177) ("Richtigkeit des Vernehmens und Aussagens," [231]) brings with it is a certain desire for possession: a striving for acquisition or "achieving of a correct view of the ideas" (179) ("die Gewinnung des rechten Ideenblickes," [234]).

90. See Bloom, *The Republic of Plato*, 471 n. 13.

91. See Voegelin, *Order and History*, 52ff.

92. There is much that could be said about the question of necessity here in Hades, linked to turns and revolutions and especially to plentiful contradictions of a variety of sorts in Er's narrative of moral consequences. None of this is irrelevant to the general argument, but it would be complicated to the point of getting us off track.

93. The tale of Gyges and the role of the Delphic oracle would also be relevant.

94. One sees the complexity as well when Socrates makes a slip while insisting on the analogy of city to man: he all but forgets that individuals are tripartite when he ascribes to all individuals of particular regions the characteristics of just one of the classes:

"Isn't it quite necessary for us to agree that the very same forms and dispositions as are in the city are in each of us?" I said. "Surely they haven't come there from any other place. It would be ridiculous if someone should think that the spiritedness didn't come into the cities from those private men who are just the ones imputed with having this character, such as those in Thrace, Scythia, and pretty nearly the whole upper region; or the love of learning, which one could most impute to our region, or the love of money, which one could affirm is to be found not least among the Phoenicians and those in Egypt." (435e–436a)

95. It is only in Book V (454a) that we discover the name to put to this shift.

96. The creation of the city might seem a mere steppingstone on the way to viewing the structure of justice in the individual, but, on the other hand, there is "more justice in the bigger" (368e) city and the polis goes on to occupy much of the dialogue.

97. Bloom (*The Republic of Plato*, 311) and Sallis ("The Upward Way," 318) rightly suggest that at the very beginning of the dialogue (in which Socrates finds the performances of the Thracians at the festival of Bendis as good as that of the Athenians) the border between the polis and the foreign is already uncertain.

Chapter 4. Hamann Is a Nomadic Writer

1. The text from Isaiah is as cited by Gwen Griffith Dickson, *Johann Georg Hamann's Relational Metacriticism* (Berlin: Walter de Gruyter, 1995), 444. Unless otherwise noted citations from the Book of Judges are from *The New Oxford Annotated Bible* (New York: Oxford, 2001).

2. Johann Wolfgang von Goethe, *Aus meinem Leben, Dichtung und Wahrheit*, Pt. III, Bk. 12 (Frankfurt: Deutscher Klassiker Verlag, 1986), 561, and *The Autobiography of Johann Wolfgang von Goethe*, trans. John Oxenford, vol. 2 (New York: Horizon Press, 1969), 137. Goethe prefaces this passage (and this is relevant to what is to follow) with: "In my collection there are several of his printed pages where in the margin, in his own hand, he cites the passages to which his hints refer. If one looks them up, there is . . . " (ibid.; *Aus meinem Leben*, 561).

3. Unless otherwise noted all references to Hamann's work are from the historical-critical edition of Josef Nadler, reprinted as Johann Georg Hamann, *Sämtliche Werke* (Wuppertal: R. Brockhaus) (Tübingen: Antiquariat H. P. Willi, 1999). They are marked by N, followed by the volume and page number.

4. See Hamann's letter of June 1, 1759 in J. G. Hamann. *Briefwechsel*, ed. Wal-

ther Ziesemer and Arthur Henkel, 7 vols. (Wiesbaden: Insel-Verlag, 1955–79) I, 334–36. The letters will hereafter be referred to by ZH followed by the volume and page number. See also his letters of August 18, 1759: "My letters are perhaps difficult because I write elliptically like a Greek and allegorically like a Levanter. A layperson and nonbeliever can only explain my way of writing as nonsense, because I express myself with many tongues. . . . " (ZH, I, 396); October 12, 1759: "I am no match for truths, fundamentals, systems. Scraps, fragments, caprice, whims. Each according to its fundament and ground" (ZH, I, 431); and May 21, 1760, where he speaks of "Disorder, the general fundamental error of my disposition" (ZH, II, 2).

5. See Sven-Aage Jørgensen, ed., *Sokratische Denkwürdigkeiten, Aesthetica in nuce* (Stuttgart: Reclam, 1968), 163–64. See also Hans-Martin Lumpp, *Philologia crucis: Zu Johann Georg Hamanns Auffassung von der Dichtkunst. Mit einem Kommentar zur 'Aesthetica in nuce',* Studien zur deutschen Literatur, vol. 21 (Tübingen: Max Niemeyer Verlag, 1970).

6. On this issue see Eric Blackall's excellent essay "The Mystical Approach," in Eric Blackall, *The Emergence of German as a Literary Language 1700–1775* (Ithaca: Cornell University Press, 1978). He writes of Hamann "reiterating that opposition to all rationalistic criteria which he had expressed some twenty years before in 1763, when he had spoken of 'the chimeras of beautiful nature, good taste, and healthy reason. . . . Lying is the mother tongue of our reason and wit,' he wrote to Kant on 27 July 1759" (426). "In the Bible we find precisely the regular disorder that we discover in Nature. All methods are to be regarded as walkers of reason and as its crutches" (ZH, I, 229–30), cited in Blackall, "The Mystical Approach," 431.

7. See for example Werner Kohlschmidt, *Geschichte der deutschen Literatur vom Barock bis zur Klassik,* vol. 2 (Stuttgart: Reclam, 1965), 444f. Also Dickson, *Johann Georg Hamann's Relational Metacriticism,* 16–17; Lumpp, *Philologia crucis,* 4, 6, 8, 174–86; Rudolf Unger, *Hamann und die Aufklärung* (Jena: Diederichs, 1911), 263; James O'Flaherty, *Hamann's Socratic Memorabilia: A Translation and a Commentary* (Baltimore: Johns Hopkins University Press, 1967), 18 and 128. See also Jørgensen, *Sokratische Denkwürdigkeiten,* 191, for a pointed critique of such historical simplicity and 84 for his suggestion that Lowth's lectures were of great importance for the development of the genetic approach to literature.

8. Translations of "Aesthetica in nuce" are taken from Dickson, *Johann Georg Hamann's Relational Metacriticism,* 409–31. Since Dickson also numbers her pages according to the German edition, the German pagination suffices here.

This is a monumental work that does great service to the English-speaking reader, containing as it does translations of some of the major works, detailed notes to the translations, as well as highly intelligent expositions and analyses of each text. Without the scholarly work of Dickson and many others, this essay would have been impossible.

9. See Lumpp, *Philologia crucis*, 3, and Jørgensen, *Sokratische Denkwürdigkeiten*, 183.

10. O'Flaherty makes this point with respect to the "Socratic Memorabilia" (*Hamann's Socratic Memorabilia*, 70–71).

11. See Blackall, "The Mystical Approach," 437–38, who has a good sense of the complexity of Hamann's practice of allusion, and O'Flaherty, *Hamann's Socratic Memorabilia*, 68–70. There are moments when the biblical references seem to clarify (see, for example notes 12, 13, and 14 [N II, 200]) and others when a rapid-fire series of allusions leaves the reader as blank as before.

12. See Dickson, *Johann Georg Hamann's Relational Metacriticism*, 132ff.; Lumpp, *Philologia crucis*, 3; Blackall, "The Mystical Approach," 430; Jørgensen, *Sokratische Denkwürdigkeiten*, 170–72, who is excellent on typology's parallels to concepts of history; Karlfried Gründer, *Figur und Geschichte: Johann Georg Hamanns "Biblische Betrachtungen" als Ansatz einer Geschichtsphilosophie* (Freiburg: Karl Alber, 1958), 118–19 and 127–31, and others.

13. Dickson, citing Volker Hoffmann's *Johann Georg Hamanns Philologie: Hamanns Philologie zwischen enzyklopädischer Mikrologie und Hermeneutik* (Stuttgart: Verlag K. Kohnkammer, 1972), sums it up as follows: "Hoffmann's understanding of Hamann's use of typology is along these lines: typology produces a relationship between the Old Testament and the New Testament on the foundation of a salvation-historical continuity and the tension it contains between promise and fulfillment" (*Johann Georg Hamann's Relational Metacriticism*, 133).

14. See also: "God reveals himself—the creator of the world a writer" (N I, 9). "Writing can only speak to us humans in images (*Gleichnissen*), because all of our knowledge (is) sensual, figural, and understanding (*der Verstand*) and reason (*die Vernunft*) make the images (*Bilder*) of external things everywhere into allegories and signs of abstract, spiritual, and higher concepts" (N I, 157–58).

15. "Des Ritters von Rosencreuz letzte Willensmeynung über den göttlichen und menschlichen Ursprung der Sprache." ["The Last Will and Testament of the Knight of the Rose Cross on the Divine and Human Origin of Language."]

16. See Dickson, *Johann Georg Hamann's Relational Metacriticism*, 76–77.

17. "The title of this ill-mannered collection is a provincial joke and is related to the [going] back and forth in this realm (Prussia) in the labyrinth to be found there, and its meaning . . . owes its origin to the deception of the former brothers of the order and crusaders" (ZH, II, 195).

18. Something similar takes place in the "Sokratische Denkwürdigkeiten":

On this occasion Socrates spoke of **readers** who could **swim**. A confluence of ideas and feelings in that living **elegy** of a philosopher made his statements into an archipelago, perhaps, for whose communication **bridges** and ferries of method were lacking." (Dickson, *Johann Georg Hamann's Relational Metacriticism*, 379)

Bey dieser Gelegenheit redete Sokrates von **Lesern**, welche **schwimmen** könnten. Ein Zusammenfluß von Ideen und Empfindungen in jener lebenden **Elegie** vom Philosophen machte desselben Sätze vielleicht zu einer Menge kleiner Inseln, zu deren Gemeinschaft **Brücken** und Fähren der Methode fehlten." (N II, 61)

19. Many of Hamann's readers speak of "Aesthetica in nuce" as a cento: see for example Jørgensen, *Sokratische Denkwürdigkeiten*, 189; Dickson, *Johann Georg Hamann's Relational Metacriticism*, 83; and Blackall, "The Mystical Approach," 438. The *OED* defines the cento as "a piece of patchwork; a patched garment," but also, citing Johnson, as "a composition formed by joining scraps from other authors."

The question the cento raises, of course, is the question of authority, who is speaking. It is at once the voice of the original texts as well as that of the gatherer of textual fragments. One might think of the cento as gathering and preserving a multiplicity of voices. Still, Proba Falconia, in his Cento Vergilianus, told Bible stories by citing lines of Virgil: this suggests that the cento might also be thought as shredding the intentions of the authors it cites. Let us remember that if Virgil can be made to speak in the voice of the Bible, the Bible, as Hamann cites it, might yet be made to say . . . we are not yet sure what.

20. See Jørgensen, *Sokratische Denkwürdigkeiten*, 7, and Dickson, *Johann Georg Hamann's Relational Metacriticism*, 82–83. Here and throughout her intelligent exposition Dickson speaks of interpretation as Hamann's overriding concern in "Aesthetica in nuce."

21. In addition to Dickson, Jørgensen, and Lumpp, the work of Fritz Blanke and Karlfried Gründer, *Johann Georg Hamanns Hauptschriften Erklärt* (Gütersloh: Mohn, 1962) should be mentioned, although there is no volume on "Aesthetica in nuce."

22. See for example N II, 213–14.

23. To be sure, Hamann ascribes this role to the title of his works (rather than to his epigraphs). In a letter to Jacobi of November 12, 1785, he writes that for him "the title is not a sign (*Schild*) to merely hang out, but the *nucleus in nuce*, the mustard seed of the whole growth" (C. H. Gildemeister, *Johann Georg Hamann's, des Magus im Norden, Leben und Schriften* vol. 5: *Hamann's Briefwechsel mit Friedrich Heinrich Jacobi* [Gotha, 1868], 137–38), cited by O'Flaherty, *Hamann's Socratic Memorabilia*, 67.

24. See Dickson, *Johann Georg Hamann's Relational Metacriticism*, 84n, for a discussion of this.

25. Robert Lowth, *Lectures on the Sacred Poetry of the Hebrews,* vol. I (London: Ogles, Duncan, and Cochran, 1816), 290.

26. "Aesthetica in nuce" at its most polemic often poses itself as battle or contest. The second sentence of the text proper presents the essay as a race against Michaelis. "Hail to the archangel on the relics of the language of Canaan!—on fair asses he triumphs in the race, but the wise layman of Greece borrows Euthyphron's proud stallions for the philological debate" (N II, 197). Hamann, as "the wise layman of Greece," will triumph with borrowed stallions over the "archangel" Michaelis who rides "'on fair asses.'" This last phrase, as Hamann's footnote reminds us, is also from the Song of Deborah. And here is where the confusion continues. For the phrase Hamann borrows from the Song of Deborah for his philological debate, "on fair asses," would place Michaelis in the original biblical text among the triumphant Israelites. Here as elsewhere one traces Hamann's allusions only at the price of disrupting their original intention and thus destroying the logic of his own assertion, a warning, then, from the beginning, about the enterprise of following footnotes to their source.

27. Lumpp, *Philologia crucis,* 33; Marie-Theres Küster, *Inhaltsanalyse von J. G. Hamanns "Aesthetica in Nuce, eine Rhapsodie in kabbalistischer Prose"* (Bottrop: Wilh. Postberg, 1936).

28. Dickson, *Johann Georg Hamann's Relational Metacriticism,* 84. Blackall sees the spoils of the motto as Hamann's "Aesthetica in nuce," although he also seems to identify Hamann's voice with that of the prophetess ("The Mystical Approach," 439–40).

29. John Gray, *Joshua, Judges, Ruth,* New Century Bible Commentary (Grand Rapids: Eerdmans, 1986), 203 and 280.

30. *Judges,* Introduction, Translation and Commentary by Robert G. Boling (Garden City: Doubleday, 1975), 105.

31. The first version is that of the *New Oxford Annotated Bible.* The other alternatives are taken from a number of translations in George Foot Moore, *A Critical and Exegetical Commentary on Judges,* The International Critical Commentary (New York: Charles Scribner's Sons, 1900), 168, who gives his own translation and those of others. He adds: "In the general disorder of the text in this verse, it is impossible to feel much confidence in any restoration" (168). Due to the corruption of the text, these lines have a lot in common with "Aesthetica in nuce," at least in its legendary unreadability.

32. Lowth, *Lectures on the Sacred Poetry of the Hebrews,* 1:293.

33. See Dickson, *Johann Georg Hamann's Relational Metacriticism,* 102.

34. A footnote warns us with respect to this passage and with respect to prosopopoeia in general: that "the art of personification opens a much less limited and more fertile field than ancient Mythology" (N II, 201). The breaking of limits in

the prosopopoeia of the nut leads us again to the implicit admonitions of Judges V, 30 about a misplaced thirst for spoils in this text.

35. Lumpp cites *Meyers Lexicon*, 8th ed. (1936) 1:460, entry. "Apostille" as saying: "verified postscript to a document" (*Philologia crucis*, 105).

36. Jørgensen, *Sokratische Denkwürdigkeiten*, 146.

37. In Proverbs the merchant ship that brings nourishment from distant lands is a simile for "a virtuous wife" (Prov. XXXI, 14). Here, as so often elsewhere in "Aesthetica in nuce," one traces the ostensible referent only to find that it does not work, or that one has to rethink the biblical meaning.

38. In the first German edition the word *Asterisken* is followed by [*] which leads the reader to a footnote. In the modern edition of Nadler, the numbered footnote 64 appears.

39. This is set typographically as it was in the first edition (Lumpp, *Philologia crucis*, 234).

40. Jørgensen (*Sokratische Denkwürdigkeiten*, 146) suggests both Ecclesiastes XII, 11 and Isaiah LIV, 2 ("Enlarge the site of your tent, and let the curtains of your habitations be stretched out; do not hold back; lengthen your cord and strengthen your stakes." Dickson points to Isaiah but gives us the passage from Ecclesiastes as: "The sayings of the wise are like pegs of a tent."

41. "Today I began with God to read the Holy Writ for the second time" (N I, 7, first sentence of the *Biblische Betrachtungen*).

42. Hamann, in his "Gedanken über meinen Lebenslauf," recognizes his acts of identification as he reads and rereads the Bible, but he writes of an identification with Israel, not its enemies: "I recognized my own crimes in the history of the Jewish people, I read my own life's record and thanked God for his patience with this his people, for nothing but such an example could entitle me to a hope such as this. . . . " (N II, 40; O'Flaherty, *Hamann's Socratic Memorabilia*, 52).

43. How can it be a coincidence that the phrase from the Song of Deborah, precisely that from the motto, translated by Lowth as "A spoil of needlework of divers colours" appears in the OED's definition of the cento: "1610 HEALEY *St. Aug. City of God* (1620) Centones are peeces of cloath of diuerse colours. . . . "?

44. And did not Hamlet's father and Sisera both die a similar death, attacked from the side of the head in sleep?

45. From "erteilen—was man erteilt"—what one apportions.

Chapter 5. What Does It Mean to Count?

1. All citations of *The Emigrants* are from W. G. Sebald, *The Emigrants*, trans. Michael Hulse (New York: New Directions, 1997) and *Die Ausgewanderten: Vier lange Erzählungen* (Frankfurt am Main: Fischer, 2002). Page numbers from the translation are followed by an "E," from the German edition are followed by a

"G." Occasionally the English translation has been altered. The quotation in the epigraph appears in *Logis in einem Landhaus* (Frankfurt am Main: Fischer Verlag, 2002), 184.

2. To be sure, in the second of the chapters Sebald has Paul Bereyter engage in similar activities:

> It was only in the last decade of his life . . . that reconstructing those events became important to him. . . . [He] spent many days in archives, making endless notes. . . . (54E)

> Erst während seines letzten Lebensjahrzehnts . . . war ihm die Rekonstruktion jener Ereignisse . . . wichtig . . . geworden. [Er habe] tagelang in Archiven gesessen und sich endlose Notizen gemacht. (80G)

And the narrator also seems to take his cue from photographic documents:

> Mme Landau put before me a large album which contained photographs documenting not only the period in question but indeed, a few gaps aside, almost the whole of Paul Bereyter's life, with notes penned in his own hand. (45E)

> [Mme. Landau] legte mir . . . ein großformatiges Album vor, in welchem nicht nur die fragliche Zeit, sondern, von einigen Leerstellen abgesehen, fast das gesamte Leben Paul Bereyters fotografisch dokumentiert und von seiner eigenen Hand annotiert war. (68G)

3. An article in the *Partisan Review* 68, no. 4 (2001), a publication that surely has no interest in selling books (which may undercut my cynicism in reading the Fischer Verlag blurb) makes a similar claim, speaking of "the stories of four twentieth-century Germans of Jewish descent who left their country" (cited from http://www.bu.edu/partisanreview/archive/2001/4/krauss.html). But Henry Selwyn was not German and Ambros Adelwarth was not Jewish.

4. We read of "the fact that . . . old Bereyter was what was termed half Jewish, and Paul, in consequence, only three-quarters an Aryan" (50E, 74G).

5. Sebald changed the name to Ferber in the English translation.

6. Or are the inhabitants of Sebald's tale, Jews and non-Jews alike, already lost to us? Of Manchester, in general, he writes: "One might have supposed that the city had long since been deserted, and was left now as a necropolis or mausoleum" (151E, 223G).

7. And these, in turn, perhaps have something to do with the advice of Paul Bereyter's doctor that "peaceful absorption into the moving leaves would protect and improve his eyesight" (58E, translation altered; 85G).

8. One might compare in this regard the scene in *Vertigo* (*Schwindel. Gefühle.*) in which the narrator goes into the past with another gesture. He touches the centuries-old uniform on an old tailor's dummy only to watch it turn to dust: "But when I stepped closer, not entirely trusting my eyes, and touched one of

the uniform sleeves that hung down empty, to my utter horror it crumbled into dust." W. G. Sebald, *Vertigo* (New York: New Directions, 1999), 227; *Schwindel. Gefühle.* (Frankfurt am Main: Fischer Verlag, 1994, 248).

9. The sections that close *Nach der Natur* (*After Nature*) and *Schwindel. Gefühle.* (*Vertigo*) also engage figures of the author.

10. "I came across a sign on which TO THE STUDIOS had been painted in crude brush-strokes. It pointed the way to a cobbled yard. . . . " (160E, 236G).

11. Just as the return of Naegeli's body takes place on the way to Lake Geneva.

12. In the closing chapter, when the narrator arrives at the hotel Arosa, Mrs. Irlam asks: "And where have you sprung from?" (152E, 224G), making him and perhaps Sebald himself something of a Butterfly Man.

13. And yet this is not total obliteration, for we are left haunted by the sense, if not of an individual, then of a long line of ancestors: "Thus it had for the onlooker the semblance of having evolved from a long lineage of grey, ancestral faces, rendered unto ash but still there, as ghostly presences, on the harried paper" (162E, translation altered; 239–40G).

14.

During the winter of 1990/91, in the little free time I had (in other words, mostly at the so-called weekend and at night), I was working on the account of Max [Aurach] given above. It was an arduous task. Often I could not get on for hours or days at a time, and not infrequently I unraveled what I had done, continuously tormented by scruples that were taking tighter hold and steadily paralyzing me. These scruples concerned not only the subject of my narrative, which I felt I could not do justice to, no matter what approach I tried, but also the entire questionable business of writing. I had covered hundreds of pages with my scribble, in pencil and ballpoint. By far the greater part had been crossed out, discarded, or obliterated by additions. Even what I ultimately salvaged as a "final" version seemed to me a thing of shreds and patches, utterly botched. (230–31E)

Über die Wintermonate 1990/91 arbeitete ich in der wenigen mir zur freien Verfügung stehenden Zeit, also zumeist an den sogenannten Wochenenden und in der Nacht, an der im Vorhergehenden erzählten Geschichte Max Aurachs. Es war ein äußerst mühevolles, oft stunden- und tagelang nicht vom Fleck kommendes und nicht selten sogar rückläufiges Unternehmen, bei dem ich fortwährend geplagt wurde von einem immer nachhaltiger sich bemerkbar machenden und mehr und mehr mich lähmenden Skrupulantismus. Dieser Skrupulantismus bezog sich sowohl auf den Gegenstand meiner Erzählung, dem ich, wie ich es auch anstellte, nicht gerecht zu werden glaubte, als auch auf die Fragwürdigkeit der Schriftstellerei überhaupt. Hunderte von Seiten hatte ich bedeckt mit meinem Bleistift- und Kugelschreiberkritzel. Weitaus das meiste davon war durchgestrichen, verworfen oder bis zur Unleserlichkeit mit Zusätzen überschmiert. Selbst das, was ich schließlich für die "endgültige" Fassung retten konnte, erschien mir als ein mißratenes Stückwerk. (344–45G)

Moreover, already in 1989, before he finds Aurach's paintings in the Tate, the narrator says: "I never succeeded in really picturing him properly to myself. His face had become a mere sketch" (177E, translation altered; 264G).

Ambros Adelwarth is no less an artist of this sort. A photograph of his diary shows his letters layered over one another (132E, 194–95G). In the German edition the image of Adelwarth's "Agenda" overlays the double pages of Sebald's book in a gesture of coincidence. See both 194–95G and 200–201G.

15. This returns us as well to the scene in *Vertigo* cited in note 8, reminiscent as well of Aurach's enterprise.

16. The narrator, too, speaks of "fragmentary recollections" (42E) ["meine eigenen, bruchstückhaften Erinnerungen" (63G)] as does Luisa Lansberg (208E, 312G).

17. This follows on a scene in which the passage of time is carefully marked out. Here as in *Austerlitz*, conventional and inevitable measures of narrative time are juxtaposed with reminders of their artificiality (see, for example, the temporal guideposts that follow Austerlitz's long disquisition on arbitrary concepts of time: W. G. Sebald, *Austerlitz*, trans. Anthea Bell (New York: Random House, 2001), 100–102E, and (Munich: Carl Hanser Verlag, 2001), 145–48G.

18. The play on *Staub* (dust) and *Bestäubung* is mine, but in the chapter on Ambros Adelwarth, at the site of those whose thoughts go wild, one can almost imagine hearing it. The narrator visits the now decaying mental institution in which his uncle had passed away, tortured to death in the name of science by an electric shock assault that passed for therapy. Here Dr. Abramsky lives on in regret, no longer practicing institutional violence. He keeps bees and acknowledges his own madness (110E, 161G): and in his role as apiarist his thoughts cannot be far from pollination/*Bestäubung*. The impending collapse of Samaria Sanatorium will take place with the help of the "mouse folk," the "woodworm and deathwatch beetles" (112E, 165G).

And that is precisely what does happen in my dream, before my very eyes, infinitely slowly, and a great yellowish cloud billows out and disperses, and where the sanatorium once stood there is merely a heap of powder-fine wood dust, like pollen. (113E)

Und so geschieht es dann auch, vor meinen Traumaugen, mit unendlicher Langsamkeit, und eine große, gelbliche Wolke steigt auf und verweht, und an der Stelle des ehemaligen Sanatoriums bleibt nichts als ein Häufchen puderfeines, blütenstaubähnliches Holzmehl. (166G)

That *Bestäubung* might coincide with a certain liberation, despite its obvious destructive thrust, is something with which one must come to terms.

19. The names of characters transgress not only the chapter divisions, but also the individuality of Sebald's works. (In this Sebald's practice is not unlike that of Werner Herzog who in elaborate acts of cross-film citation carries over his ac-

tors and sometimes his characters from film to film.) Thus a Bereyter appears in
Vertigo and, does so, tellingly, in the context of one person standing as a cipher
for many others.

> La Ghita, who reappears a number of times on the periphery of Beyle's later work,
> is a mysterious, not to say unearthly figure. There is reason to suspect that Beyle
> used her name as a cipher for various lovers such as Adèle Rebuffel, Angéline *Bereyter*
> and not least for Métilde Dembowski, and that Mme Gherardi, whose life would eas-
> ily furnish a whole novel . . . never really existed, despite all the documentary evidence.
> . . . (*Vertigo*, 21–22E, emphasis mine)

> Diese Ghita, die am Rand von Beyles späterem Werk noch einige Male in Erscheinung
> tritt, ist eine mysteriöse, um nicht zu sagen geisterhafte Gestalt. Es gibt Grund für die
> Vermutung, daßBeyle ihren Namen als Chiffre für verschiedene seiner Liebhaberin-
> nen wie Adèle Rebuffel, Angéline *Bereyter* und nicht zuletzt für Métilde Dembowski
> einsetzte und daßMme Gherardi, deren Leben . . . leicht einen ganzen Roman aus-
> machte, allen dokumentarischen Angaben zum Trotz in Wirklichkeit gar nicht existi-
> ert hat. . . . (*Schwindel. Gefühle.* 26G, emphasis mine)

20. The scene haunts each of the volume's stories. Paul Bereyter and Lucy
Landau have also been in the mountains and have seen the landscape of Lake
Geneva. It passes by less perceptibly elsewhere as well: as when Adelwarth works
in a hotel in Montreux, near the Grammont (77–78E, 113G) and returns to Lake
Geneva in 1911 with Cosmo (91E, 132G); as when Aurach returns to Manchester
after the war and looks down on the city with a bird's-eye view (168E, 249–50G),
which is not unlike a scene we are about to encounter in Herzog's film *Kaspar
Hauser*. Moreover, Nabokov, already an important figure in the opening chapter,
spent the last seventeen years of his life in Montreux.

21. Figures 5.1 (mountain panorama) and 5.2 (newspaper clipping, detail) are
reproduced from W. G. Sebald, *Die Ausgewanderten* © Eichborn AG, Frankfurt
am Main, 1992, 25, 37.

22. The twinned image makes its appearance even before the opening lines
of the first story. We see the photograph of a great tree spreading its branches
among the tombstones of a cemetery. A remarkably similar tree appears in the
final chapter, the reproduction of Courbet's *The Oak of Vercingetorix*, which the
narrator speaks of as "the point of departure for [Aurach's] study of destruction"
(180E, 268G). This tree, so very similar to the first, lacks, however, the grave
markers. Twinned images, once again, like the two glacier scenes in which the
version marked by death precedes the double that restores the departed (in a
newspaper photograph) or eradicates the remembrance of their loss (in a painting).

23. Other guides, notably blind, traverse these tales: the blind guide who
shows Ambros and Cosmo er-Riha (142E, 210G) and the blind Berber leader

in Kaspar Hauser's final story, though the latter is never explicitly mentioned by Sebald's narrator.

24. It may be coincidental, but not irrelevant, that the word for screen here, *Leinwand*, is that used in the story of Aurach for canvas.

25. Sebald changed the name Edward Ellis to Edwin Elliott in the English translation.

26. This is not quite possible, since Nabokov was there, not in spring of 1971, but in August of 1971, as the actual appearance of the photo in the Swiss press shows.

27. Hersch was the original name of Henry Selwyn before he changed it to Henry (20E, 33G).

28. Mirages reappear throughout the stories.

29. This is a phrasing that appears elsewhere in *The Emigrants* (for example 179G, 261G). Kaspar dreams a scene he could not possibly have known in reality ("in Wirklichkeit") and returns the narrator to a Crete he has also never known.

30. *Kaspar Hauser* opens with a scene of writing in which a young man with no identity learns without understanding to write his name. This is its point of origin. An unnamed figure forces the inmate to write his name (for he writes by himself as little as he later dreams for himself): "Write, Wrr-ite. Note this: write!" These are the first distinct words uttered in the film entitled *Kaspar Hauser*, about whom we are reminded repeatedly: "The riddle of his origins remains unsolved to this day."

31. Flickering images run throughout *Austerlitz* as well, often the sign of ghostly presences.

32. This is the same alternative, almost, as that we read of before: "as if the dead were coming back *or* as if we were on the point of passing away into them" (46E, emphasis mine, translation altered; 69G).

33. This is a reappearance of the desert caravans of which Cosmo and Ambros speak (97E and 141E, 141G and 209G) and the caravan of Kaspar Hauser's tale.

34. *Litz* as heddle—a part of the weaver's loom.

35. Sebald's description refers to the exhibition at the Jüdisches Museum Frankfurt am Main (the Jewish Museum in Frankfurt) to which I extend my gratitude for permission to use the images they provided. These were also gathered in the catalogue: "*Unser einziger Weg ist Arbeit*": *Das Getto in Łódź 1940–1944* (Vienna: Jüdisches Museum Frankfurt am Main and Löcker Verlag: 1990). The photograph of Genewein is on 76, that of the weavers on 119.

36. Ibid., 66–142.

37. The Austrian-born Walter Genewein eagerly joined the NSDAP early in 1933 and worked in the Łódź ghetto from 1940 until its *Auflösung* in 1944. In 1943, when ordering five hundred slide frames, he described his project as ar-

chival documentation. Still, he clearly regarded his photographs not only as a service to the German cause but also as an aesthetic accomplishment that placed him in the avant-garde of color photography. His correspondence with IG Farben Berlin, with its insistent complaints about the disappointing quality of the color of their film, attests to his artistic aspirations (ibid., 54).

In 1947 he was brought before the Austrian Volksgericht for his role at Litzmannstadt. In addition to being starved, worked to death, and deported for annihilation, with Genewein's help the Jewish population was continuously charged for the services and provisions they received and in other ways systematically robbed of the little they had in goods and funds (ibid., 22–23 and 45). Genewein denied that the ghetto was a concentration camp, denied ever having shown the photographs, denied profiteering from his position in the ghetto administration (ibid., 54). The 1998 film *Photographer* directed by Dariusz Jablonski documents Genewein's slides and his trial statements along with the counternarration of a ghetto survivor, Arnold Mostowicz.

38. The difficult light through the window, the obscurity, bring us back to Aurach's studio where contact with the past is equally problematic: "where [Aurach] had set up his easel in the grey light that entered through a high north-facing window layered with the dust (*Staub*) of decades" (161E, 237G).

39. The German racial laws concerning *Mischlinge*, if nothing else, would have taught him that.

40. The narrator's mother, like Sebald's, was Rosa (76E, 110G), one of several echoes of the name in the text. Aurach's mother, whose diary occupies so many of the last pages, was Luisa.

41. The English translation anglicizes the name to Luisa, but the parallel world of Poland's Łódź Ghetto is important to maintain in its difference. If the Nazis germanified Łódź, the text pays them back in kind, transforming the German names Rosa and Luisa, to the Polish Roza, Lusia, and Lea. And lest we get caught up in the specificity of national identity, the narrative shifts to the mythic dimensions of the three Parcae.

42. One need only think of Ambros Adelwarth who, in an institution removed from the eye of the public, willingly gives himself up to the cruel pseudo-experiments of a maniacal Eastern European doctor and his "annihilation method" (114E, 168G).

43. There is a geographical version of this in which the structure of one thing becomes that of another—in which, suddenly, one terrain, Constantinople, becomes associated with the terrain of Allgäu, of Switzerland, and of the Judenviertel, the place where Jews are quartered (130–31E, 192–93G).

44. This essay has no pretensions to being a profound theoretical reflection on the political implications of either the Holocaust or identity politics. It offers the beginnings, rather, of a meditation on the implications of Sebald's *The*

Emigrants in this regard. A highly nuanced and careful reflection on the related issue of multiculturalism and the implications of identity politics is to be found in Werner Hamacher's essay "Heterautonomien—One 2 Many Multiculturalisms—," in *Gewalt Verstehen*, ed. Burkhard Liebsch and Dagmar Mensink (Berlin: Akademie Verlag, 2003), 1157–1201. There too the question of counting comes up, though in a rather different context.

Chapter 6. Playing Jane Campion's Piano

1. The opening line of the epigraph is from Jane Campion, *The Piano* (New York: Hyperion, 1993), 146. Citations from *The Piano* are a difficult matter. To begin with, the dialogue of the film and that of the script are not always identical. Moreover many scenes in the script never appeared in the actual film and some dialogue from the film does not appear in the script. Spoken text in this chapter is usually from the sound track (unless the script offers a telling variation). Where the passage does not appear in the script, the citation is followed by "(film)." Otherwise the page number given refers to the place in the script where some version of it appears. Scene descriptions are from the script.

Page numbers higher than 123, however, refer to the notes on "The Making of *The Piano*" at the end of the volume. There illuminating commentary by Campion, Chapman (the producer), Dryburgh (the cinematographer), the actors, and others is offered.

2. Two of the most telling reviews appear in the conservative *National Review* and the liberal *New Republic*. Such symmetric attacks from putative right and left that, to boot, are so (unwittingly) hilarious makes one almost suspect Campion of ghost writing. The outrage that John Simon expresses returns over and over to a betrayal of reality. Still he is equally exercised by Campion's historical accuracy when a scene or image seems jarringly unlikely.

Yet, in other ways, Miss Campion is a stickler for accuracy, especially when such accuracy looks or sounds ridiculous to us, e.g., people wearing London street clothes and shoes to slosh through jungle mud. (John Simon, "Praise Jack, Shoot 'The Piano,'" *National Review*, 27 December 1993, 67)

Stanley Kauffmann is only a little less silly. What threatens him about the film, no doubt because he begins to understand it, is its challenge to easy concepts of sense.

> At the end she and Keitel leave together, and en route the piano is hurled into the sea. Wow. What a symbol—the piano on the ocean floor. Only a clod like me would ask what it's a symbol *of*—since, at the last, Hunter is still mute and is playing another piano, her injured finger tipped with metal.

Every moment is upholstered with the suffocating high-mindedness that declines to connect symbols with comprehensible themes. (Stanley Kauffmann, *The New Republic*, 13 December 1993, 31)

The Piano . . . is an overwrought, hollowly symbolic glob of glutinous nonsense. The New Zealand writer-director Jane Campion, who made an appealing film of Janet Frame's autobiography . . . here reverts to the thick, self-conscious poeticizing of her first film, *Sweetie*. (Ibid. 30)

It seems that Kauffmann is more comfortable with stories about thoroughly passive "madwomen" like Janet Frame, and prefers the Campion film that breaks conventions least of all, to the "non-sense" in both form and content of *Sweetie* and *The Piano*.

3. Mary Cantwell, "Jane Campion's Lunatic Women," *New York Times*, 19 September 1993, 40.

4. Ibid., 30.

5. *Pakeha* is the Maori (and New Zealand) term for white man.

6. The final version of the film, in contrast to the script, omits the most explicit commentary on the colonial rapaciousness with respect to Maori land. What is left is a far more abstract commentary on the relation among nature, humankind, and death.

7. "Many of the MAORIS have coughs, running noses and sores. (They have no immunity to European diseases.)" Note II, iii, 128.

8. The MAORI GIRLS are part of the mission's good works. They are dressed in European style and while their training is in polite, proper, domestic behaviour they constantly corrupt it with their demonstrative displays of affection, and their clay tobacco pipes to which they are addicted. (38–39)

(A description which, in the actual film, is less carried through with respect to the girls than to other figures.)

9. Ada, too, cannot escape her shadows, who like the famous natives of Lévi-Strauss's *Tristes Tropiques* mimic her signing and writing. (See Claude Lévi-Strauss, *Tristes Tropiques*, trans. J. and D. Weightman [New York: Atheneum, 1974], 294–305. [Campion, who did her undergraduate work in anthropology, might well have known this passage.] See also Jacques Derrida, *Of Grammatology*, trans. Gayatri Chakravorty Spivak [Baltimore: Johns Hopkins University Press, 1970], 101–40. Derrida's commentary on ethics in this chapter, on morality and immorality [139–40], has much to say of what we are doing here.) The humor of *The Piano*, in fact, is often produced by a theater of doubling. The Maoris double the whites, Flora mimics Ada, and the chirpings of Nessie echo the endless chatterings of Morag.

10. The ballad the children sing is "Barbara Ellen." It tells a story of unrequited love with obvious parallels to Baines' love for Ada. The second scene, it goes without saying, prefigures Ada's relation to Stewart.

11. The politics of the scene are feminist and anticolonialist at once. The

mode of rectification as revenge would be like that in *Sleeping with the Enemy.* But Perrault's *Bluebeard* is itself strange in its insistence on the blueness of the evildoer's beard—a not so veiled racism.

12. It is a matter of a key falling into the hands of the husband in both stories.

13. Along with such works as the stories of Isak Dinesen or Heinrich von Kleist's *Penthesilea*, which, like *The Piano*, side by side offer also a tamer definition of feminism as well.

14. Torn strips of sheet are wrapped around the piano's legs and stool in preparation for the journey across the sea in the opening scene, covering every inch of what seems, therefore, a wondrous, wounded creature. Prefigurations of the bandage wound around Ada's stump of a finger, a bandage that unravels on her underwater descent (as though one needed yet another indication that woman and instrument are somehow one). And like the fabric around the wound is the cloth that Ada wraps around the fateful, disembodied piano key, which in turn is mimicked by a handkerchief around the amputated limb, that macabre substitution that Stewart performs, sending the finger in place of the key as a warning to Baines.

But it is the clothing, above all, that redoubles the complexities found in the Bluebeard melodrama, cloth not only as protection from a future violence or dressing for a past one, but also as translucence.

15. This is just one of several winged creatures that inhabit the film—from the cupid-like statue in Ada's Scottish home, to Flora in ominous angel wings, made for the performance, and which she still wears when least angelic, to the bird into which Stewart transforms Ada by referring to his violence as having "clipped [her] wing" (112).

16. Not only of Flora's story but, immediately thereafter, of a silent story that Ada tells.

17. Similarly, the theatrical performance at the school is preceded by eyes peering out at the audience from behind many holes in the stage curtain.

18. Beaumont Newhall, at least, places the autochrome rather at the beginning of the twentieth century, *The History of Photography* (New York: Museum of Modern Art, 1964), 192.

19. Ibid., 12.

20 Ibid., 17, 14–16.

21. Campion's fidelity, if one can speak of such, is less, of course, a fidelity to reality than to such famous photographs as the calotypes of the Scottish photographers Hill and Adamson. One finds frequently in their work paired figures of women similar to Ada and Flora, for example "The Sisters," "The Birdcage," and "The Misses Grierson," in David Octavius Hill and Robert Adamson, *Photographs*, ed. Graham Ovenden (London: Academy Editions, 1973), 20, 21, 27.

22. See Susan Sontag: "To photograph is to appropriate the thing photographed. It means putting oneself into a certain relation to the world that feels like knowledge—and, therefore, like power" (Susan Sontag, *On Photography* [New York: Farrar, Straus and Giroux, 1973], 4). In a more obvious moment, later in the film, we see Stewart with an album of *"pressed botanical specimens"* (85).

23. That the photo fails as "the pencil of nature" becomes evident when Stewart first encounters Ada. The look of immense disappointment on his face is unmistakable and he announces the disparity between imitation and reality with: "You're small. I never thought you'd be small" (22).

24. This is the title of a famous book by William Henry Fox Talbot published in 1844, the first showbook of photographs which also gives an account of Talbot's photographic method (Newhall, 33).

25. Many of the reviews of *The Piano* return to a certain, narrow question of reality. Could the piano really have survived the trip to New Zealand? Is Michael Nyman's music really thinkable as the composition of a nineteenth-century woman? Why does Campion insist on certain historical veracities such as oily hair, and cast others to the winds? Still, the question of representing the real is far more complex than that.

26. Annette Michelson ("Toward Snow," *Artforum*, June 1971, 32) speaks of "the entire tradition of the independently made film" as follows: "Grounded in the experience of Surrealism and Expressionism, its will to destroy narrative was an attempt to situate film in a kind of perpetual Present, one image or sequence succeeding another in rapid disjunction, tending, ultimately in the furious pace of single-frame construction, to devour or eliminate expectation as a dimension of cinematic experience." (See in this regard also Maya Deren, "Cinematography: The Creative Use of Reality," *Daedalus* [Winter 1960]: 167.) This is not what Campion does. *The Piano* is, from beginning to end, a coherent narrative, and its political gesture has as much to do with the maintenance of continuity as with its disruption. The point here is not one of how to radicalize the medium of film in general, but rather how the moments of its radicalization in *The Piano* relate to a complex of other issues.

27. "FLORA: My REAL father was a famous German composer. . . . They met when my mother was an opera singer. . . . " (30).

28. Unreadable, as language often is in the film: not only in those scenes where no subtitles illuminate the finger talk of Ada and Flora or the Maori commentary, but also in the insistence on Baines' illiteracy. Thus Ada prepares for him an engraved message on the piano key that he in any case cannot possibly read. The script, if not the film, will insist on this in a long scene of deciphering.

29. In the iconography of the script and film, freeing oneself from a single shoe (or putting on but one) already has a history, from the early scene in which

Ada, oddly, cuts one skate from the foot of her sleeping daughter to an insistence in the script on the Maori as only half-shod. For at the opening of the story are three enigmatic and brief vignettes in which the "shoes" in question are those of roller skates. The scenes take place as Ada's "mind's voice" tells of the coming journey to New Zealand, and one cannot help sensing that the image of the skate, first going nowhere, then cut free, has something to do with the displacement to come.

We see a small girl skating down a very narrow, dimly lit hallway, and then coming toward us. We see her next wearing the same skates as she sits on a small pony that refuses to move. But then in a third scene in which Flora lies fast asleep "*still wearing her skates*" (10), Ada cuts the laces of one of them, removes the boot, and sets "*one disembodied skate [to roll] across [the floor]*" (10). Ada has then only to play her piano and with the next shot we are under water with the boat traveling rapidly above us.

Strange that the laces have to be *cut* and that the script speaks of the skate as "disembodied." One cannot but think of the disembodied finger—and yet it is thus in a sense that the skate, and Flora perhaps, take off. One shoe off and one shoe on—as when Ada rises up under water from the rope that bound her to the piano. It is with this disbalance of the shoes, a split of sorts that leaves an obvious mark on the subject, that the transitions of the various journeys take place.

Campion repeats this image of the half-shod a number of times in relation to the Maoris.

> *Through a dense bush walk a party of fourteen* MAORI MEN *and* WOMEN *and two* EUROPEAN MEN. . . . *Two of the* MAORIS *share one pair of shoes and all of them are clothed in a mixture of native and European costume.* (17, script only)

To be fully civilized one needs two shoes and the Maoris always have but half the measure. The script makes this evident by describing the natives come to observe the play within the play, just at the middle of the film.

> *Two of the* MAORI PARTY *share one pair of shoes so that only one may be in the hall at a time, while the other waits barefoot outside.* (64)

30. We take Perrault's morals here more or less at face value, but there are obvious ironies, hard to miss, in the relation between the morals and the story they are meant to comment on.

31. Charles Perrault, *Perrault's Complete Fairy Tales*, trans. A. E. Johnson (London: Puffin, 1999), 77.

32. Ibid., 77. Is the moral of the story, then, that Bluebeard's wife would have done better not to have looked and to have lived unknowingly with a murderer?

33. Ibid., 78.

34. Unable to imagine the kind of expenditure in which George and Ada are engaged, Stewart reacts with fury toward Ada who, he thinks, has cost him his eighty acres of land.

> STEWART (*Still from some distance.*): Stop right there! This isn't yours . . . What are you doing with the piano?
>
> *The women exchange looks.*
>
> . . . .
>
> STEWART (*Out of breath.*): Hah, you're very cunning, Ada, but I've seen through you. I'm not going to lose the land this way. (77)

35. And yet, in another sense, of course he does envision it, or at least sees it. For as Ada and Baines abandon themselves to one another Stewart observes it all.

> *He has found a spyhole where he can see ADA and BAINES kissing, undressing.*
>
> *He reels back, angry, but just as we might expect him to burst through, he steps up to look again; the fatal second look, the look for curiosity. . . . STEWART watches . . . as BAINES buries into ADA's skirt. He does not seem to notice the dog licking his hand. Suddenly he pulls his hand away and looks at it, wet with dog saliva; he wipes it on the boards and continues watching as if mesmerized.* (83)

It is Stewart's curiosity that deflects the seemingly inevitable violent retribution, curiosity once again that forestalls simple narrative predictability and closure. In the cruel and witty doubling that makes the dog to Stewart as George is to Ada under her skirt, the scene also leaves Stewart considerably more complicated than the purely adversarial figure he may soon seem to be.

36. In a scene cut from the final film version, Campion has the blind piano tuner say this of the relation between marriage and perfect musical expression:

> BLIND MAN: My wife sang with a bell-clear tone. After we married she stopped. She said she didn't feel like singing, that life made her sad. And that's how she lived, lips clamped closed over a perfect voice, a beautiful voice. (49)

37. Simon, "Praise Jack, Shoot 'The Piano,'" 66.

38. But also by a key inscribed long before she had met George Baines, with desire for another lover, "A heart D," a key we discover only as she decides to go to George.

39. The logical conclusion to a dualistic understanding of the relation between nature and culture in this film would have had George and Ada join the Maoris (if they had been the idyllic versions of the interrelation between nature and humankind). The script sets the penultimate scene in the drawing room, without George and Flora. The film shifts it to the more questionable locus of the garden just outside the house, as an ironic double of the scene on the beach in which Flora also performs her cartwheels.

40. The earlier dialogue emphasized the relation of possession. Thus Flora on translating Ada's response when she hears of Stewart's agreement to trade the instrument to Baines:

FLORA: She says it's her piano, and she won't have him touch it.

. . . .

ADA's *breathing becomes heavy with anger, she writes furiously on her pad:* 'THE PIANO IS MINE! IT'S MINE!' (42)

41. In an exchange about *The Piano* Campion speaks of it as her attempt to "write a proper story with a narrative." She follows with a commentary on her discomfort at such an enterprise. David Sterritt, "Jane Campion Directs on Instinct," *Christian Science Monitor*, August 17, 1993.

42. Walter Benjamin, "Theses on the Philosophy of History," in *Illuminations* (New York: Schocken, 1969).

43. It is hard to resist reflecting on the name Hood, with respect to a poem cited just after Ada is seen with a dark cloth over her head.

44.

DRYBURGH: Part of the director's brief was that we would echo the film's element of underwater in the bush. "Bottom of the fish tank" was the description we used for ourselves to help define what we were looking for. So we played it murky blue-green. . . . (141)

45. Just as unexpected is the typographical insistence in the script. The very last lines are Ada's voice-over of the verse printed at the top of the page, all in capitals. These are followed by an asterisk, its counterpart at the bottom of the page—"*Thomas Hood (1799–1845): 'Sonnet: Silence.'" In between the poetry and the reminder of the poet's silence, is a photograph of the piano abandoned at the water's edge, a version of the film's beginning linked to its end. And then some thirty-four pages of notes and commentary later, once again those same lines at the very end of the book, this time occupying a full page—"Thomas Hood (1799–1845)," and a page later, again the photograph.

46. Thomas Hood, *Selected Poems of Thomas Hood*, ed. John Clubbe (Cambridge: Harvard University Press, 1970), 63.

47. Walter Benjamin, *Gesammelte Schriften* (Frankfurt: Suhrkamp, 1972), I.3.1232.

48. It is hardly a question of theorizing cinema per se in this essay, but rather of giving one reading (if such literacy were possible) of *The Piano* in relation to the question of the political. That relationship is, of course, a much-pondered and much-debated subject in film theory. Susan Sontag reminds us of a tradition that sees the "political-moral position" of cinema allied to an "apotheosis of realism" ("Theatre and Film," in *Styles of Radical Will* [New York: Farrar, Straus and

Giroux, 1966], 102). Annette Michelson sees the radical position as more often related to narrative dislocation ("Film and Radical Aspiration," in *Film Culture Reader*, ed. P. Adams Sitney [New York: Praeger, 1970], 404–21).

What I have traced here is a political questioning in *The Piano* that plays both on the disruption of narrative in cinema as medium (as in Flora's tale to Morag or the opening frames of the film) and also on a disruption that may be read from conventionally mimetic statements: for example the notions of passion and will or the disruptiveness of the concatenation of three, individually tame, endings.

Index

Crossing Aesthetics

Jacques Derrida, *Eyes of the University: Right to Philosophy 2*

Maurice Blanchot, *Lautréamont and Sade*

Giorgio Agamben, *The Open: Man and Animal*

Jean Genet, *The Declared Enemy*

Shosana Felman, *Writing and Madness: (Literature/Philosophy/Psychoanalysis)*

Jean Genet, *Fragments of the Artwork*

Shoshana Felman, *The Scandal of the Speaking Body: Don Juan with J. L. Austin, or Seduction in Two Languages*

Peter Szondi, *Celan Studies*

Neil Hertz, *George Eliot's Pulse*

Maurice Blanchot, *The Book to Come*

Susannah Young-ah Gottlieb, *Regions of Sorrow: Anxiety and Messianism in Hannah Arendt and W. H. Auden*

Jacques Derrida, *Without Alibi*, edited by Peggy Kamuf

Cornelius Castoriadis, *On Plato's 'Statesman'*

Jacques Derrida, *Who's Afraid of Philosophy? Right to Philosophy 1*

Peter Szondi, *An Essay on the Tragic*

Peter Fenves, *Arresting Language: From Leibniz to Benjamin*

Jill Robbins, ed. *Is It Righteous to Be?: Interviews with Emmanuel Levinas*

Louis Marin, *Of Representation*

Daniel Payot, *The Architect and the Philosopher*

J. Hillis Miller, *Speech Acts in Literature*

Maurice Blanchot, *Faux pas*

Jean-Luc Nancy, *Being Singular Plural*

Maurice Blanchot / Jacques Derrida, *The Instant of My Death / Demeure: Fiction and Testimony*

Niklas Luhmann, *Art as a Social System*